GETTING RID OF PATIENTS

TERRY MIZRAHI

Getting Rid of Patients
Contradictions in the Socialization of Physicians

RUTGERS UNIVERSITY PRESS

New Brunswick, New Jersey

TO EVE TOVA AND JOSHUA AVRAM,
who were born during different phases of this work,
but who inspired rather than tired me.

Library of Congress Cataloging in Publication Data

Mizrahi, Terry.
  Getting rid of patients.

  Bibliography: p.
  Includes index.
  1. Physician and patient. 2. Hospitals—Medical
staff—Attitudes. 3. Internal medicine—Study and
teaching (Graduate). 4. Social medicine. 5. Internists—
Attitudes. 6. Residents (Medicine)—Attitudes. I. Title.
[DNLM: 1. Internship and Residency. 2. Physician–Patient
Relations. 3. Socialization. W 62 M6845g]
R727.3.M59 1986   610.69'6   85–2284
ISBN 0–8135–1128–3

Contents

Contents

Tables

Acknowledgments

It does not seem possible to thank adequately all the people who provided direction, criticism, advice, and support in my long, arduous, rewarding journey during these last few years—so many mentors, colleagues, and friends who made themselves available to me.

First and foremost, I must acknowledge that this project would never have been undertaken, and certainly never completed, without the guidance and encouragement of Jeffrey Hadden and Diana Scully. They helped in ways far more significant than in their official capacities as chairman and member of my dissertation committee. Their availability, ideas, and participation were invaluable. I am also appreciative of the input and reactions from Franklin Arnhoff and Thomas Hunter, who served as committee members.

I must thank Edward Peeples, David Rosner, Milton Ogle, Robb Burlage, Harold Lewis, Michael Madison, Theodore Long, Mill Roseman, Sam Bloom, and especially Ralph Larkin, and many others who shared and shaped my experiences and offered concrete as well as emotional support at various critical junctures during my research.

I also want to thank the number of people who helped in the collection and analysis of the enormous amount of data generated during the course of this study. Among them are Carol Logue, Phillip Erickson, Charlotte Sloan, Patricia Hein, Nadine Bullion, Chip Byrd, and Eugene Zitkus. I am especially grateful to Marion Kelly, who moved beyond the role of research assistant to become a sounding board and at times a collaborator.

I want to acknowledge the grant I received from the Professional Staff Congress of the City University of New York in 1982, which allowed me to follow up the former Southern Area Medical School house officers now in academic and community practice across the United States of America.

I owe a public debt to the interns and residents at SAMs who allowed me to observe, question, and interpret their world. Many of them became informants, confidants, collaborators. Protocol dictates that they and the institution remain anonymous, but their candor and honesty are most gratefully acknowledged. Likewise, I am most appreciative of the cooperation extended by the Department of Medicine at SAMs and all the faculty, most particularly, Dr. G., chair of primary internal medicine, who served as a facilitator, interpreter, and mediator and without whose visible support the research effort would have been far more difficult, if not impossible. I am especially grateful to the former SAMs house staff who welcomed me into their homes and offices five years later and who so readily shared their disappointments as well as visions.

To the patients at SAMs, who put up with yet another intruder, I extend my sincerest thanks. I hope that the findings of this study ultimately make a difference in their lives.

To Patricia Stevens, Elizabeth Addis, and especially Ina Salzman, I express my thanks for their excellent typing assistance. They turned my scribbles into readable prose and made this massive manuscript a physical reality. I would like to express my appreciation of the enthusiastic help and support I received from Marlie Wasserman, Rutgers's Editor-in-Chief.

Finally, I want to express my love to my sister, Phyllis Mizrahi Cohen, who was there every time I needed her.

GETTING RID OF PATIENTS

"What we need is a sick and salvageable patient who will walk away and say thank you."
 Attending faculty Kirk, intensive care unit, a general hospital

"The only good [patient] admission is a dead admission."
 The House of God (Shem, 1978), quoted by several house staff

There "are new strategy-oriented board games like . . . INTERN. Your object in INTERN is to get the patient out of the hospital (still breathing) fast."
 New York Magazine, November 23, 1981

Chapter 1

Introduction

In the critical years of internship and residency in internal medicine that constitute the transition between medical school and practice, new doctors liken their experience to being ordered into the trenches as the first line of defense against disease and trauma. It is an experience that shapes their beliefs about and attitudes on the practice of medicine and the nature of patients. Learning takes place in situations that range from chaotic emergency rooms to faculty-sponsored symposia. Burdensome work loads encompass everyday patient management as well as theories and diagnosis of rare and poorly understood diseases. These years of training forge a professional consciousness. This tough initiation into the practice of hospital-based and clinic medicine to which new doctors must submit themselves in order to become fully certified members of their specialty within the medical profession is also their period of first employment in that profession. They are paid to provide services to large numbers of the indigent and, increasingly, to the middle class. Hence their role has been characterized as a structurally ambiguous one that complicates both the process of patient care and that of physician socialization.[1]

Crucial as the internship and residency years are for the socialization of doctors into the medical profession, medical sociologists have largely neglected them until recently (D. Levine et al. 1974).[2] Yet, Bloom (1963, 1979) notes it is highly probable that doctors' perspectives on the doctor-patient relationship are shaped in this final phase of formal education. This book examines the context in which young doctors are socialized into the specialty of internal medicine and how this socialization process affects the doctor-patient relationship. It concentrates on how interns and residents learn and carry out their roles and functions as internists and how their social relationships

3

with peers, faculty, and others affect their relationships with and perspectives on patients. It also presents a retrospective view of internal medicine training five years later by a group of former house staff members who are practicing medicine in a variety of academic and community settings. This longitudinal perspective, rare in field research, also provides some insights about professional development and patient care beyond graduate medical education.

Historically, internal medicine has been viewed as virtually synonymous with the profession of medicine. It is the largest and one of the most prestigious specialties in medicine today (Wechler 1976).[3] It has evolved with a dual and at times conflicting heritage (Pellegrino 1974; Regelson 1978). The main influence was the German scientific and academic tradition (Bloomfield 1959), which concentrated on understanding bodily systems and diseases. Internal medicine was far removed from the then-developing world of the practicing German doctor. A second influence was the clinical scholarship that evolved under the leadership of Sir William Osler in this country around the turn of the century (McGovern and Burns 1970). Internists differentiated their training from the basic education for general medical practice with the founding of the American College of Physicians in 1915. Yearly professional conferences were held; required internships were established; research was encouraged; and standards for education and practice were proposed. As specializations proliferated, the American Board of Internal Medicine was founded in 1936, in part as a way of retaining many of the subspecializations that were rapidly evolving.[4] Together with its scientific orientation, internal medicine claims clinical competency for the "whole" adult patient; hence it has been involved in developing primary care and generalist tracks within internal medicine residency programs. Some view this as a move to compete with emerging family practice residency programs (Petersdorf 1975a, 1978; Stevens 1971) and to counter criticism of overspecialization (Petersdorf 1976). Despite this important and long history, there are very few comprehensive studies of the process of socialization of novice internists, especially as it affects their relationships with patients during or after training.[5] My hope, in selecting internal medicine as the context for this study, is to begin to fill some of this gap.

The research for this book was done over a three-year period. It is multimethodological, using participant observation, in-depth interviews, and self-administered questionnaires. I interviewed a total of sixty-five different subjects, randomly selected at the beginning and end of internship and at the end of residency. Ten were reinterviewed as ending interns, and thirteen were reinterviewed at the end of the training cycle. I also reinterviewed an additional twenty-six residents five and six years later as practicing physicians. Hence the study includes longitudinal and cross-sectional data. In addition, I interviewed seven family practice interns who spent four months of their training in the internal medicine services. They directly experienced the world of internal medicine training without being *of* it. Overall, a total of 109 interviews were conducted, which represents approximately 30 percent of each of the cohorts. I also spent one full year observing the 102 internal medicine house staff (or house officers) who were in training during that year, approximately 34 at each of the three levels: internship, junior residency, and senior residency.[6] (For a full discussion of the methodology and analysis of the field experience, see the Appendixes.)

THE HOUSE STAFF

The subjects of this study were the house staff in the department of internal medicine of a large southern university medical center that I have pseudonymed Southern Area Medical School (SAMs). The largest specialty for which new doctors were being trained at SAMs was internal medicine, reflecting its status as the largest in the medical profession. The interns who entered the internal medicine program during the years of the study (the late 1970s and early 1980s) came from at least twenty-five American medical schools located around the country.

The department of medicine had the dual responsibility of maintaining training programs for medical students and house staff and operating medical services at three sites: a large public general hospital (GH), a smaller private hospital (PH), and a Veterans' Administration hospital (VAH).

The house staff characterized the standard three-year training program as "middle of the road," with a good reputation, but one that emphasized clinical rather than research aspects of medicine. They considered it a "big city hospital" program (in contrast to smaller, community hospital internships and residencies) but less competitive than the more academic university medical centers.

By and large, internal medicine is still predominantly a male specialty, although the number of women entering it has been slowly and steadily increasing.[7] The number of women in internal medicine training at SAMs increased from approximately 5 percent to 20 percent during the years of the study. The more than one hundred faculty members (known as attendings) were, however, virtually all male.

The SAMs house staff was an all-white enclave. During the years of this study there were a very few blacks in training. The SAMs program was probably slightly underrepresentative of training programs nationally, due to its southern location, although the percentage of black medical students has been declining nationally (Strelnick 1980).

The age of the house staff was typical for such programs: the mean at the beginning of internship was around twenty-six years old. Virtually all of the house officers were American born and pursued the typical uninterrupted path from medical school to graduate medical specialization. Almost all the physicians in the study expected to take the internal medicine certification boards, even those few who were not intending to practice internal medicine immediately or ever but who were using internal medicine as basic training for subsequent specialization in other areas.

THE ORGANIZATIONAL SETTING

The SAMs Department of Medicine had responsibility for staffing the internal medicine inpatient services in all three hospitals. It also had responsibility for staffing the emergency rooms (ERs), intensive care units (ICUs) for critically ill patients, and outpatient (OPCs) clinics for adult ambulatory patients at both the GH and the VAH. An additional responsibility was providing general medical consultation to all the other non–internal medicine adult services (e.g., surgery, psychiatry, neurology, obstetrics/gynecology, etc.) in all three hospitals. If there were suspected medical problems on those nonmedical services, senior residents and attendings were assigned to evaluate the patients.

All services in the three hospitals were staffed through a system of rotations, each one lasting approximately one month. House officers were assigned randomly to required rotations; no negotiations were allowed. During the internship year there were no electives; all twelve rotations were required. The interns' time was divided among the inpatient medical services in all three settings, ICUs, and the ERs. Ten JR (Junior Resident) rotations were mandatory; the remaining two were electives. In addition to rotations through all inpatient medical services, where they supervised interns and medical students, the JRs staffed the VAH emergency room. The time of the SRs (Senior Residents) was more flexible. All but four of their rotations were in subspecialty internal medicine electives, such as cardiology, endocrinology, and nephrology. Their required rotations included the critical care emergency room, the ICUs, and the general medicine consultation service. Additionally, all house officers were assigned one-half day per week to the outpatient clinic beginning in internship.

Staffing an inpatient service was done by a team arrangement whereby (from top to bottom of the organizational hierarchy) attendings, residents, interns, and medical students all had differential responsibilities for the patients assigned to them:

Attending is the title given to those faculty members who have assigned patient care responsibilities in addition to their assignments in teaching, research, or administration. Reflecting to some degree a national trend, almost all the faculty who directly attended in the GH and PH were full-time employees of the department of medicine. There were few "part-time" and "voluntary" faculty at SAMs. The attendings, though the titular heads of the patient care teams, shared administrative responsibility for the patients with the resident in charge of a team.

The *resident* was the actual manager of the service, the supervisor of the interns, and the teacher of the medical students. It was the resident who had the final authority to accept, reject, discharge, or transfer patients and who made the major therapeutic and medical management decisions.

While the resident was the overseer of the ward and its patients, the *intern* was the implementer of decisions. Interns were responsible for carrying out the day-to-day decisions made for each patient and for handling most patient management problems. In the language of the house staff, the intern was the "scut man," performing all the services (e.g., nursing and transportation as well as technical and supporting activities) the patient needed, whether or not those services were part of the official job description. In the everyday world of graduate medical training, roles and responsibilities among attendings, residents, and interns were actually more complex and often blurred, as Mumford (1970) and Miller (1970) also discovered.

Third- and fourth-year medical students also rotated through internal medicine services and were assigned to the team; it was however, the intern, and not the medical student, who was at the official bottom of the hierarchy. Although patients were assigned to medical students and the care they gave was evaluated by the resident and the attending, they did not have any official patient management authority. Hence, theirs was more a learning than a service role.

Also part of the administrative—but not the patient care—hierarchy of the department of medicine were the *chief residents*. The daily responsibility for managing the internal medical settings in all three facilities was the major role of the chief residents, each of whom (on a rotating basis) was in charge of one of three hospitals. The chiefs, who in the previous year had been senior residents, served as political troubleshooters (responding to complaints by and about the house staff), educators (making presentations at conferences), and attendings (for one or two months in GH). They also oriented and evaluated the interns. Because chief residents have traditionally been accorded high status, they were also presumed to be in leadership positions and thus serve as role models for junior house staff and medical students.

While I gathered no formal demographic data on the patients, from observation and from house staff reported data, most of the patients seen at GH were black and poor. Patients at the VAH, in addition to being virtually all male, were racially mixed and were predominantly from the lower and working classes. At PH the patients were racially mixed but tended to be more middle class than at the GH and the VAH. These differences proved to be important in the house staff's evaluation both of those services and of the patients admitted to them.

The *general hospital* was considered the "public" facility and functioned as a city hospital. All patients admitted to the GH were assigned to a team of physicians that usually consisted of an intern, a JR, an attending, and sometimes a medical student. They were usually hospitalized directly from the ER or the OPC. The faculty attending was the doctor of record, although the residents had virtual autonomy in deciding who was admitted and when. The assigned intern, however, was considered to be the patient's primary physician.

The route to hospital admission at the *private hospital* was more complex, for it functioned as both a private (nominally, at least) and a tertiary care facility, which means that community health providers (institutions and practitioners) could refer to the PH those patients for whom they could not or would not care. At the house staff's discretion, patients also could be admitted to the PH directly from the ER or OPC.

Patients admitted to the *Veterans' Administration Hospital* were also assigned to a team of physicians similar to that at the GH. At the VAH no organizational distinction was made with respect to whether the attending on the team was a SAMs or a VA employee.

THE DAILY ROUTINE

On each medical service, regardless of hospital, interns had a specified number of assigned patients. The average load was ten to twelve patients, but depending on the nature of the service, interns could have as many as fifteen to twenty patients under their care. Hence, the attending and the resident, who usually supervised two interns, could be responsible for as many as forty patients. The number of beds allotted to the service, the census rate (the rate of occupancy), and the medical and social problems of the patients all helped determine the volume of work to be done each day.

When assigned to any of the inpatient services, house officers were on call every third night, responsible for admitting and working up all new patients to the service. On the ICUs they were on call every other night. On the days when they were not on call, the interns and residents would sign their patient group out for the night to their respective peers for coverage.

Interns traditionally have worked from 80 to 130 hours each week, and SAMs was no exception. Considering that a week has only 168 hours, interns often worked nearly to the point of physical exhaustion. Interns' days began early, usually 7 a.m., if they were not on call. The day would blur with the night before if they were on call and had additional new patients to treat. Work days often would not end until late in the evening, even on off-call nights.

Task rounds, held daily between 8 and 9 a.m., officially opened the day. This was the time when all the team members except the attending reviewed the status of each patient for whom they were responsible. They usually walked to each patient's room and sometimes went inside. They discussed the patients briefly and sometimes greeted them perfunctorily. Between 9 and 10 a.m., while the resident attended a scheduled conference (residents' rounds), the interns were busy scheduling tests, reading records, obtaining consultations, and writing orders.

Attending rounds, where all the patients would be reviewed a second time by the team—this time with the attending present—were scheduled from 10 a.m. to noon each day. Any new patients admitted to the team from the night before would be formally presented to the attending by either a medical student or an intern. Each presentation could take from fifteen to forty-five minutes or more, depending on the complexity of the case and the interest or knowledge of the resident or attending. Frequently, the attending also accompanied the house staff to examine and question the patient (known as conducting the "history and physical").

For each new patient, interns also conducted an extensive history and physical examination, which could last as long as two hours. After the clinical work-ups, interns would turn to the technical aspects of their diagnostic work on their new patients: ordering, overseeing, or conducting procedures, the list of which was extensive.[8] Diagnosis usually involved, first, deciding on which tests to conduct, often in consultation with or at the suggestion of the resident; second, ordering the tests or procedures, including contacting the appropriate technical people and entering the orders into the computer and onto the chart; third, transporting the patient to the sites where the tests were to be conducted if they were not to be done at the bedside; fourth, witnessing, assisting, or performing the tests; fifth, retrieving and interpreting the results and discussing the findings; and sixth, entering the results and interpretations into the computer and the medical record. In addition, whenever a malfunction occurred, interns were compelled to repeat all or part of the procedures. If, for example, the laboratory lost a specimen, test results were inconclusive, the patient was improperly prepared, or the forms were incorrectly completed, the process would have to be repeated. Sometimes interns had to obtain permission from the patient and report back briefly to the patient or the family. Afterward the interns had to analyze their findings and write them up in detail in the patient's medical record for their own as well as their superiors', colleagues', and possibly consultant physicians' review.

Besides this work on new patients interns and residents had to keep tabs on all their ongoing patients to be sure that the orders given were carried out correctly, that the implemented patient management decisions were having the desired effect, and that patients who were ready could be appropriately discharged or transferred to make room for the new patients always awaiting admission. Additional work was created by the medical-subspecialization and university-hospital environment. The consequent variety of professionals that usually saw a patient generated seemingly endless suggestions as to what was to be done for the patient. This often meant that house officers had to spend time mediating different opinions as well as attempting to reconcile past and present views on the patients—all of which were entered in the patient's medical record. Hence, much energy and time went into reading, reviewing, and writing in patients' charts and negotiating with superiors about the scope of patient management.

Responsible house staff, especially the interns, never seemed to catch up. Physicians (attendings, other house officers, physicians from other services or from other institutions), nurses, social workers, the laboratory, the family, and ultimately the patient clamored for their attention. The pace was frenetic. Telephones were constantly ringing or occupied. The paging system never ceased. House officers seemed chronically fatigued, harassed, and inundated. They ate on the run and never sat down without having a specific reason for doing so.

With the exception of their months in the ERs and ICUs, all house officers continued their outpatient clinic responsibilities one-half day per week. The clinic was universally viewed as periodically interrupting inpatient responsibilities. Since interns had the most work to do on the inpatient floor, they seemed to resent it the most. They especially dreaded the possibility of having a clinic patient sick enough to require an extensive work-up or hospitalization. Junior and senior residents also intensely disliked clinic because they viewed it as intruding into their educational or personal agenda when it was not interfering with their inpatient duties (Mizrahi 1984b).

The resident's daily role on the inpatient services was less intensive than the intern's. In the beginning of the year and on some services, however, the pressure did not lighten appreciably or automatically. Depending on the attitude of the resident and on the perceived competence of the intern, residents could still be involved in direct patient management, because the efficiency with which the service or unit functioned was now their responsibility. The important difference, however, was that it was not the structured role of residents to be directly available to the patient. They were now the supervisors or the managers of the team.

Residents were also required to be involved in educational and teaching responsibilities. One of the two regularly scheduled didactic conferences—*residents' rounds*—was reserved exclusively for them. Rarely did a resident miss one. Each day different attendings and residents were assigned to present some medical topic for discussion. These sessions also served as an informal social hour. For example, those house staff who moonlighted in the various community hospitals would discuss their "horror stories" or "great saves" with each other. Information about fellowships would be shared. Following task rounds every day, this important educational and social function was often responsible for the frenzied pace of the former activity.

The second regularly scheduled didactic session was weekly *grand rounds,* a formal and traditional ritual that all attendings, internal medicine house staff, and medical students were expected to attend. It usually consisted of a lecture by a distinguished professor about some new and usually esoteric development of interest to the discipline of internal medicine. Faculty, medical students, and residents were present more often than were interns, whose work on the service usually kept them too busy to attend.

The afternoon of the residents varied depending on the type of service, number of patients, and amount of trust in their relationships with the interns. If called for, they would assist their interns with the procedures that had to be done on the patients; if they wanted the experience, they would do the procedures themselves. Junior residents were also responsible for teaching medical students, which took up some time each day. They also spent time away from the service—in the library, at teaching conferences, or in personal or extraorganizational activities such as moonlighting.

Senior residents had administrative patient management responsibility for the ERs and ICUs for a total of three months during the year and were responsible for supervising the interns assigned to them on those services. Because of their critical nature, the patient volume, and the inexperience of the interns, these were considered to be highly pressured and stressful rotations. Decisions had to be made rapidly as well as expertly. The rest of the year the SRs were on elective rotations, with the exception of one month of required general medical consultation to the rest of the hospital system. These rotations were considered to be principally educational in purpose and entailed little patient management responsibility, for the senior residency was considered to be a period for fine tuning of diagnostic skills and for acquiring further in-depth medical knowledge and procedural skills in a variety of internal medicine subspecialties. Senior residents were on their own, and most considered the year to be the "payoff" for the previous two years and for the three months on critical care as well. Most SRs would absent themselves from the house staff culture to moonlight and prepare for the next phase of career development: fellowship or medical practice.

EMPIRICAL CONNECTIONS

Both the socialization of physicians and the physician–patient relationship have been subjects of empirical as well as theoretical scrutiny. The popular and social-scientific literature abounds with commentary on and growing criticism of medical training and practice, albeit with differing perspectives on the causes and consequences of the many problems documented. The increasingly sophisticated and skeptical consumer public shaped by the social protest era of the 1960s and the antigovernment, antielitist movements of the 1970s clearly has had an unsettling effect on the American health system (see, e.g., Ehrenreich and Ehrenreich 1970; Haug and Lavin 1983; Haug and Sussman 1969; Reeder 1972).

Criticism of professions in general continues to mount amid charges of laxity in concern for public service; overzealousness in pursuing the self-interest of their members; and promotion of unaccountable, inefficient, and inequitable modes of service delivery. The very concept of professionalism has been characterized by many as fostering elitism, monopoly, conservatism, mystification, dependency, and self-aggrandizement (see, e.g., Daniels 1971; Gaylin et al. 1978; M. Gross 1978; McKnight 1977; J. Roth 1974a).

Medicine, as the quintessential model of professional service, has received especially intensive scrutiny (see, e.g., Alford 1975; Freidson 1970a; Greenberg 1965, 1971; Illich 1976; Jonas 1978; Navarro 1976; Rayack 1967; Waitzkin 1983; Waitzkin and Waterman 1974). Many commentators have pointed to the phenomenal growth of costly, technologically sophisticated, institutionally-based medical care, which they have characterized as contributing to the depersonalization of the entire system (see, e.g., Starr 1982; Waitzkin 1983). Concomitant with criticism of the rise in corporate medicine is the increasingly common criticism of overspecialization, or "trained incapacity," and the focus on disease and organs rather than on the whole patient (see, e.g., Howard and Strauss 1975; Kendall 1961; Levin 1974; Petersdorf 1976; Stevens 1971; R. Strauss 1978).

These critiques are reflected in a growing body of social science research that depicts a disquieting sense of dissatisfaction and conflict in the relations between the seekers of health care and professional providers. They identify a variety of social, demographic, and medical characteristics of patients that contribute to alienation between doctors and patients. For example, the advancing average age of the population with the concomitant increase in chronic disease is resulting in fewer opportunities for dramatic intervention and requiring more patient participation, often with a negative effect on the traditional doctor–patient relationship (see, e.g., Cambridge Research Institute 1975; Sorenson 1974; Zola and Miller 1971). The literature reflects the realization that, at some level, the problems arising between practitioner and patient are rooted in the nature of the professional–lay relationship. Moreover, there is definite evidence that the dehumanization many patients experience is exacerbated for the poor, the elderly, the working class, minority groups, and women, all of whom must also contend with discrimination, inequity, inaccessibility, and soaring costs (see, e.g., Adams and McDonald 1968; Duff and Hollingshead 1968; Howard 1978; Kennedy 1972; Kosa and Zola 1975; J. Roth 1975; Scully 1977; Seham 1973; Sudnow 1967; Zola 1963). Mutual dissatisfaction between more affluent health consumers and providers has also been documented. It is important to understand the novice physicians' attitudes toward middle-class patients for a more complete perspective on the socialization of physicians to private practice and mainstream American medicine (see, e.g., Donabedian 1978; Duff and Hollingshed 1968; Freidson 1973; Osofsky 1968; Scully 1977; Solon 1966; Wartman et al. 1981).

Much of the research done to date on the doctor–patient relationship has been limited to the practicing physician's doctor–patient relationship or else has ignored the larger training milieu in which, presumably, these physicians are being or were socialized (see, e.g., M. Davis 1971; Duff 1975; Ford, Ort, and Denton 1967; Friedson 1975; Hagner, LoCicero, and Steiger 1968; Hulka et al. 1975; Ima, Tagliacozzo, and Lashof 1970; Korsch, Gozzi, and Francis 1968; Pratt, Seligmann, and Reader 1957; Sorenson 1974; Stewart and Buck 1977; Stimson 1978, and R. Strauss 1978). Duff (1975) and Petersdorf (1978) are among the few physicians who have identified the impact of physician training on the physician–patient encounter. The research on the training environment has measured mainly medical student attitudes toward patients or toward a humanistic dimension of patient care and has seldom focused on advanced trainees who have direct patient care responsibilities. The existing research has used mostly survey methods, effectively preventing comparison of espoused attitudes with actual observed behavior. Furthermore, these studies rarely have described the process by which these student attitudes are acquired.[9] This body of research documented that students acquire negative attitudes toward many types of patients (see Brandt and Kutner 1957; Fredericks and Mundy 1976; Fredericks, Mundy, and Lennon 1971; Geertsma and Stoller 1966a, 1966b; Gottheil, Hassenfield, and Gronkiewicz 1969; Gray, Moody, and Elton Newman 1965; Maguire and Rutter 1976; Parker 1960; Reynolds and Bice 1971).[10]

On the other hand, most major studies of professional socialization have been concerned primarily with the development of physicians and have not fully analyzed the individual and collective impact of professional training on the novice physician's understanding and treatment of the patient (see Becker et al. 1961; Bloom 1973; Bosk 1979; Bucher and Stelling 1977; Chaiklin 1960; Coombs 1978; Merton, Reader, and Kendall 1957; Miller 1970;

Mumford 1970). Light (1980) and Scully (1977) are among the few researchers who identify the negative impact which the socialization of psychiatrists and obstetrician/gynecologists has on patients.

Evidence now accumulating indicates that the problems between doctors and patients in training and practice settings are having an adverse effect on the doctors as well as on the patients. The devaluation by society of the physician's status, together with the increasing problems of modern medical practice, are being linked to physician alienation and impairment (Schieber and Doyle 1983). The manifestations are visible signs of stress and tension in medical school (see Coombs 1978; Gerber 1983; Rosenberg 1979), internship and residency (see Light 1980; McCue 1981; Nadelson and Notman 1979; Pfifferling 1978, 1983; Shapiro and Driscoll 1979; Tokarz, Bremer, and Peters 1979; Werner and Korsch 1979), and practice (see AMA 1977; AMA Council 1973; Kahn-Hut in Light 1980; Lipp 1980; Mawardi 1979; McCue 1982; Preston 1981; Scheiber and Doyle 1983; Waring 1974).

Absent almost entirely from the medical socialization literature are longitudinal studies that move across status boundaries from medical school through graduate medical training and into practice settings, though these transitions are acknowledged as critical in the medical career. The studies that have followed one or more cohorts of medical students usually use a limited survey method, do not focus on the patient care implications of their subjects' career development, or both (see Erdmann, Jones, and Toneski 1978; Fredericks and Mundy 1976; Langwell 1980).[11]

Several critical but neglected dimensions of house staff training and post-training experiences that affect the physician–patient relationship are, then, addressed here: potential conflicts between the educational function and the provision of primary health care, the influence of the hierarchical arrangements of the medical profession, the increasingly technological orientation of medicine, and the potential conflicts generated out of the differential social locations of internists and patients.

THEORETICAL CONNECTIONS

Theoretical perspectives provide a framework for making sense of empirical data. Two basic orientations—functionalist and symbolic interactionist—can be found in the literature on the professional socialization of doctors. Each imposes different, and at times conflicting, meanings on the findings of research.

The functionalist school views professional socialization as a relatively ordered process of learning whereby what is learned functions to help the learner assume the role of the "professional." The physician-teacher serves as the interpreter of the moral ideals of the profession. Mentors are viewed as role models who transmit values, knowledge, and skills to essentially passive novices (Goode 1957; Greenwood 1957; Merton, Reader and Kendall 1957). In the extreme, this conceptualization of professional socialization assumes that appropriate values are internalized during the formal training period and that these values presumably guide future professional conduct. They are immutable across situational or organizational contexts.

The symbolic interactionists, on the other hand, perceive socialization as a process whereby people are shaped and molded by social institutions while simultaneously creating their own identities (Becker et al. 1961; Bucher and Stelling 1977; Meltzer 1975). This theory emphasizes the dual role of persons as both products and producers. Significant action is the product of interaction with self and others and can only be understood from a situation that is meaningful to the actors. The interactionists focus on the emergent and negotiated character of socialization (A. Strauss 1978).

The contradictory conclusions of Merton, Reader, and Kendall in *The Student-Physician* (1957) and Becker et al. in *Boys in White* (1961)—two major studies of medical students—continue to be debated. The points on which these classic studies differ are not primarily empirical; indeed their substantive finding are similar.[12] Despite substantive differences, the contradictory conclusions of the two studies seem to stem mostly from divergent theoretical assumptions. Merton and Becker differ in their conceptions of the principal determinants of social behavior and social order. Simply summarized, Merton believes that the social order of any collectivity is sustained primarily through the internalization of the group's values and norms in socialization so that they become a permanent guide to behavior. By contrast, Becker sees behavior as largely an adaptation to the demands and constraints of particular situations. Neither study fully describes the process of socialization: how medical culture is presented to students and how they respond to that presentation (Hadden and Long 1978).

Two major, now-classic studies of the internship phase of medical training extend the theoretical dichotomy: Mumford (1970) and Miller (1970) demonstrate that important role learning continues in post–medical school training. Both, however, leave unanswered many questions about how this learning takes place. Mumford's conceptualization of role learning as a gradual process mediated by the setting in which it occurs mirrors the perspective of *The Student-Physician*. Miller's presentation of situational learning, with actual physician status deferred until training is completed, follows the orientation of *Boys in White*. There have been so few comprehensive studies of physicians in practice that it is difficult ultimately to resolve the question of whether socialization occurs by situational adaptation or by acquiring a more internalized and permanent value system.

There are differences, too, in how functionalists and symbolic interactionists conceptualize the doctor–patient relationship. The functionalists (Moore and Tumin 1949; Parsons 1951, 1975) characterize it as a competency or knowledge gap between professionals and clients that creates an asymmetric, stratified relationship in which professionals occupy superordinate positions in relation to patients. The functionalists believe that the imbalance in power, rooted in the therapeutic relationship between the doctor and patient, is justified and necessitated by the patient's adoption of the "sick role." The doctor, in regulating access to the sick role, permits limited deviation for individuals who experience strain in their customary roles in order that social stability may be preserved. The functionalists posit that, to induce change, the professional must have leverage, which is generated by the prestige and situational authority of the professional and the situational dependency of the patient (Bloom and Wilson 1972). The patient's acceptance of this professional dominance rests on the principle of *credat emptor,* "let the buyer trust" (Moore [quoting Hughes] 1970), rather than *caveat emptor,* "let the buyer beware." Protection for the patient is presumably assured by a collectively enforced set of standards laid down by the profession itself, in other words, its collectivity orientation. The functionalists (e.g., Fox 1977; Moore and Tumin 1949; Mumford 1970) believe that real and presumed differential knowledge and skill between professionals and consumers are inherently necessary to maintain mutually satisfying relationships.

The symbolic interactionists believe that therapeutic relationships are situationally and structurally, as well as culturally, derived. Freidson (1961), J. Roth (1963), and Sudnow (1967) describe the process of negotiated patienthood, which is based on encounter bargaining rather than homeostatic adaptation. Freidson (1961) further characterizes the doctor–patient relationship as a clash of perspectives rather than an interaction based on the common reciprocal needs of a professional–client system (Bloom and Wilson 1972). Other sociologists (Kirsch and Reeder 1969; McKinlay 1975; J. Roth 1974a) suggest that in order to maintain control over their knowledge and skill, professionals must cultivate an ideology that stresses the client's inability to evaluate professional performance. This ideology is supported by the media and maintained through the manipulation of certain status symbols. Stimson (1976), for example, uses the concept of the "idealization of ignorance" in characterizing the doctor–patient relationship. These critics assert that functionalist analysis has tended to confuse statements about ideal patterns of practice with empirically observable activity. It is interesting to note that neither perspective negates the presence of inequality in the doctor–patient relationship. Their point of departure concerns the issues of values and pragmatism: should social arrangements be that way, and do they necessarily have to be that way?

NEW DIRECTIONS IN SOCIALIZATION THEORY

There have been some attempts to address some basic inadequacies in both functionalism and symbolic interactionism as they relate to professional socialization. Olsen and Whittaker (1970) discuss the conceptual inadequacy in the study of professional socialization; they believe no adequate theories exist. They state that theory building must include three streams of sociological thought: the study of professionalization in occupations; the analysis of individual growth and change rooted in the process of enculturation and lateral role socialization; and the scrutiny of social institutions. They denounce both the routinization of the concept of social origin and the divorcement of attitudes from the social context in which they occur. In their important but little-cited study of nursing, *The Silent Dialogue* (1968), Olsen and Whittaker investigate how to assess validly the interactions of self, role, and situation.

Shuval (1975) emphasizes the role of ancillary personnel, patients, peers, and faculty as agents of socialization during early clinical training. Although she seems to accept the internalization model, she identifies additional dimensions. For example, she suggests that even though physician-teachers enjoy the highest status and legitimation as role models, one cannot assume that their role as socializers is more critical or more far-reaching in its effects than those of other agents. She is also aware of the importance of the organizational structure in a socialization process characterized by considerable conflict and ambiguity in messages delivered and received between socializing agent and novice.

Bucher and Stelling (1977), in a comparative study of four groups of professional trainees (including trainees in internal medicine), delineate the essential features of a model of socialization: organizational environment (setting), persons, and interaction. Their data demonstrate an indelible "program effect" on the trainees. Outcomes of socialization are in large part determined by the nature of the training program, yet at the same time, the trainees exercise considerable autonomy in developing work styles and in constructing personal identities.

For Bucher and Stelling, the interaction between structural and situational aspects of a training program accounts for the professional characteristics of graduates, a conclusion they base on analysis of, first, the organizational context of training; second, the structure of the curriculum (e.g., the number and timing of requirements); third, peer influence; fourth, the nature of faculty supervision; and fifth, the responsibility and autonomy given students. In their view, the earlier in training the novice gains responsibility for the central activity of the profession, the earlier identification with the profession occurs. Peer group contacts and role-playing opportunities arise from the structural arrangements and requirements of training programs. Bucher and Stelling identify the actual interaction among peers and the playing of professional roles as situational rather than structural variables, however, and it is here they locate the *process* of socialization. Role playing is the central situational variable, with peer groups and faculty supervision secondary. Only when the novice can play the professional role realistically and has acquired a sense of mastery can that novice assume the identity of a professional.

Light (1980), in his discussion of the nature of professional socialization, has also branded the classic theories of socialization as incomplete. He believes that, while situational perspectives abound, enduring values and ways of acting are learned as well. While disagreeing with the concept of socialization as role learning, he nevertheless points to the power differential between the socializers and the novices, mentors having more experience, longevity, and stake in the system. For him, negotiation lies at the heart of socialization, not because trainees work out important arrangements and deals, but because the process of negotiating actively involves the trainees in their own transformation.

> Professional socialization is, to use (Anselm) Strauss's term of a structural process, where the process not only has its own structure but the larger structure of the profession is built into the process, which in turn recreates that structure, altering it as forces of change affect both. (Light, 1980, 311)

Hadden and Long (1978) have attempted systematically to delimit the process of socialization and to define its dimensions. They reject the traditional functionalist perspective that assumes that professional values permanently guide professional conduct. They also assume socialization activity is delimited and distinguishable from other forms of human action. According to Hadden and Long socialization is the social process of creating nonmembers and incorporating them into a group. From a member's perspective the aims of socialization are to create persons who can sustain confidence that they meet the requisites of knowledge, skill, and commitment and to incorporate them into membership. Members' creating activities include "showing" and "shaping." *Showing* means the demonstration of knowledge and skill; *shaping* involves the application of sanctions. Members' incorporating activities are recruiting, provisional and final certifying, and placing. Hence Hadden and Long view socialization as a confidence-building activity that justifies to both members and the general public the novice's claims to membership in the group.

Hadden and Long state that it is important to separate the socialization process from its outcome and to assume that the socialization outcome is problematic. For example, what the faculty teaches and what the students learn are not synonymous, nor does either replicate what physicians actually do in practice. Student interpretations of and responses to faculty teaching are variable, and therefore the identification of both members' and novices' personal goals is essential. Moreover, students are exposed to a variety of other potential socializing agents. These agents, including other house staff and ancillary personnel, among others, wittingly or unwittingly indoctrinate them with different ideas, which add to or substitute for what they are taught by the faculty—a process the faculty cannot control. Also, the relative maturity of novice physicians enables them to shape the process toward their own ends and makes them somewhat selective in their responses to socializing action.

My study examines the socialization of graduate internists by focusing not only on interaction between mentors and neophytes but on collegial processes within the house staff and on house staff interaction with patients. In addition it examines situation and context during and after formal training, including, but not limited to, effects of bureaucratization, technology, stratification, culture, economics of health care delivery, and politics.

OVERVIEW

The following chapter introduces the reader to the career and culture of the internal medicine house staff. It presents house officers' collective expectations about graduate medical training and details their prior experiences with patients, physicianhood, and the practice of medicine. It also describes *what* house officers encounter in graduate medical education and patient care and the repercussions of those experiences: the acquisition of a *Get Rid of Patients* (GROP) perspective.

Chapter Three analyzes the structural, professional, and normative factors that inform the GROP perspective. *Why* the house staff develop a GROP orientation is presented along with the circumstances under which the house staff cannot or will not GROP.

Chapter Four depicts the criteria by which the house staff evaluate various characteristics of patients and calculate their social and medical worth. The processes of selecting *who* to GROP intervenes between the structural factors that produce the GROP perspective and the implementation of GROP. Chapter Four describes the house staff's system of social categorization.

Chapter Five enumerates the variety of strategies used by the house staff to implement the GROP perspective. It examines *how* they use techniques of negotiation; manipulation of the bureaucratic hierarchy; and avoidance, omission, objectification, and intimidation of patients for the purposes of GROP.

Chapter Six explores barriers to acquiring optimal skills in doctor–patient relations at each stage of medical training. It presents a perception of house staff reality that No Time Is the Right Time for experiencing a positive interaction with patients.

Chapter Seven focuses on the outcome of the training for the house staff and on their future orientation toward patients and the practice of internal medicine. It also provides a framework for analyzing their career choices.

Chapter Eight presents follow-up data on a randomly drawn subsample of the original cohorts five years beyond their residency. Data on retrospective views of graduate training; current career positions; and views on patient care, the profession of medicine, and contemporary house staff are presented.

Chapter Nine presents the conclusions, which include a discussion of the relationships among training, career setting, and patient care.

Chapter 2

Career and Culture of the House Staff

Socialization is a process whereby nonmembers are ushered through a set of experiences regarded by members as necessary for gaining inclusion into the collectivity. Upon completion of a period in which the neophyte's status is liminal, he or she is accorded membership with rights, privileges, and status as a publicly identified member of the group. Part of the socialization process is the learning of what defines a group member: adherence to rules, regulations, and internal systems of stratification and the sharing of a system of meanings (Hadden and Long 1978). In this chapter those involved in the socialization of the SAMs internists are examined along with the culture of the house staff as a collectivity.

EXPECTATIONS AND EARLY ENCOUNTERS

The new SAMs recruits arrived, full of tension and excitement, to begin their internships on July first. They had just completed four grueling years of medical school, and the experience had, by their own accounts (confirmed by sociological ones: Becker et al. 1961; Coombs 1978; Lesserman 1981; Merton, Reader, and Kendall 1957; and Shapiro and Lowenstein 1979), begun to shape their professional identity, career choice, and perspectives on patients. As medical students they had for the most part been exposed to and participated in patient care as practiced in large teaching hospitals. They had acquired beginning medical knowledge and skill. They had also been exposed to the values or moral dimensions of the system as well as to the meaningful and distributive dimensions (Hadden and Long 1978). Now, graduate medical training actually offered the opportunity to become internists with their first full responsibility for patients. This was to be the critical juncture at which not only did their status change but their fundamental orientation toward their practice and their patients would be reinforced or modified.

They entered internship recognizing how far they had come as well as how special they were as a group. The following comments by a junior resident are typical.

JR ARI:
Your acceptance by your peers is whether they accept you as a person and not so much for what you know. Most medical house staff are pretty smart. They're the guys that really did well in college and they really did well in medical school. . . . Most are in the top 10 percent of graduating medical class. As you go up the ladder people start falling away, so when you're near the top you're surrounded by people of exceptional ability and it's pretty impressive.

Another house officer described the weeding-out process and the elitist perspective it engendered:

JR SUTTER:
First of all in order to get in college and be pre-med you're probably top 25 percent of the population—intellectually, money-earning capability . . . however, you measure it. . . . Then to successfully complete pre-med and get into medical school, that only makes you more of an elitist . . . and people who didn't meet certain standards are dropping out along the way. . . . Who's left? Those who knew every last formula in chemistry and who did research and who had great study habits. . . . [Whatever else you are] . . . if you got a *D* in organic chemistry you better give it up.

Professionally they had already been certified as "doctors" after receiving their M.D. degrees and having completed the national boards.[1] They had already begun to think of themselves as doctors. They had (as Coombs [1978] and others have also found) a sense of beginning mastery and confidence. Nevertheless, they also realized that they still had a long way to go to become competent and confident internists, although almost all believed they would achieve that result at the end of three years of graduate training.

They had chosen internal medicine in a large urban public medical center after exploring various programs in the previous two years.[2] Their rationale for their choice formed the basis for their future comparisons of expectations to experiences. The choice of SAMs resulted from the following criteria:

How they were going to learn (by knowing or doing)
What they were going to learn (a research or clinical orientation)
How much they were going to learn
How much service they would have to provide (the nature of the trade-off, known as the "scut/skill" ratio)

How much cooperation there would be among the house staff (the nature of collegial relationships)

In the main they had chosen SAMs because it had a good reputation; it had a clinical rather than a research orientation; there was lots of "good pathology"; there was little serious competition among the house staff; and they would be given a great deal of responsibility and autonomy. They would learn by doing and practicing; the term they most frequently used was "bread and butter" medicine. Finally, although it would be a difficult routine, they believed that some programs were even more stressful. Hence, along several dimensions, they characterized SAMs as a "mainstream" clinical program.

Upon arrival, most interns defined their first professional goal as to learn basic patient management of sick people, that is, to learn the "hows" of internal medicine, their second goal being to learn the "whys." They expected, namely, to acquire skill first and knowledge afterward. They were prepared to acquire practical knowledge as well as skill, but (to varying degrees) they recognized that the process would be long, hard, and at times diversionary, as Intern Tony's comment indicates:

> The most important thing about being an intern is being able to make a diagnosis. I'll learn that by seeing patients with as many diagnoses as I can. . . . You see a lot of pathology at SAMs so that's the main thing. The other thing—is just learning how to cope with doing a ton of work and stand up under it. . . . It's hard getting there.

This intern's comment reflects the importance the house staff place on the intellectual aspect of internal medicine (the making of diagnoses); it is, in fact, a prime reason for choosing the specialty. A related reason was the opportunity, at least initially, for broad and full responsibility for the whole adult patient. Two more intern comments illustrate:

> INTERN CHAREN:
> I chose it [because] it's one of the only specialties of medicine where you feel like a doctor [not a technician]. . . . It's where you use your brain. . . . You need to be able to take a good history to tell if a person is sick or not.

> INTERN WEND:
> [I chose it because] you think and do a lot. I like to think and I like the patient contact.

Although most house staff viewed internal medicine in terms of its broad patient management and its inclusiveness as a specialty (as opposed to more exclusionary and segmented specialties such as surgery or neurology), their concept of patient involvement was rather narrow from the beginning of their internship. They usually expressed the concept merely as the ability to have

23

contact with patients, in contrast to non–patient-contact specialties such as radiology or pathology:

JR Sing:
I chose internal medicine because it's the most interesting field intellectually and I wanted to choose an area of medicine where I dealt with patients—which left me out of radiology.

With this background they arrived for orientation. Their first formal encounter with the specialty, after the greetings and general orientation to SAMs and the VAH, was with the internal medicine chief residents, who served as bridges between the house staff, faculty, and hospital administration. These chief residents, who had just completed their internal medicine training, were now officially representing the department of medicine.

From a sociological perspective orientation is important because it provides newcomers with their initial impressions of the norms and values emphasized (as well as omitted) by the socializers; in other words, it conveys, what formal or legitimizing messages the members wish to communicate to the new recruits. Whether those messages are in fact received and, if received, whether and how they are internalized are empirical questions to be inferred from future attitudes and behavior. One chief's opening remarks reveal much about the social organization and culture of SAMs:

Welcome to SAMs. This is a big city hospital. There's a lot of "scut work"—so carry a clipboard. This is an intern's hospital. I know you'll feel like you have too much to do but after a while you'll love it. There's so much "great pathology" here. . . . With regard to charts, remember the problems list . . . flow sheets and yellow sheets . . . . (Field notes, orientation week)

The themes of the orientation speeches are critical to comprehending the environment in which the internal medicine interns were to function. They are, first, the objectification of the patient, that is, the patient as pathology; second, the importance and use of the chart as a communication and evaluation device reflecting the technological base of medicine practice; third, the contending norms of self-reliance and humility, as in "this is an intern's hospital" versus "work will be reviewed and evaluated by us, attendings, consultants, and resident"; and fourth, a recognition of the drudgery and frustration of internship and the anticipation of resentment and depression.

With laughter and mumblings, the new recruits acknowledged the situation: "We are not totally novices; we know what's in store [to some degree]. We've been on the wards and in the clinics already as third- and fourth-year medical students." The gap between the fourth year of medical school and the first year of graduate training was, however, uniformly perceived as enormous. Critical distinctions were noted by all of the new interns within the first two months. Typical of the comments contrasting internship with medical school was this statement by JR Kots:

> As an intern you're responsible for everything. . . . Mostly [it is] learned through trial and error. Initially, you're overwhelmed and you don't know where to begin. When you come out of medical school you don't know more than the man on the street about how to be a doctor in terms of everyday care of patients.

The fourth year of medical school was usually described as one with little responsibility and more personal choice. The reality shock (Schmalenberg and Kramer 1979) of internship was extreme and overwhelming regardless of medical school preparation and the new interns' former exposure as medical students to the structure and routine of house staff training.

JR FABLE:
> You get all kinds of advice [before beginning internship] but it's hard to even imagine what it's like being an intern until you've done it. . . . It's an incredible learning experience. . . . There are times when you're absolutely frustrated because you can't get something done and are absolutely exhausted. When you figure you work 100 hours—some weeks 120—and the amount of "scut" work—the new interns are not going to believe you . . . and looking back I still don't believe a lot of it myself.

Observing the scene is qualitatively different from experiencing it directly. The critical distinguishing variable is responsibility. The change was described as making a quantum leap. Junior Resident Ari summed it up thus:

> [Being a fourth-year medical student is] one of the more enjoyable times you'll have. You're sort of being spoon fed as far as learning goes and you have time to learn and you don't have the responsibility to make the decisions. The difference is when you're an intern you're the one who's responsible at all big hospitals. The intern is a transport service, nursing service, pharmacy . . . and now and then he's the resident . . . so he's everybody!

And in hindsight SR Rogers concurred:

> I didn't appreciate how hard the interns work . . . even though I saw them working hours and hours and hours. I never realized how much of my personal freedom I had to give up to get the job done. I'm not sure people realize how difficult internship is.

Most significant, both the expectations the new interns had about the difficulty of internship and any doubts they harbored about their own capability and willingness to withstand it were quickly compounded by the social conditions with which they were confronted from the first day. Typical of the house staff reactions were the following comments presented in hindsight:

SR MELON:
> I opened up my internship at the VAH, and that was the most dismal place I have ever seen in my life. The smell of urine and all sorts of people who should be in

nursing homes. . . . That was incredible because I wasn't prepared for that—God knows who would be and—after my first month there I was ready to leave. . . . This place was a fairly miserable dump.

JR FABLE:
There were a lot of things this year that have just blown my mind. For example, you see patients that are sent in from nursing homes. The "crap" they get—the "stuff" they send. . . . It's almost criminal.

Hence, the first year—and to a lesser degree, all three years—of graduate medical training were a series of continuing conflicts. First, there was the traditional conflict between the role as deliverers of service and the role as advanced learners, between being practitioners and being students. The house staff are paid salaries to deliver patient care at all three hospitals and as such are employees of and responsible to both the SAMs and VAH administrations. They are at the same time responsible to the department of medicine, with its educational and patient care hierarchy. What quickly emerged was a discounting of accountability to both, or to the dual authority structure. The so-called professional–bureaucratic dilemma identified in the literature (Blau and Scott 1962; Etzioni 1964) seemed to dissipate quickly, replaced by an attitude of resentment toward both sources of conflict.

Second was the underlying conflict between short situational and long-range personal goals, the former always characterized in terms of survival, the latter as becoming competent and confident internists. Third, there were conflicts with respect to how to behave and what one needs to know to become an internist, that is, how one acquires, and is assessed as acquiring, the norms of professional conduct, norms that include, for example, both compulsiveness and efficiency.

As far as the first conflict was concerned, the interns attempted to cope by defining their learning in practical terms from the beginning:[3]

INTERN SHU:
There is no time to be a student. No time to learn about disease processes. . . . Here service comes first. . . . There's not always much time to read. . . . There's a conflict as far as time is concerned and how much time one wants to spend doing both.

While the interns accommodated themselves to this dilemma they did so with resignation. Their acceptance was largely temporary and conditional upon the assumption that the education/service ratio would shift during their three-year tenure.

It was principally the experience with and response to the second and third categories of conflict that produced, in house staff, patterns of behavior that ultimately affected their orientation toward patients and their practice. They described their situation as follows:

INTERN GARNEY:
I'm looking for the whole thing to be over more than anything else in the world because it's affected every facet of my life. . . . I'm looking forward to the end and not looking forward to its taking so long to end.

Intern Shu noted that the demands of the work place were dehumanizing:

I'm not looking forward to not being able to live as a human being. . . . I think that's the regret that all interns have. It's a big sacrifice in that one gives up a whole year to devote to taking care of patients. This cannot be an enjoyable experience.

As a result, interns began to redefine for themselves both the processes and outcome of their work according to the normative structure conveyed to them by their more experienced peers, as these two assessments respectively indicate:

JR WHITE:
Basically what I look for in an intern is someone who is efficient and fast and gets his job done quickly because that's what my goal is. I don't like having a lot of patients on my service, and the more efficient and fast the intern is the more I admire him.

INTERN TONY:
I think an intern is usually evaluated by how he gets his work done and mostly how conscientious he is in working. The evaluation of his knowledge is a secondary component, at least this year. If you can manage to get your patients organized and get the work that needs to be done, done—that's it.

What emerged were mechanisms allowing for sheer endurance that were antithetical to optimal relationships with patients.

While it has been found elsewhere that an antihumanistic orientation emerges among beginning physicians upon completion of medical school,[4] medical students were viewed almost unanimously by the house staff as more caring than house staff:

INTERN SMOTH:
I think the majority of house staff are limited in the amount of time they spend with patients by the amount of work they had [*sic*] to do. . . . I would like to spend more time with patients but I can't—unless I want to stay to midnight every night. . . . I think medical students at first tend to be more sympathetic [to patients than house staff].

INTERN GISER:
Medical students as a whole are much more idealistic than house officers. I suppose they have the time to be idealistic and get to know the patient in a way that an intern

can never do. . . . He can't sit down and talk over a problem and realize that behind this "gomer" [pejorative slang for a patient] is a depressed individual.

Furthermore, in describing this largely adverse orientation toward patients, many of the new interns were already justifying, if not exonerating, it:

INTERN JOVERS:
At my former hospital, house staff were so harassed, so bothered with doing rinky-dink stuff that they hardly had time or interest to care for their patients for the most part—just because the whole hospital was so impersonal.

INTERN SHU:
I would say on the average the attitude toward patients at [County Hospital] was fair and that's because it's a city hospital and you get lots of indigent people who don't take care of themselves, so it's difficult to be sympathetic with these people. . . . A lot of times one would see the house staff be abusive toward them or make fun of them.

The frustration and dissatisfaction were not to be reduced as the new interns became familiar with the SAMs environment, as this typical graduate of medical school at SAMs indicates:

INTERN LIGHT:
The general attitude [at SAMs] toward patients is probably appropriate for people who totally abuse their bodies . . . and if people [patients] get angry at you, it's natural to feel a little resentment toward them and a large part—80 percent—of the population is that way.

PEERS AS PRIMARY SOCIALIZERS

The tentative negative attitude toward patients among novice interns derives primarily from the house staff who taught them as medical students. They had spent the last two years of their clinical hands-on training principally in the company of, and being taught (hence socialized) by, interns and residents.[5] Their daily activities had generally been supervised by the house staff, not by attendings, who were usually not as accessible or available.

Almost all the new interns remembered those house staff supervisors as having had negative attitudes toward patients, sometimes worse ones than those encountered among the SAMs house staff:

INTERN FERST:
There's a much better attitude here at SAMs. I was a little surprised to hear how little "gomer" or "vet" or "dirtball" or other derogatory [patient] terms were used here. . . . You heard that all the time [where I went to medical school].

The extent of anticipatory socialization to a negative doctor–patient relationship was revealed in the theme of one of the SAMs senior medical school class annual shows (held during the time of this study). It was based on the best-selling satirical novel about internship, *The House of God* (Shem 1978). These senior skits were characterized by abusiveness toward patients that was couched in sardonic and sarcastic humor. No doubt these images were presented to the medical students by the SAMs house staff, since the intensity of feelings and experiences portrayed went beyond their own limited exposure to the SAMs system. Intern Cory provided an explanation for such an adverse medical student reaction to so many patients even before specialty training began:

> It's simple. They learn their views from disgruntled interns and residents. When they went out into the wards the first time, they didn't know anything about those patients. They were just human beings to them, flesh and blood, until they heard the house staff say, "Oh, here comes a gomer!" and they'll probably be like that when they're interns, too. You inherit the attitudes. They're all pervasive. (Field notes, VAH)

Because of the embattled position in which interns and (to a lesser extent) residents found themselves, the peer group emerged as the most important source of support and validation. As a result of the structural situation whereby interns and residents supplied the everyday nuts-and-bolts health care in the hospitals according to a rotational structure of services, the peer group became socially isolated from other groups in the hospitals. Thus it developed its own self-validating system of meanings that excluded those outside the house staff, including, to a large extent, attending faculty. Although interns and residents worked with other members of the health care team, the peer group became encapsulated so that its members came to view themselves as "special," "different" from other groups. They perceived their own behavior as occurring under such special circumstances that it could be evaluated only by those simultaneously undergoing the same experience. Hence they excluded and devalued evaluation by others, including the attending faculty members, who were formally accountable for the work of the house staff but who were socially and structurally distanced from them. (Bucher and Stelling 1977 also identify this phenomenon.)

As the first year became defined as one of endurance and survival, the house staff seemed to become increasingly alienated from more and more groups of people. They perceived themselves as unappreciated or misunderstood by ancillary staff, administration, attendings and other physicians, family, friends, and ultimately, patients. Withdrawal, even from significant others, was described on several occasions. For example, SR Mendel recalled the death of a patient that resulted from a fellow resident's negligence; the patient had been labeled pejoratively and subsequently avoided so that certain treatment had been omitted. In an attempt to exonerate his fellow house officer to some degree, Mendel blamed the patient and the system and then added:

We have all used those [slang] terms for patients. At home my wife thinks I'm a monster because I may talk about those problems. . . . But she doesn't realize all the reasons for it.

The house staff retreated into its own subculture, as SR Deren's comment indicates:

There is no way to describe the feeling of being an intern. Nobody at all is more hassled. You feel like the whole world is dumping on you all the time. You work very hard and every third night or every other night the entire year. And you develop a special bond with the people you experience that with.

Others likened it to indoctrination and to an almost total conversion experience—a baptism under fire.[6] It was the fellowship among the interns that allowed them personal relationships, validation, a sense of humor, and sharing of feelings. Senior Resident Filps summed it up:

I didn't anticipate doing as much "scut" and I didn't anticipate I would enjoy and appreciate the house staff as much as I did. . . . If it hadn't been for that, I would have left for sure.

Filps echoed the comments of other interns and residents that without such social support from the peer group, they would never have survived the internship. The new interns recognized this early on, as Intern Tony commented:

Residents are kind of your security. If you have any questions you can always ask them. It's fun to discuss cases with them . . . but attitudes toward patients—I don't learn that much from residents. I think they are hassled and patients are kind of ignored sometimes . . . but I think that's to be expected.

It is generally accepted that, the more involved members are in a group's activities, the more interdependent they are for job performance, the greater their exposure to the group's norms, and thus the greater their susceptibility to having their values and norms changed or reinforced (Hyman and Singer 1968). The peer group had its own world view, which was far removed from that of the attending faculty or outsiders, and it was forged out of the everyday shared experiences of its members. It had its own system of beliefs and normative structure to which members had to conform if they were to survive.

While it has been demonstrated that other novice professionals experience dissonance and alienation, which can lead to moral outrage, rejection, fatigue, and perceptual distortion (for example, nurses in the Schmalenberg and Kramer 1979 study or rehabilitation counselors in certain settings in Wiseman's 1970 study), those trainees in other disciplines appear to respond to their situations individually and in relative isolation. Physicians-in-training move into the work world with, and perceive themselves to be part of, a protective cohort.

DISCOUNTING OF FACULTY

It has been assumed in medical education that the faculty are the main social-izers of the interns and residents. Yet this was clearly not the case at SAMs, where their participation in the education and training of the house staff was limited for a variety of reasons. For one, faculty were much less involved in the day-to-day management of patients, a circumstance almost universally as-serted by the house staff, regardless of whether they thought it appropriate or not. Most faculty, furthermore, were viewed by the house staff as uninterested in patient care or as preoccupied with other interests. For example, according to JR Patty:

> You know the faculty attending comes by for just two hours. The attending has more patience because he doesn't have to deal with something at 3:00 in the morn-ing. . . . They are more distant from the actual patient care.

Junior Resident Jovers' reaction seems extreme, but nevertheless expresses the prevalent sentiment:

> Some of them [faculty] never really talk to the patients. All they do is write a note, and some of them don't even write notes. They just sign the intern's notes. . . . They are totally worthless to anybody.

Exceptions were made for the younger faculty, particularly those who had re-cently completed their training at SAMs or comparable institutions. House staff assumed that the younger attendings commiserated with, if they did not actually condone, house staff behavior.

Given the distance of the faculty from the house staff, it is not surprising that the house officers learned from each other. More often than not, attending faculty were not consulted about everyday decisions. Most deliberations, such as discussions of whom to "code" (resuscitate), were conducted when faculty were not present. Faculty were usually apprised after the fact of house staff decisions made mainly between the supervising and junior house staff.

Corroboration of this observation occurred when a new attending appar-ently violated this accepted norm and committed a breach of professional con-duct by chastizing a JR about the latter's decision not to "code" a patient. The gossip that ensued among the house staff demonstrated "the norm of noninter-ference." Upon overhearing some informal discussion between SRs and in-terns that same day, another attending told the group:

> I would have been furious if it was any of my residents, but to be honest, most attendings don't give a damn. [Attending] Stretch [the one who got upset] must be a new breed. (Field notes, PH)

When asked from whom he learned the most, SR Silverman replied:

31

I'll put house staff first. . . . The house staff know each other better than anybody else. We've seen each other in stressful and nonstressful situations. We try to generate definite frameworks and no attending has ever seen that. No attending is here at 3:00 a.m. watching me trying to work with somebody who's sick.

Another reason that house staff discounted the role of most attendings was that, overall, they did not believe many faculty were capable of teaching them general, acute, or critical patient management (which is what they were primarily there to learn). After two or three years of training, most house officers believed they knew as much if not more than most attendings except in the latter's specific areas of subspecialization. The following perceptions of two SRs were typical:

SR WALTERS:
[Acceptance by faculty professionally] . . . varies from attending to attending. I think if a lot of them were put in the position of dealing with the patients in GH now, they would be a lot more inept than the house staff, in my point of view. So I think we have their respect there. I think they couldn't switch roles with us.

SR LYNCH:
You realize that you know probably more about the day-to-day management of a patient in the hospital wards than do most of the faculty members, so you feel in that regard as though you have something to offer them. . . . And you feel as though you are teaching your faculty members something that they do not know.

This discounting of faculty input results not only from the encapsulated meaning system of the interns and residents but from a certain amount of resentment of the privileged status of the faculty. The faculty occupied a paradoxical position in relation to the house staff. They were peers, in that all were certified physicians. Yet, within the structure of social relations maintained in all medical schools, faculty had greater leisure, higher compensation, and superior status. Boundaries were erected between house staff and their privileged professional peers, and the faculty acquiesced to those boundaries by maintaining a distance between themselves and the house staff.[7]

For faculty to intervene would have meant taking time away from other matters, only to incur the resentment of many house staff, who, submerged in everyday pressures of long hours, scut work, and holding the line against disease, did not want faculty to second-guess them medically or morally. While house officers made individual exceptions, in terms of the collective impact, they viewed faculty as worlds apart from, if not above, them.

THE GROP PERSPECTIVE

The terms the internal medicine house staff used to describe their experience were those applicable to combat. They portrayed themselves, figuratively and literally, as doing battle. The patient, the embodiment of a recalcitrant and impenetrable system, many characterized as the ultimate enemy. Apathy about, if not antipathy toward, patients was expressed by most of the cohort completing the internship:

JR McGEE:

You start regarding them [patients] as the enemy and you really don't care. The patients who don't respect you . . . you write off because you haven't any time to invest energy in them if they are going to fight you. . . . In the beginning of the year a patient signs out AMA [against medical advice] and you're devastated. Toward the end of the year if the patient says he wants to leave, you go back to the room with the AMA form in your hand and say, "Here—off you go." That's one less patient you have to take care of.

JR EDWARDS:

You can't examine [obese patients]. You can't hear their heartbeat, you can't put an IV [intravenous line] in. . . . *They get you before you get them.* . . . *They just destroy you* and you don't even want to deal with them.[Emphasis added.]

They identified a series of offensive and defensive strategies in order to "win," with "victory" redefined as survival; that is, what they most hoped for was to complete training without being permanently wounded in the process. Battlefield metaphors abounded in their speech:

SR PAUL:

This is really a combat zone hospital. . . . Everything is on such a large scale that you always are fighting.

JR KOTS:

By the middle of your internship, you may be more conversant about trench warfare medicine. . . .

JR SING:

If attendings think I'm good because I present well on rounds. . . . It doesn't mean as much to me as a JR who has seen me working in the trenches nightly.

Their collective descriptions of patient-related encounters included such violent and aggressive terms as "hits," "crashing and burning," "under fire," "getting killed," "time bombs," "trainwrecks," "killers," "under the gun," "going down the tubes"—all of which connoted siegelike, assaultive circumstances. This overwhelmingly shared perspective on their training experience appeared to promote a style of behavior toward patients that was self-protective, distancing, and sometimes outwardly hostile. This view of the patient was defined as part of the necessary survival mechanisms of residency by JR Grotts:

[There are] thousands of negative experiences [here] . . . when you see shifts come and go and you haven't taken a shower, changed your clothes or gone to bed, and

33

you say, "What the fuck is this?" "What for?" You just wonder why you're sub-
jecting yourself . . . to so much distastefulness and misery . . . and the fact that
three-quarters [of the patients] don't fit the ideal image . . . it's clearly a negative
factor. I can't see how it would be a positive except insofar as you're allowed to disparage patients and objectify them and to care less about them as people as a result
of your hostility toward them. When you turn them into something other than human, you don't have to care about them. Slang terms for patients reflect the anger
and hostility that people feel about the situation—the cynicism. You see this "piece
of shit" in the middle of the night that you know has been here 50,000 times. . . .
It's going to be a waste of time and money and you think "*Get out of my* emergency
*r*oom, you gomer [a pejorative slang term for detested patients].[8]

The extensiveness of this view emerged immediately. Once the house
officers knew they were the subjects in my study, many referred me to the satirical novel *The House of God* (Shem 1978), a fictionalized account of internship training ostensibly occurring at a large urban teaching hospital in Boston,
which paints a bizarre and brutal picture of the world of the intern in a com-
edy-of-the-absurd style. To many house officers, it was not even an exaggerated account of the experience:

SR WALTERS:
That was one of the funniest, truest books I ever read. . . . I guess someone not in
medicine might think it was revolting. You could tell it was written by a doctor and
[there was] a lot of truth to it, especially the slogans, "the fat man's rules." With
most of your patients here you're either a veterinarian or a pediatrician in the way
you treat them.[9]

SR FABLE:
The House of God accurately depicts the internship experience. Anyone of us could
have written that book. It is fairly close. . . .

SR FILPS:
I wrote *The House of God*! . . . It's extremely accurate. I've passed it all around.

In *The House of God* the patients are the interns' nemesis and the bane of
their existence. Patients are abused, ridiculed, manipulated and feared. More
important, the book identifies a sense of profound disillusionment and despair
about the whole experience. The house staff at SAMs would not allow me to
avoid this interpretation,[10] as noted here:

SR PAUL:
There's a book that's just come out called *The Kingdom of God* [*sic*]. . . . It talks
about what it's like to be an intern in a "combat zone hospital." . . . From the ex-
cerpts I've read, it's just like the [SAMs] experience. They even use the same slang
terms for patients, like "gomer." . . . You should read it because you might understand a lot more of what's going on here.

The House of God became an important piece of datum because it verified the overall detachment and dehumanization resulting from the training process. It substantiated a world of contradictions wherein the patient was oppressed while being characterized as the oppressor.

Because house staff training in internal medicine at SAMs was perceived as extremely harrowing and frustrating, their mutually shared and supported goal and the organizing principle of their everyday life, regardless of service rotation or patient population, became, paradoxically, to *get rid of patients*: to GROP.

LEARNING TO GROP

The actual process of acquiring and perpetuating a GROP orientation occurred as part of the dynamic day-to-day interaction among house staff. An informal behavior system not only encouraged the GROP perspective but provided the norms for both its justification and, within limits, its implementation. There was active commiseration, reinforcement, and reassurance among the house staff for GROP behavior.

The GROP perspective was manifested in the house staff's private and shared perceptions; in its slang, jargon, and adages; in its articulated norms; in its preoccupation with its many variations; and at times, in its behavior and actions. The GROP perspective was an explicit and integral part of the house staff's everyday activity.[11] In evidence were all three modes of interaction—modeling, sanctioning, and symbolic structuring (Hadden and Long 1978)—reinforcing this attitude.

Every patient admitted to an intern and his or her team, or to the service, was characterized as a "hit." The number and types of hits seemed to be the major preoccupation of those house officers involved. A typical observation illustrates house staff attitudes:

> A good deal of informal conversation among the interns and residents had to do with whether or not they were going to get any "hits." Everyone commented they hoped the rain continued so there wouldn't be as many people coming into the ER and therefore not as many potential admissions. The slang term they used was "gomer repellent" weather. (Field notes, ER)

One new resident corroborated the collective sentiment:

> "When you're an intern, you always dread 'hits.' You dread them especially on 'on-call' nights. You can contrast that with surgical residents who want 'hits' because that means they can operate, but we don't." (Field notes, VAH)

Another beginning resident identified the especially negative tone set by the incessant use of "hit":

JR PATTY:
There's always an overtone of cynicism in any conversation you have [with your peers]. It's "I got this new 'hit.'" "You ought to see it." It's the "hit" not the patient; I got this "hit!"

The figure of speech "hit" for an admission is revealing of house staff attitudes. *Hit* is a verb that obviously connotes violence and recalls military air strikes and battles. The subcultural notion of a "hit" not only reduces the patient to an enemy but further reduces him or her to a piece of enemy material. Hits in battle refer to tanks, planes, ships, and so forth. Yet whereas in battle, hits are prized, in the hospital they are feared.

Another dimension of the term *hit* is found in black speech in the form of "hit on," meaning an aggressive form of social interaction in which the person who "hits on" another person is the initiator, as when a panhandler "hits on" a potential soft touch or when a person who delivers an insult to another "hits on" him. In a similar sense, patients can metaphorically "hit" back at staff: they create work; they can "crash and burn" or create other unforeseen problems.

Maintaining a light and, hence, manageable service was extolled. Those house staffers who could lessen and lighten their service by discharging or otherwise getting rid of patients were admired by their colleagues and were humorously labeled "dispo (for disposition) kings." The following is one of numerous examples of the GROP perspective being discussed.

Two female interns sought out Intern Cory in order to sign out to him for the evening. It was rather early in the afternoon, and they both joked about how early they were getting out on their day off. They both kidded Cory about the fact that women were better than men. . . . Intern Floss said, "I get them [patients] in and out fast, one door or the other" [meaning by death or discharge]. She laughed. (Field notes, GH)

In another instance there was a lot of kidding throughout rounds, with the term "dispo-ing" often used. Intern Charen, who apparently had a reputation for getting patients off the service, was admired and applauded. Junior Resident Johnson from time to time made a kicking motion with his feet in reference to getting the patients out. In the middle of those rounds, Intern Charen said to me:

"Boy, you can really see the changes that have occurred over this year, can't you? In the beginning we were bright-eyed and bushy-tailed, now we can't wait to get them [patients] out." (Field notes, GH)

In the following comment a JR identified the evaluative component for self and others in GROP action:

JR WHITE:
There's no great competition [here] but I think there is some. . . . I think it's manifested in the little things, such as how big is your service. You know, "I have fewer patients than you do; therefore, I've done a better job of getting rid of people."

This comment reveals an unspoken truth about the hierarchy of internal medicine: status within the profession is determined by distance from patients and the freedom to choose among them.

Certain times and circumstances were especially dreaded by house officers because they interfered with their ability to maintain control over patients: "getting killed the last day of the month," patients "going bad" just as they are ready to go home, a colleague's patient "crashing" when one is covering for him or her, or someone "burning" in the clinic. An example of the first:

There was a lengthy discussion on rounds about a patient who was admitted for impending dt's. At this point, JR Cap said, "We should spend no more than two minutes on this man, that's all" [meaning he was disgusted with him]. . . . JR Jovers commented to me, "It's the last day of the month. That's why he went into dt's. Catch my cynicism?" (Field notes, VAH)

An example of patients going "bad" occurred on a day spent with Intern Zorab on oncology. He told me when I joined him that two patients had "crashed":

"That was so bad, just when you're trying to get out." . . . Junior Resident Cape concurred: "It never fails, when you need or want to leave early, that's when things go bad. I had a woman patient when my family was expecting me, who went 'down the tubes' . . . and I didn't leave until late." (Field notes, VAH)

An example of the fourth circumstance was related to me by JR Sing:

Now there's a negative experience, the general medicine clinic. I dreaded that every other week. That would be the service I preferred the absolute least. . . . It often reaches the point where you sit there and hope nobody is sick, because if they're sick you don't know what you're going to do because you don't have time to deal with it. Your one goal is to get their prescriptions filled and get them out, so you can get back to your work.

This last comment illustrates the ultimate distortion of what the house staff is supposed to be doing for patients while learning medicine: they often dreaded sick patients, especially in the clinic setting.

JR PAUL:
[With regard to the clinic], we don't have enough time to see patients. We hope to God that when a patient comes in, he's not sick because that's going to blow the afternoon.

The process of shaping permissible GROP conduct began from the first day of exposure to patients on the wards as interns (and medical students) were continuously exposed to GROP-related discussions. In addition, they were often rebuked by senior colleagues if they manifested an anti-GROP orientation toward many types of patients, as in the following observation:

> In the Emergency Room, JR Weiss asked the medical student, "Why is that man still here?" referring to an elderly, somewhat disheveled, alcoholic-looking man. The medical student said, "I want to observe him. It's not too busy and he's not taking up any room." Weiss said in a rather loud and annoyed tone, "Get him out of here It's not his home. . . . We'll have 250 of 'them' sitting here if the word gets out." (Field notes, ER)

At the VAH the language and actions of the house staff were even less guarded, as in the following observations:

> Junior Resident Beach was annoyed because the nurses didn't move a patient around and he was getting bedsores. Every time a patient seemed ready to go, Beach made some elaborate gesture to the interns and medical students like waving his arms wildly, implying "get him out! Let's get going!" . . .
>
> Over lunch that same day there was a lot of discussion about a patient who was belligerent. Beach said, "I have no sympathy for him. If he wants to go AMA [against medical advice], I'll hand him the papers and show him the door." (Field notes, VAH)

In all ERs the behavior of most senior house staff with regard to GROP was also clearly evident. The structure and function of that service tended to support the GROP perspective, but the house staff's disdain for many of the patients who came into the ER exacerbated that orientation. Almost without exception, the SRs in charge set a tone of permissiveness with respect to the callous treatment of many patients seeking help:

> In the ER one day, SR Fable was observed commenting to Intern Kots, loudly enough for everyone to hear, "Let's get that fucker out of here!" referring to the same patient who had been called a "turkey" by someone else earlier. "Let's get moving. Why can't we get those winos out?" When someone told him they couldn't because he [the patient] was still wheezing, Fable told the interns, to their faces, "You're all slow as shit. Let's get moving!" (Field notes, ER)

The following exchange indicates the speed with which interns absorbed the continuously reinforced message. In this typical situation one can identify a variety of GROP criteria at work—social, disease, structural-technological, professional, and cultural—as well as the type of negotiations involved in the "GROP-ing" process (all discussed further in the following chapters).

> In an earlier discussion about the demented lady, SR Flips described her speech through imitation. She made a point of saying that the patient was not malicious and

kind of cute [social criterion]. Intern Kots offered to start the patient's IV. Senior Resident Fable caught Kots and said, "I wouldn't do that unless Intern Big could watch her constantly. You'll pump her full of fluids and she could go into [heart] failure" [structural-technological criterion]. Someone else said, "So we'll send her to the ICU Unit," and SR Winn responded, "No way, no way would the Unit [house staff] take her" [demographic and disease criteria]. . . . There were further comments about the few patients with interesting diseases [professional criterion] and the fact that beds weren't opening up [structural criterion] so they had to keep patients out of the hospital. (Field notes, ER)

Finally, a major incident occurred during the year that demonstrated the collective house staff defense of GROP behavior when it was evidenced by one of them. It became known as "Walter's Affair," and the scenario was played out as follows:

Senior Resident Walters had sent a patient out of the VAH ER. He told the patient that he did not need to be in the hospital for his symptoms and that he did not need an ambulance to drive him home since he came in a car. Walters told his peers:

> The next thing I knew both the VA police and the city police were involved, for the patient's wife was a reporter from the [local newspaper]. I'm waiting for a call from the department chairman. . . . I don't care how they [patients] get out of the ER—by magic carpet, by Concorde jet—as long as they get out of my emergency room!" There was much laughter and sympathy from the group about his plight with the gomer! (Field notes, VAH)

The next day, an article appeared in the local paper condemning the VAH for prohibiting a patient from being admitted. For many weeks afterward there were informal discussions similar to the following:

> Fellow Batt (who was an SR the year before) said to his colleagues during lunch, "It's all a bunch of crap. They're all alcoholics [at the VAH]." Junior Resident Zimmerman said, "If the public knew what comes through that door, rather than complaining about someone's not getting admitted, they'd holler bloody murder at the waste!" . . . Intern Kots concurred angrily, "The VA's are the same all over. I had a month's experience as a medical student at the VA [in another city]." (Field notes, VAH).

The Walters Affair was just one critical incident highlighting the prevalence of GROP action. Moreover, it was clear that most faculty and the administration neither sought actively to prevent GROP action nor openly criticized it when it was expressed, which constitutes yet more evidence that the house staff culture was structurally self-contained, operating at some social distance from the formal authority figures and the larger socializing environment.

Further, in what seemed like attempts to demonstrate conviviality, faculty on occasion supported the GROP norm more overtly, as illustrated by these observations:

The next patient discussed was identified as a demented patient. Junior Resident Levitt colorfully described how he found the patient wandering around outside the hospital. . . . He proceeded to bring the patient upstairs, dressed in his pajamas, apparently wandering around waiting for the bus. Jokingly, Attending Baumgarten said, "You should have let him go." (Field notes, GH)

Intern Sully mentioned that she was talking to neurology about "turfing" a patient. Attending Zietz asked for a brief explanation. There was laughter and the comment that "turfing means getting rid of a patient by transfer. It refers to a phrase from the *House of God*." Sully's comment on "turfing" led Attending Zietz to tell a story of how when he was an intern on this service he got it down from twenty-three to one patient, which he said, with pride, was a record. (Field notes, VAH)

JUSTIFYING GROP ACTION

The key to such a seemingly counterproductive perspective lay *not* in the normative structure of the profession, where such behavior would ideally be classed as deviant (but may in reality be the norm), but in the structure of social relationships. The interns and residents were used in the hospital system as sources of easily exploitable labor, and they were aware of that fact:

FAMILY PRACTICE INTERN DANET:
I think that perhaps the hours that we do have to work, you know, when you're so tired that you really can't think straight, they say, well, that's when you learn because in situations you'll get to the point where you don't have to think, you'll just react. You make mistakes, too, when you're tired. I'm not sure it has to be every third night. I mean, we're cheap labor, let's face it. I mean, we're not even making minimum wage, so they've got a good thing going.

Their human needs were largely disregarded in the allocation of work and responsibility. As they saw it, there was little they could do but accept their burden, especially since they expected endurance to bring them such compensatory gains as the acceptance, power, esteem—and ultimately, material benefits and status—that accrue to the medical doctor. Thus, overall the house staff seemed to suffer from an acute form of the disease of the middle class, status inconsistency (Stub 1972). They were in a political structure in which they were powerless to change the conditions of their labor. Feeling exploited, they often projected their perceived dehumanization on the only group who was less powerful—the patients—especially when those patients were members of a stigmatized social category: poor, black, derelict, drug addicted, alcoholic, street dwelling, and so forth. The remarks of Intern Smats, who came from another large urban medical school, reflect the pervasiveness of this reinforced behavior beyond the SAMs environment:

There's something that goes on with house staff. They get desensitized or disillusioned. Yet they can't deviate from it because pressures are so great they can't quit. But they are frustrated—people die, no good facilities, the amount of work—it's efficient not to get involved. . . . You could ignore the emotional things if you have a group of peers that accept that sort of thing and joke about the alcoholic patient at his bedside. It's insulting to the patient and therefore to the physician who's taking care of him. But it's a city teaching hospital and it's accepted.

While social distance (Kadushin 1962) certainly encouraged GROP behavior, it is not sufficient to explain it. The house staff attitude toward middle class patients, and more important, their observed behavior in the PH, indicate that the GROP dynamic was fundamental to house staff–patient relations regardless of the social condition of the patient.

CONCLUSION

"Gomers," "hits," "trainwrecks," "turkeys," "scumbags," "dirtbags," "crocks," "garbage," "junk," "SHPOs" (*s*ub *h*uman *p*ieces *o*f *s*hit) were terms repeatedly used to characterize patients, at times within an earshot of the patient. The pejorative attitudes reflected in these terms result in a distortion of the presumed professional goals of physician socialization. Although I observed that some attending faculty and an occasional chief or senior resident attempted to communicate concern for certain patients by work or example, most house officers viewed these colleagues as an exception to the norm and also made it plain to me that within the house staff community the paramount norm was peer allegiance. This often meant giving patients short shrift because the peer culture supported such skills as "GROPing," "turfing" (guarding your territory against the incursion of new patients), and "dumping" (finding a reason to get a patient assigned to another service). The peer culture valued this GROP orientation because it allowed for the release of pent-up anger and hostility, served to intimidate abusive patients, and conferred upon those who GROPed skillfully a certain amount of status and esteem from peers. The immediate outcome of this socialization experience was adverse consequences for many of the physicians and patients under their care.

Despite the prevalence of the GROP orientation in everyday interaction, certain structural, professional, and normative conditions at times precluded action on that basis. These restraints, rather than weakening GROP orientation, simply produced tension and, at times, conflict. Difficulties in determining how, why, and when to GROP affected house staff behavior toward colleagues as well as toward patients. House officers learned they had to be simultaneously compulsive and efficient. Fear of making mistakes as to when they could and could not GROP was omnipresent, as the following chapters show.

The complex dynamics of the GROP process do not, however, negate the salience of the principle around which house staff organized its work and its culture; that is, when an anti-GROP perspective appeared, it was generally because there were social forces at work that house staff could not resist. In fact one cannot discount the possibility that this pervasive GROP orientation occurred precisely because the house staff knew they could not GROP most patients. Perhaps the inevitability of a continuous inundation of patients left them collectively free to articulate a norm that if carried out in the extreme would, of course, be detrimental to their own personal goals: learning to be competent internists.

Within the mutually shared, supported, and reinforced house staff GROP perspective, there were, of course, individual differences in degree of hostility and alienation and in how strategies were applied. These differences seemed to be based in part on the level of training and also on individual expectations about and actual experiences with training. Hence, socialization ultimately was a result of interaction between the individual and the social environment.

Chapter 3

GROP Dynamics
Structural, Professional, and Normative Factors

The structural, professional, and normative variables simultaneously propelling and restraining GROP action create a series of antinomies that surround the house staff's everyday activity and interaction. It is in adjusting to these conflicts that house staff refine their ability to GROP. In analyzing *why* the house staff adopts a GROP orientation, both external conditions and organizational context of the socializing environment provide explanations. Working conditions, administrative and policy mandates, the ramifications of new technology, and the priorities of internal medicine as implemented in a public urban medical center all contribute to the shaping of the GROP initiative.

STRUCTURAL LIMITATIONS

Patient Overload in the Public Hospital

The most fundamental structural limitation on health care delivery in public institutions is the magnitude of the work load that confronts the house staff, which is regarded as a source of cheap and easily exploitable labor. Their tradeoff for undergoing the frustration consequent to their work load during internship and residency is education and certification. Within the house staff culture, this tradeoff is expressed as the "scut/skill" ratio.

The problems at GH are typical of this type of public facility (Dowling 1982; J. Roth 1970; Sudnow 1967). House staff continuously complained about—and came to resent—the pressures created by the need to take care of too many patients at once in what they asserted were antiquated facilities with

43

inadequate ancillary staff and insufficient supporting services. Almost universally they complained about administrative and environmental obstacles to rendering patient care that always frustrated and at times angered or depressed them. The term *scut work* is collectively defined as activities or tasks that, in the trainees' judgment, do not contribute to their education as physicians. It is a dynamic term, varying to some degree in relation to level of training and personality. In public hospitals the amount of scut work encountered seemed to reach a tipping point; that is, at some time during internship the cumulative effect of the overwork and attendant frustrations eventually distorts the perspective of physicians-in-training and skews their sense of purpose. The heavy patient load and scut work cut into the time to learn about the things that they think are important. Disillusionment can set in, helping to justify the GROP perspective.

Many house officers were quite outspoken about the negative repercussions of work conditions on themselves and their patients. Several described as repugnant the training and service environment, in the vein of SR Mahoney:

> The usual problems with a big city hospital [are here], which is a lack of ancillary services, pains in the neck with the lab, and stuff like that . . . and the nursing service in GH, making incredible errors, not telling the doctor what was going on with a patient when something was going on. . . . I'd get so "p.o.'d" all the time. I don't think you could function as effectively . . . if you're walking around seething all the time, and I was steaming as an intern. It's improved now. I don't think there are nearly as many complaints now.

The change for the better described by that SR was, however, contradicted by similar complaints from other house officers at all levels. Therefore, it may be inferred that the structural conditions negatively affecting the operation of public hospitals remain constant and perennial, especially when contrasted with the private sector,[1] as SR Jones, who became a chief resident, noted:

> It's impossible just about [to do your job as an intern] because of the way radiology is run, the way everything is run. There are always high obstacles to everything. Being a public institution as SAMs is, the people that work here are just not the best people. I think it's the caliber of people you hire, number one, and the amount you pay them, and the system itself is just that once it's set into motion it's hard to get out of. It's totally different when you work at a private hospital and you see how friendly everyone is . . . being a physician here, you're no different than a person who sweeps the floor at SAMs. You rate no more with most of the people. Half of them make the same salary as I did as an intern. If you call a lab tech to do something, they say, "I don't want to do that, I don't have to do that," and you have no authority to tell them what to do.

This perceived status of the house staff in the authority hierarchy was explicitly mentioned by several others as well ("In terms of power, the interns are at the very bottom," SR Curren told me), and naturally resented.

Some house officers perceive a measure of compensation for the working conditions in the autonomy they are granted and the amount and types of pathology they see. For example, in the view of ending SR Paul, who became a chief resident one month later:

> Everything is on such a large scale [at SAMs] that you're always fighting with the labs. Labs are overworked and the staff is underpaid and the nursing care isn't what it should be. It's just the fact that this is a public institution that inhibits you from giving good care because there just isn't enough money, and I think the doctor is the most expendable person in the whole system, and we end up doing all the odds and ends that aren't covered by nursing or the labs or transport. We spend a lot of time doing "scut." It would be a lot different in a private institution or in a place like I came from, which was wealthy. . . . *The taking part* is that we see things here that we wouldn't see in any other setting and we're given responsibilities here that we wouldn't be given anywhere else [emphasis added].

Junior Resident Grots articulated the overwhelming house staff sentiment:

> SAMs is one of the harder internships, but it's by no means the hardest. There are some that are certainly worse and I'm sure many are better. I wouldn't want to indict SAMs without indicating the system that it is part of. You know, because certainly it reflects the national situation in terms of municipal hospital house staff training, and the thing is that you trade off, because when you do an internship in a private hospital, you have attendings breathing down your neck all the time and you really can't manage patients independently. As a result you can't take risks and you can't make mistakes and you can't learn the same way. And so in choosing a house staff-run program, you choose to take on a lot more bullshit than you might.

In addition to being on the bottom rung of the status structure in the hospital, house staff in public hospitals are working at the termination point of a two-tiered system of American health care, so the patients they receive have been rejected or released from other sectors of the system. The public system traditionally has served poor people and is generally recognized as underfinanced, overcrowded, and understaffed with personnel who are underpaid and who work under suboptimal conditions. Further, the public sector (which includes city, state, and federally sponsored medical facilities) is often a victim of policies and practices that permit private health care providers (practitioners and institutions) to choose their patients and to establish fees unencumbered by any effective regulation.[2] The private system selects, with some exceptions, only those who can pay. This biases them against the most elderly, poor, and to a large extent, racial minorities. Historically, permission has been granted to private institutions and physicians to exclude patients, either initially or at some point during the treatment process. As a result, public hospitals and clinics traditionally have been inundated with patients who, for a variety of reasons, are unwanted elsewhere. According to house staff, these private community providers (doctors, hospitals, nursing homes, etc.) continuously "dump" their undesirable patients on the public facilities, and it is the internal medicine services within the public system that receive most of those "rejects":

SR MAHONEY:
I think [internal] medicine is the dumping ground. I think that more services dump on medicine than anywhere else. Medicine doesn't really have any place to go. You can't send [many patients] home. . . . They're going to have to go to a nursing home but you can't pop them into a nursing home. So we call it a "dump admit" and it's very uninteresting.

There is an ironic aspect to house staff's observations on the behavior of other institutions and medical specialties. Because of their position of responsibility for patient care in the public system, they were experiencing the consequences of GROP behavior by outside institutions or physicians. This precipitated intense feelings of resentment and frustration, causing house staff in the public facility to disparage not only the patients themselves but the providers of private health care for their neglect or abuse of patients. Collectively, they recognized that these public institutions (SAMs and the VAH) were viewed as institutions of last resort, or they characterized them, "dumping grounds."

One manifestation of the way in which this institutionalized relationship of inequality between public and private medical systems (Milner 1981) affected the house staff was the presence of an official referral book in the ER at the VAH that was actually entitled *Dump Admits*. The house staff regarded dumping as an abuse of the system, a waste of money and time, and they were appalled at its extent. For example, SR Miney recalled:

I guess the thing that irked me the most since I've been in this program happened on a few occasions at the ER at the VAH: getting calls from outside physicians about patients they were sending in that we would deem inappropriate and the patient would show up two hours later. It happened personally to me on two or three occasions.

House staff expressed vehement anger at the VAH system precisely because it required the admission of most patients, many of whom in its judgment should not have been hospitalized. The VAH, by and large, would not turn away eligible patients, and since the house staff could not usually from the VAH system to anywhere, they were especially resentful:

SR ROGERS:
At the VAH there is such a waste of money that it's phenomenal. They [patients] get their medication free. At the VAH they get good follow-up, probably the best medical care in the country, plus there are extras, like they get travel pay. It's ridiculous when you are paying them to come to the clinic. There are far too many people out there on disability that aren't disabled. And I think that there is a tremendous waste.

They come in the emergency office and just give the physicians verbal and physical abuse because they are so demanding. They think they should get everything handed to them on a silver platter. . . . You order a lot of tests. *You* learn from every patient, but it's such a waste . . . [emphasis added]. The average length of stay at the VAH is fourteen days, where at SAMs it's probably five to seven.

The pace at the VAH did compensate, however, for the perceived wastefulness. Also, when at SAMs, the house staff could transfer ("dump" or "turf" in their vernacular) those undesirable patients who met VA eligibility to the VAH.

A second, related structural limitation is the neglect of preventive, primary care, and rehabilitative services at the neighborhood level in favor of centralized, institutionally based medical centers with their emphasis on high technology, research, and complex illnesses. The resulting gaps in services place additional strain on already crowded public and tertiary-care institutions. For the poor, the socially diseased, and many old people, the port of entry—the ER—has become, by default, the substitute physician's office, as described by this family practice intern:

The routine ER is always absolutely swamped with patients. It's basically an outpatient clinic, and you can see as many as seventy patients a day during the eleven hours you're there. And you're trying to work on three or four different patients at one time and there's this whole row of patients sitting in front of you . . . getting more and more angry. . . . You know by the time you see them they're going to be out of sorts and you're not feeling so hot yourself. So it doesn't make for a good doctor–patient relationship.

While some house officers did demonstrate sympathy, on a selective basis, for the wretched lives or circumstances of some of their patients, many showed hostility toward families they considered to have abdicated their familial responsibility by placing unwanted relatives in the public system. House staff often referred to this behavior as "social dumping" and identified as "social admissions" those patients for whom they were then forced to care. The typical reaction was to blame the families, often without sufficiently recognizing the relation between the families' behavior and structural barriers to alternative courses of action. House staff rarely placed individual private behavior in a larger systemic context that might reveal a lack of the financial or social supports that make it possible to keep relatives (or themselves) at home, as these typical comments reveal:

JR PATTY:
You feel pressure at the VAH because it functions as a social institution. You know, "Take my father. I can't take him anymore." A lot of pressure to admit patients who have social problems. . . . [You] try to control the rage that you feel about the demands being made. It makes me very angry to see families dump their loved ones. A

lot of times I'm not very sympathetic. . . . I don't explore it. I'm learning to handle it by controlling my anger and trying to get them to contact social workers.

JR ZIMMERMAN:
Another major frustration was the fact—I think it's inherent in the system—that the intern and the people essentially in the hospital are getting dumped on constantly with disposition problems more than acute medical problems. The patient is brought in by the families who don't want to take care of him any longer. . . . And we're stuck as social workers as much as doctors. . . . I don't think it's my place to always find a nursing home placement. . . . I think that should be more their [the family's] role.

The house staff did need many of these referrals, of course, to learn about pathology and for exposure to a variety of disease processes. Like most workers, however, they wished to have more choice in their assigned work.[3] Predictably, the patient overload in public hospitals spills over into the organization of work. In the immediacy of house staff reality, it was experienced as a chronic bed shortage.

Shortage of Beds

Among the most important structural features giving impetus to the desire to GROP was the lack of available beds. The enormous volume of sick patients needing admission contributed to a critically high bed census. This created additional pressure both to GROP and to prevent patients from being admitted in the first place. The issue of beds was the major preoccupation of those house staff involved in admitting and receiving patients.

There were numerous times during the year when the bed shortage became the critical theme of the day in the ER:

Junior Resident Archer examined a man with a knee problem. He and JR Lovell considered admitting him. They tried to suggest ways that she could get him admitted to other floors since the bed situation in both GH and PH was terrible. Somebody commented that they felt like "bed administrators." (Field notes, ER)

On another occasion:

Intern Berg, after examining a patient, deliberated further with a medical student and said, "This is a 'family dump.' There are no changes in him except for hydration." Junior Resident Olat came down from GH to consult with Intern Berg. She was very exasperated by the lack of beds and tried for at least fifteen minutes or more to ascertain where there were empty beds. (Field notes, ER)

The house staff viewed their ability to change the conditions of their work as very limited. Given these systemic barriers to the delivery of high-quality medical service during training, they asserted that they had no choice but to treat patients as objects and to get rid of them as quickly as possible in order to survive:

CHIEF RESIDENT NOLAND:
There's always a push to get the patients out . . . particularly now with the bed problem. That's the problem, the lack of beds for the number of patients we're serving. [As a result] . . . I think people [house staff] have had conflicts when they send patients out early.

Feeling abused and neglected, many house officers appeared to become demoralized and adopt the perspective "If no one else cares, why should we?":

JR SAUL:
You're on every other night or every third night without good ancillary help and [they're] treating someone who has his doctorate like he's shit. People vomit on you and abuse you and you get no sleep and yet you're supposed to think of their [patients'] needs, but nobody ever thinks of yours; nobody ever does during internship.

Their demoralization seemed to become incorporated into a hardened attitude toward patients that caused house staff automatically to calculate the disposition of cases in terms of where patients could be sent.

Traditional Limitations on the Placement of Patients

Cost, social, and structural factors affected not only whether a patient was admitted but to which service within the hospital system. House officers quickly learned from each other to identify patients as "general," "private," or "VA" types, and for the most part they were supported when they channeled a patient so labeled away from their service to another more "appropriate" one. They were extremely conscious of race and class factors traditionally associated with each facility. These SAMs traditions supported house staff designations of patients as belonging in the various facilities and allowed them some measure of discretion in deciding which patients they would take themselves and where they would route the others. To illustrate:

Senior Resident Ari was observed telling SR Farmer about a patient who was "the GH type" who was coming. . . . It was the second time the term GH *type* was used in a single day, and it was clearly a euphemism for black. (Field notes, ER)

Historical precedent permitted the house staff to justify selected GROP action. *De jure* segregation by race had existed at SAMs until 1964, and *de facto* discrimination still existed. General Hospital, which was once exclusively for black patients, was still known as "the black hospital" as well as the "poor people's hospital." Private Hospital, which was once an all-white community hospital, was still known that way and was also labeled middle class. A clinic administrator told me early on that many patients, even lower-class white ones, would rather die or wait in the wings for a bed to open up in PH than go to GH.

Faculty seemed to concur in patient-tracking distinctions based on social and financial circumstances. Race and class influenced not only the incidence of "dumping" but the facilities into which patients could be "dumped." The "black hospital" was considered out of bounds for most white patients even though the "white hospital" might be filled to capacity while the "black hospital" had extra beds. Veterans, generally from the lower half of the population in socioeconomic terms, were routinely dumped in the VAH.

Cost-Containment Policies

Because of the ever-increasing cost of hospital care and the documented inability of the medical profession and hospital associations to regulate themselves, the federal government in recent years has mandated a variety of policies and procedures for any hospital receiving Medicaid, Medicare, and other federal funds. All parties—hospital administrators, professional utilization review teams, attending physicians, and ultimately, the house staff—must justify the appropriateness and length of hospital stay for most patients (Kotelchuck 1984; Vladeck 1984). Thus, administrative pressure to GROP—to resist patient admission and propel discharge—is an additional structural factor. The importance of cost is emphasized constantly in patient care, and the house staff is goaded to speed up work. The following comments demonstrate the kind of pressure the house staff is under:

INTERN BLUM:
A lot of things that you do in the hospital, you try to speed up hospitalization, not because you want to get them out but because everyone has been made aware of the cost factor in hospitalization. Don't spend a lot of time. Try to schedule tests as closely as possible. Treat them quickly; start them on drugs right away so that they can be stabilized and gotten out. . . . When I was a medical student, a lot of things had to do with the attendings pushing for it because they were pushed on by medical review or hospitalization utilization review committees.

JR JOVERS:
Really the only thing that's taught in internship is efficiency and getting things done the quickest way and hopefully the best way possible. But the quickest is more important. . . . *How fast you can get the patient out of the hospital* [emphasis added]. It's prized by the intern, the resident, the attending and Blue Cross and Blue Shield. And especially Medicaid. They nag you from the day the patient comes in to the day the patient goes out.

Patients draw resources from a finite budget that does not readily expand or contract in relation to demand, which is invariably too high. Because of the tremendous expense of health care (partly the result of increasing technological sophistication) and the finite resources, the house staff is under continual pressure to get the patients out as quickly as possible:

SR SILVERMAN:
I think the skills most valued by the faculty are . . . how well you can keep your service in line, how well you can get people in and out and worked up, and how well you can keep your charts . . . so they can sign them and write notes in them. . . . And if you want to use a scapegoat, blame Blue Cross and Blue Shield. . . . Here the attending is forced to see every single patient, and it's ridiculous to discuss four or five patients and have the house staff learn anything from them. So the resident and the attending physician end up being administrative tools of the system.

Silverman's comments emphasize the administrative limitations (Mauksch 1973) on the current delivery of health care. In discussing this complicating organizational impact on the GROP orientation, he focused on the structurally ambiguous status of house officers, who not only provide medical care but are also students learning in a teaching hospital. Hence, faculty review practices also affected the impetus to GROP.

Faculty Review Policies

For the last several years attending faculty have been required to write a daily note on each Medicaid and Medicare patient's chart, in addition to examining all new patients personally and reviewing and signing discharge orders as well. While faculty are obviously not as heavily pressured to GROP as are house staff—in that they do not have the day-to-day management responsibility—they must share in the administrative, if not direct supervisory, responsibility for admission and discharge. Therefore, as a result of this forced involvement, it seems evident that it is in the attendings' self-interest to have fewer patients admitted to their teams and to discharge patients as quickly as possible: the fewer the patients, the less work for them and the lower the possibility of iatrogenesis (see the next section).

These regulations brought organizational changes that were viewed differently by attendings and house staff. One chief resident was ambivalent in his assessment of the effects of these new administrative procedures:

CHIEF RESIDENT LOMBARD:
We've [the department of medicine] tried to structure it so that the attendings do have a fair amount of input into patient care, such that they are not there as symbols or people to ask questions of or people who come by once a day and teach the students and residents something that doesn't have anything to do with the case. Legally now Medicare requires that the attending write notes on the chart. I think it's good that they have to look at the charts every day. I think it forces the attending to

come by and know about each patient every day and they [the attending] will be involved in the day-to-day care of the patient. . . . [However,] this business of having to write long, detailed notes is a waste of time.

While the house staff recognized that faculty implemented patient management responsibilities with varying degrees of interest and efficiency, many house officers still questioned the appropriateness of this regulation. Most house staff reacted more strongly than this chief resident and discounted the overall importance of that aspect of the attending's role, viewing it as a duplication of effort and as contributing little to the improvement of patient care, as illustrated by the more typical views of this JR:

JR TONY:
In general the attendings rarely know the patient at all. It's the intern or resident who do [*sic*] the best. Personally I think the attendings are a little bit peeved that they have to write these notes every day and write an admission history and physical . . . instead of just cosigning the intern's or resident's forms. That's just not necessary. It's the law, I guess, or regulation. Some people [attendings] just write their notes and paraphrase what you've [the house staff] said about them. I don't blame them.

House staff also disliked direct faculty input because it could potentially limit their overall autonomy; more specifically, it could affect their ability to GROP.

Technology and Iatrogenesis

Much has been written about the impact of high-technology medicine on the organization and delivery of health care (Ehrenreich and Ehrenreich 1970; Howard and Strauss 1975; Waitzkin 1983) and on the narrow career subspecialization that is the current outcome of physician training (Duff 1975; Petersorf 1976; R. Strauss 1978). Technological developments have had as well a profound impact on the training of internists. The many advances in the detection and treatment of acute diseases as well as chronic and degenerative disorders have had their own side effects, which have affected the structure and outcome of house staff training. When medical technology is applied to the age and type of patient population seen by internists, it can and often does create serious risks for the patients. Therefore, these often invasive medical interventions contribute to an increasing fear of iatrogenesis (diseases or problems caused by physicians or the medical system).[4]

From the very first attending rounds I witnessed on the first day of the new academic year, I observed the concern about iatrogenesis:

Attending Baumgarten, in response to discussion of a patient, said, "She probably has 'Hospitalitis'" [a nonscientific term for the ill effects of hospitalization]. Apparently they had done some damage to the patient. Attending Baumgarten asked, "Who's going to pay for it?" . . . He finally commented, . . . "It really isn't clear why she's in the hospital. What are we going to do? *If we're lucky, we won't do her much harm!"* [emphasis added]. (Field notes, GH)

By the end of my first month of observing, I was surprised by the large number of potential iatrogenic illnesses and by the preoccupation of house staff and attendings with them. The longer a patient stayed in the hospital, the greater the possibility of something going wrong, either naturally in the course of a disease or from interventions—a drug therapy; procedures such as spinal taps, catheterizations, and lumbar punctures; or laboratory tests—all of which were extensive. I noted then that this seemed to be one reason why there was a lot of joking about getting patients out quickly. The house staff was afraid of iatrogenesis.

Fear of iatrogenesis was evident in many of the formal presentations—on residents' rounds, grand rounds, and attending rounds—and explicitly communicated in informal settings as well. The theme was continuously being articulated in both serious and humorous veins. The fear of things going wrong permeated everyday existence and seemed to influence significantly the entire house staff perspective on patient care so that the very purpose of hospitalization sometimes seemed to be undermined. For example:

> A ninety-four-year-old patient was referred by a nursing home. The case was discussed on task rounds. Junior Resident Patty said, "He can stay here as long as he's afebrile [without fever]. Otherwise get him out of here." (Field notes, VAH)

A similar instance occurred with a patient in renal failure:

> Junior Resident Edwards said to the team on rounds, "He shouldn't be on our service, and it's not clear why he's with us." . . . Edward finally concluded after some discussion, "Let's get him out of here before he gets sick!" (Field notes, VAH)

A paradox was thus manifested by house staff and attendings alike: a patient would be cared for if well, but dumped if ill.

Jargon was commonplace about patients who were "crashing and burning" or "going-down-hill" or who were "time bombs" and about house staff who were "getting killed" or "getting bombed" when their patients "went sour." The reality was that patients often worsened or did suddenly die. House staff fears were rooted in their collective experiences. For example:

> Senior Resident White recalled, "I had a patient who 'crashed' [died] unexpectedly during my internship. I've been afraid of that disease ever since." (Field notes, ICU)

Another time:

> Junior Resident Cape shook his head and said to me spontaneously, "I always greatly fear a young person who's admitted to the floor from the ICU. They're always so dangerous." (Field notes, PH)

These fears have two components. First, doctors do make direct mistakes of commission, for example, by prescribing the wrong dose of a drug, perforating a nerve during a spinal tap, or overdiuresing a patient by giving a high volume of fluids too quickly (Mizrahi 1984a). Second, during the routine course of hospitalization, problems arise for which staff are formally responsible but over which they often have little control. For example, nurses can give the wrong dosage of a prescribed drug; IVs can run out, resulting in hemotomas; decubitus ulcers appear because patients are too infrequently rotated; infections are contracted and spread. The longer the hospitalization period and the more comprehensive the diagnostic and therapeutic measures prescribed, the greater the chance that expected problems and unanticipated calamities may appear, a fact about which the attending faculty continuously cautioned the house staff. One case in point was an alcoholic patient with a complicated problem:

> Attending Carl asked, "Is he a vet? It sounds like it." There was an affirmative nod. Carl smiled at the apparent meaning: "We might be able to transfer him." There was some discussion of the fact that he had been "tapped" (given a spinal tap) and it was a "traumatic tap" (meaning iatrogenic) because of the way the needle went in. . . . Carl made the comment, "This is a time-consuming patient who should really be elsewhere, not in the ICU. . . . He could 'go bad' at any time." (Field notes, ICU)

Knowing when a patient is "really" sick is an essential competency of the house staff. It is defined as acquiring enough medical judgment to predict whether a patient is going to worsen or die and to be able to establish priorities for care accordingly. Most of the house staff believed that they would learn this most critical skill within the three years of training, but meanwhile they lived in some degree of fear of patients taking an unexpected turn for the worse:

> Junior Resident Zimmerman signed out on the telephone to another JR, who was covering for him. He gave him status reports on his patients and said about one of them: "He may crash. He's set up for something to go wrong." (Field notes, VAH)

The circumstances in the ER and ICU were especially stressful for the house staff. On countless occasions I witnessed interactions like this one between senior and junior house staff that showed the perpetual tension:

> With regard to a patient who had had a heart attack, SR Filps told SR Roger and Intern Gary, who came down from the ICU, "He's making me nervous." Later on she told the RN, "He's a 'hot potato.'" (Field notes, ER)

Hence the fear (and actuality) of doing harm, so contradictory to a basic tenet of the profession, helps shape the GROP perspective. Not only does increasing technology mean more work for the house staff with each patient admitted, but the outcome of that heavy work load can be detrimental to the health of many patients.

There were also times when the house officers, even the interns, found themselves conflicted about their GROP perspective when their own learning needs were introduced into the equation. The need to acquire technical as well as analytical skills can, it appears, mitigate the GROP perspective. The acquisition of skill in the performance of procedures (or in the analysis of the results of tests performed by others) is promoted by peers and mentors. Unlike surgeons, however, who always need patients in order to gain experience and perfect their craft, internists have less impetus to acquire patients *solely* for the purposes of practicing these technical skills since they themselves assign them a lower priority than medical knowledge and clinical judgment, which, with the constant inundation of patients, they had ample opportunity to practice:

SR KOTS:
If you ask the interns they might [at first] place a higher value on [technical things], but by the time you've done all these things so many times it's sort of devalued by the time you get to the end. You're not impressed that someone can put in a Swan-Ganz catheter because it's pretty easy once you've seen it and done it yourself. What I value most highly is the person who can figure out a complicated problem . . . just the good puzzle-putter-togethers. I think we probably value that more than anything else.

Interns were clearly the most conflicted group. They desperately wanted to GROP while at the same time they wanted to acquire all the necessary patient management skills, which included learning diagnostic and therapeutic procedures. Because interns also bore the brunt of coordinating and implementing the decisions of many other physicians, however, they often wanted to do less for the patient. Ultimately, to the interns, there seemed to be "no such thing as an interesting patient." In their eyes, it was the residents and occasionally the attendings who had the luxury of sharpening their intellectual prowess and clinical acumen. Hence, position in the medical hierarchy helped shape the perspective of when and whom to GROP, but not in one uncontradicted direction.

While the need to learn how to do procedures can mitigate the overriding tendency to GROP, the impact of educational concerns depends on several additional variables. The first is the amount of experience of the house officer. The second is the definitiveness of the indication for the procedure. The third is the assessment of the social status of the patient (see Chapter Four). The second variable is very elastic. Among the guiding principles in internal medicine are that there are no absolutes and that each case is different (Bucher and Stelling 1977; Freidson 1970b; Miller 1970). House staff thus had the ability to expand or contract guidelines and parameters for tests. Doing or not doing a procedure was open to negotiation and justification. (Scully [1977] also discovered the same principle in operation among obstetric/gynecologic residents with respect to acquiring skills). For example:

> During the course of a lecture on steroid drugs, it was mentioned that there were iatrogenic problems. The lecturer also said, by way of giving some general guidelines, "You have to go by each individual case. There are no hard and fast rules." (Field notes, GH)

> [In discussing a patient who died] fellow Meister said, "I wish I hadn't done this fellowship in cardiology. As an SR I was so sure of everything. Now I'm more confused than ever—when to 'Pace' [use a pacemaker], when to 'Cath' [use a Swan-Ganz catheter], when to give certain drugs. It comes down to this: You do what you want to do. I comb the literature—one says yes, one says no. Then my attending says, 'All the literature is five years old.' I give up. I need a vacation." (Field notes, VAH)

House officers learn to use the literature selectively to support their cases. They can usually find corroboration when necessary for either a "conservative" or an "aggressive" approach, as they characterize it. House staff also learn from faculty and colleagues that it is acceptable and even necessary at times to negate or discount research findings in favor of one's own clinical experience or perhaps that of significant others:

> Attending Hern interrupted attending rounds to give an autopsy report. . . . He said, "The test everyone said was so accurate didn't show the pulmonary embolism, which was what was found. You know the intern guessed it on Saturday night." Attending Poll responded, "Well, it shows that old clinical judgment is better than tests." (Field notes, ICU)

The increasingly sophisticated technology in the field thus creates countervailing pressures on the house staff. Its application creates more work, requires coordination with a variety of specialists, and carries with it the possibility of iatrogenesis. Its availability forces doctors to take closer looks at their patients and demands a more scrupulous approach, especially when test results are contradictory. The technology, in other words, emphasizes the conflict between the norm of efficiency, which impels the doctor to move the patient out as quickly as possible, and the norm of compulsiveness, which impels doctors to leave no possibility unexamined.

LIMITATIONS RESULTING FROM PROFESSIONAL ORIENTATION

The traditional professional orientation of internal medicine also contributes to a GROP perspective on health care delivery. This phenomenon is best understood in the historical context of the practice of internists, especially as manifested in the organizational context just described. Although internal medicine is an inclusive specialty with responsibility for total adult patient care, it is also reputed to be the preeminently intellectual medical discipline. Internists are considered the "thinkers" as opposed, for example, to surgeons, who are characterized as the "doers" (see Ford, Ort, and Denton 1967; Roberts 1977). But the interns' preference for an intellectually grounded discipline that incorporates care for the whole patient soon narrows, limiting the types of patients for whom they wish to care and contributing to a GROP orientation.

In the day-to-day behavior of the house staff, the emphasis was clearly on the intellectual, diagnostic process, not on care of the patient. They found the most exciting, exhilarating, and challenging aspect of their work to be diagnosis. Peers and mentors alike constantly emphasized that an essential goal of medical intervention was diagnosis. Thus it is not surprising that many house officers (especially junior and senior residents) likened their job to detective work, repeatedly describing it as an intellectual game, as solving puzzles, or as running mazes. Sleuthing was the activity they valued the most, the only one that generated observable excitement and animation. Senior Resident Ryder bluntly acknowledged:

> I don't like alcoholics but I like their diseases; that's fun for me to take care of because it's interesting to me. They have organs that have gone sick. I like playing detective.

JR DERY:
> [Internal medicine] is just a big numbers game. Maybe a game is the wrong word, but a puzzle or mystery waiting to be unraveled.

Family practice Intern Richard admitted that one way to achieve status in internal medicine was to show off one's erudition:

> [Internal medicine] does things just for completeness which I think are invalid reasons, for academic reasons, just to know, etc. Often times in internal medicine the game is to quote the *New England Journal of Medicine* and to shine on rounds. (Field notes, VAH)

Since internal medicine is valued and practiced primarily as the search for the cause of illness, and that quest is compared to unraveling a mystery, then the more complicated the puzzle, the more challenging the game. Straightforward and easy games (ones with few pieces or permutations) hold much less fascination for house staff than the more complex, bizarre, or esoteric ones. Unfortunately for patients, not that many of them meet such criteria, and most are therefore candidates for GROP.

Some house officers make significant distinctions between interesting and uninteresting patients as early as beginning internship, while most others acquire that perspective within the first year. As they progress through training, many house officers quickly lose interest in those patients whose illnesses are simple or easily understandable, and they witness their colleagues and superiors doing the same:

INTERN BLUM:
An interesting patient is someone who has something wrong or with multiple problems that relate to each other and you're left trying to figure them out. It's like a crossword puzzle . . . rather than one who comes in with a diagnosis and you sort of have a "cookbook" [routine] way of caring for [him].

Moreover, when I examined the behavior of residents on rounds, uncommon or complicated symptoms were emphasized almost exclusively. The most excited discussions were about the unusual and the complex, as in the following observation:

During residents' rounds there was a lengthy discussion on the differential diagnostic with some differences of opinion. When one of the JR's presented the final diagnosis (as if giving the answer to the puzzle) there was a round of applause. (Field notes, GH)

Once a week, residents' rounds were devoted to x-ray presentations. The house staff had to determine, from the films shown, what the patients' problems were. There was much joking and ribbing when someone did not know an answer. While some were defensive when unable to make a diagnosis, everyone was absorbed in the process.

Those faculty members and fellows who were admired by most of the house staff and whom many considered role models were those who concentrated most heavily on the intellectual aspects of medicine (the pathophysiology and "numbers," as they labeled it) or who emphasized laboratory-based diagnostic procedures:

During residents' rounds Dr. Baumgarten discussed a "horror show" presented by the SR. Everything went wrong with the patient and he eventually died. . . . Baumgarten pointed out that the patient's "numbers" were bad and not compatible with life. He put the house staff through an intense intellectual exercise. . . . After rounds I asked what people thought. They were obviously impressed. . . . Intern Cory: . . . "Incredible. . . . He really knows his stuff." Junior Resident Good: "Boy, Baumgarten is fantastic." . . . Ferst said, "I liked the session. I like intensive care medicine and playing with numbers!" (Field notes, PH)

Instances abounded where doctors discussed with one another, animatedly, the "great cases" or great pathology they saw. They spoke of "cases" and symptoms independently of the individuals who were the "cases" and manifested the symptoms. This sort of fragmented view eliminated the subjectivity of the patient, making it possible for doctors to wish for examples of pathology without much thought for the victims. Thus a patient who was gravely ill or in great pain could be a source of happiness and excitement by manifesting "interesting" symptoms.

> Intern Cory was observed to say, "I hope we see [such and such] disease on the x-ray. It would be great to make the diagnosis. I've heard about it but I never saw it before. It's a bad disease." (Field notes, VAH)

> On task rounds . . . Intern Light's comment revolved essentially around his excitement with regard to complications on two problem patients. . . . He called them "renal disasters." (Field notes, PH)

The most complicated or perplexing diseases or symptoms, and hence the ones that interested and excited the house staff most, often resulted in devastating outcomes for the patients. This dissonance between the staff's elation (especially if they made the diagnosis) and the patient's suffering further distanced them from the patients:[5]

> Intern Gloria received a call in the OPC from the floor. She just found out that the patient's bone marrow showed cancer. Junior Resident Weiss told me, "It's perverse, but you really feel good when you make the diagnosis. I remember the first time that happened to me, when I was able to diagnose the "mets" [metastatic cancer] in a patient's head when the CAT scan hadn't shown anything. I ran upstairs to my resident, all excited." (Field notes, OPC)

> SR DEREN:
> I guess it's sort of perverse, but it's really enjoyable to take care of sick people because a lot is happening . . . and when you're an SR you're comfortable making decisions, trying to figure out what's going on, trying to decipher a complex case, it's intellectually stimulating. . . . It's not saving someone or not.

Since intellectual stimulation seemed to be the principal arena in which they found satisfaction, this professional orientation created another reason to want to GROP large numbers of patients: there were just so few patients on whom they could make an interesting diagnosis or a "great save."

LIMITATIONS RESULTING FROM COUNTERVAILING NORMS OF PROFESSIONAL CONDUCT

In trying to provide health care while learning, the house staff seemed to face a series of ultimately unresolvable problems that were the result, in part, of conflicting norms of professional conduct.[6] Attempts to accommodate to the normative strains basic to the training and practice of internal medicine created varying degrees of cognitive dissonance. Progress in learning normative behavior was uneven and not automatic, and these norms, once learned, often provided contradictory expectations about GROP behavior.[7]

The norm of compulsiveness often contradicted the norm of efficiency,[8] pulling the house staff in opposite directions. Exaggerated fulfillment of one norm (i.e., being too compulsive) might negate the other (i.e., becoming inefficient). By moving too far in one direction, patient management mistakes or "social sins" against colleagues could occur.

The Norm of Compulsiveness: Afraid to Let Go

The trait the house staff identified as most essential in becoming a competent internist and as the stellar characteristic of the ideal internist was compulsiveness. Compulsiveness (defined usually as meticulousness and extreme thoroughness) permeated their approach to patient care and evolved as a norm of professional conduct. Compulsiveness in house staff behavior meant doing everything possible to (primarily) diagnose and (secondarily) treat an illness. It also had a defensive sense: *not* missing something along the way—some laboratory, physical, or medical history finding; some symptom, procedure, diagnosis, or treatment. Repeatedly, house staff would spontaneously emphasize this characteristic as the hallmark of the entire discipline of internal medicine:

SR AYRES:
[Competency as an internist is] . . . the ability to take a very detailed history and the willingness to do it and to be just nitpicky even all the way through to find the small points and to work up every problem. Most of the time when you see generalists or surgeons . . . they have tended to overlook the problems.

JR WHITE:
I think to be competent or good [in internal medicine] you need to be concerned about the patient because if you're not, you're not going to pay enough attention to the details. You need to be a little obsessive-compulsive.

When asked about their advice to new interns, almost every ending resident included the norm of compulsiveness. For example:

SR MAHONEY:
Be compulsive in everything you do—in a single word.

SR ADLER:
To keep up with your patients [that's my advice]. That may sound basic, but I think it's the most important thing to do—to be on top of everything with your patients.

The compulsiveness norm shaped how they thought about patients and what they did to and for them. In their everyday actions, they communicated to one another the profound fear of missing something:

A patient was supposed to go home, but they found some hemoglobin in the patient's GI tract. Junior Resident Olat said to the interns and medical students, "I chickened out; we're keeping him." (Field notes, VAH)

Under- or misdiagnosing could cause a patient's demise; lack of compulsiveness, or letting things slide, could result in serious errors. Scheff (1972) points out that in the medical community labeling a sick person well is a much more serious normative error than labeling a well person sick. Hence the tendency is to err on the side of overdiagnosis:

JR BINDER:
I think I'm a very compulsive person and I tend to double-check everything myself so I don't think I made any glaring mistakes. The more precise and the more you're keeping up, the less likely something will go wrong. . . . I've seen people pass through here who I thought were sloppy.

INTERN SHU:
I guess [a house officer] should be evaluated on how responsible he is and how well he takes care of his patients. Is he thorough? I guess thoroughness is a good part of it; how much work he does on his patients.

The norm of compulsiveness seemed to keep the house officers from implementing GROP behavior, and it heightened tension when they actually did GROP.

Ultimately, however, many house officers also came to believe that to be too complete, to do everything, was not only undesirable but impossible. Work was never finished. When they became inundated, they could end up delivering poor patient care. Ironically, attempting to pay attention to so many details simultaneously could produce the contrary results; namely, they might "see the trees and miss the forest" and wind up missing something important either in the patients on whom they were concentrating or in those they were neglecting. For example, one intern told me:

He [Intern Carlos] is slower . . . and therefore busier because he has sicker patients and takes so long. Also because he takes so long with his sicker patient[s], the other patients don't progress along as rapidly as they should, and this makes him and them more irritable. (Field notes, VAH)

They also soon realized that doing everything can induce iatrogenesis, as in the following example where, with one team, four instances were noted in one day.

The next patient of Intern Ralston complained of pains in her side, and Ralston said he had worked her up and couldn't locate a cause. [1] Attending Baumgarten smiled and said, "We did it, we caused it, after the stress test. It was JR Lovell's left jab!" [2] The next patient was a woman whose temperature went too low. Attending Baumgarten said, "She's another victim of the ice blanket." [3] And there was some discussion and ribbing by Baumgarten with regard to her urine output. Apparently somebody gave her too much fluid or didn't do the proper procedure and now she's putting out too much fluid. [4] Later on Baumgarten reported about a patient whom they found to be orthostatic and confused: "It's definitely a change in his mental status and I'm very concerned," Baumgarten said; "it's a bad situation." JR Lovell commented, "I think he's psychotic from his hospitalization." Baumgarten replied, "He'll die from complications of the hospitalization." (Field notes, GH)

A patient-management sin of commission, with heavy costs to the patient or the system, may occur from being overdiligent. More significantly, however, the exaggerated fulfillment of the norm of compulsiveness limits the possibility of achieving the contending norm of efficiency.

The Norm of Efficiency: Cutting Appropriate Corners

The norm of efficiency is an important cultural variable; it was continuously reinforced by the house staff until it became a basis for informal colleague evaluation. Senior house officers assessed their juniors, while junior house officers learned to assess themselves according to that criterion, among others. Efficiency was defined as being productive, doing the required work as quickly and as expeditiously as possible, and finally, appearing to have an organized approach to the tasks at hand:

JR FILPS:
The skills of an intern aren't very impressive ones. It's can you get the numbers back in time, can you move and shake? It doesn't really matter what you know as an intern. . . . They just want you to take care of patients in a very physical sense, and it's a matter of efficiency, and the resident values the intern as to his efficiency more than anything else.

SR MELON:
I think the emphasis of interns is to get things done and getting them done as fast as possible, and so the emphasis the interns get from the JRs and attendings is this and this needs to be done, go and do it. . . . The resident's life is much more think oriented . . . you supervise the interns and help them to be most efficient. You know a few more things than they do and you just are trying to help them get efficient.

The norm of efficiency is the principal norm of professional conduct that supports the GROP perspective. While in some sense this norm was a consequence of all the causes of a GROP perspective, at the same time it became an independent shaper of behavior as well as a justification for GROP among the house staff.

The house staff noticed and admitted the attitudinal transition during their internship from an emphasis on compulsiveness to one on efficiency:

JR Sing:
You learn yourself that efficiency is important after you mess around and keep four or five patients in the hospital two or three days too long and find out you have the largest service in GH and you're getting out at nine o'clock every night. You realize quickly that efficiency is very important.

Intern Charen:
I'm learning how to become more efficient, which is important, and I'm learning how to take care of patients and do a lot of "scut"; by the same token, being able to read up on my patients' problems and at the same time have time enough for sleep, etc. . . . It's damn difficult.

The demands of the system were such that house staff were constantly struggling to maintain control over their own environment, which meant attempting to keep their services from becoming unmanageable. Given the elusive definition of compulsiveness and the number of patients in their charge, they realized the difficulty—if not impossibility—of achieving completeness. Often, apathy and depression would set in. Ultimately, many attempted to do as little as possible by identifying and redefining not only what was and was not important or necessary but what they could get away with within the system and culture as well. Commented Intern Schneider:

"I leave at 2 p.m. on my 'no-call' night. It used to be on my night off. I wouldn't leave till 8 or 9 p.m. It [the change] is probably a combination of the patients not being so sick and my being efficient and not so compulsive now. You get a better feel of who will do well and who won't and what is essential." (Field notes, VAH)

Intern Garney told me:

"I'm getting more efficient plus I'm not as compulsive as I used to be. I know now that certain things are not absolutely necessary: to get on admissions at night, e.g., EKG, x-rays, urine. . . ." Intern Newman chimed in agreeing and giving his own examples: "I have learned what can wait." (Field notes, VAH)

Yet there seemed to be an extreme danger in moving too far to the other extreme. They could become overly complacent, cutting corners and leaving things undone for the next day or for someone else to pick up. Hence the exaggerated fullfillment of the norm of efficiency could lead to lazy and sloppy behavior. Implementing GROPing strategies could result in the commission of mistakes resulting from negligence in patient management and, more seriously, errors in normative conduct against colleagues—the commission of the social sin of *sloughing*. Therefore they had to justify their efficiency orientation to themselves, to superiors, to peers, and sometimes, to me:

JR Edwards:
All you have a chance to do is really survive [as an intern] and do what needs to be done. . . . The more efficient you are the better you are. It's sort of like taking a

chance. Like one of the interns who was just as smart [as everyone else but] just couldn't be good from the circumstances. . . . A lot of times he had no choice at all but to do a sloppy job, just to get any job done at all, and there is no other way he could do it.

JR TRACEY:

With regard to errors which have been made, especially after the first few months, you'll see interns won't do everything they should when they are called for a problem, just because they are fed up with the world.

Countervailing Norms and GROP Conflicts

Along with structural and professional determinants discussed earlier, these normative conflicts clearly contributed to the dynamics of GROP—especially when and whom to GROP. The differences in function and in responsibility for patients at all three levels of training affected both the degree to which the GROP perspective countered other norms and the intensity with which the house staff promoted and implemented it. The contradictions were played out intra- as well as interpersonally: interns often experienced GROP-related conflicts within themselves as well as with supervising residents.

The intern, who had most of the patient management responsibility, usually was operating from the norm of efficiency, while the resident operated from compulsiveness. Several house officers articulated feelings similar to the ones discussed by Intern Foner:

There's a natural conflict . . . in how aggressive an intern and resident is likely to be. . . . The intern may be a little less aggressive in terms of procedures just because it takes a lot more time for him to do the procedures. . . . The resident on the other hand wants to be almost compulsively complete because he is in a way responsible for how the case looks in terms of total work up. . . . And so he may be more likely to suggest those things that an intern who, if he has a lot of other things to do and if he is the one who has to do them, may wonder if they're really indicated.

The following are a few of the many GROP-related interactions I witnessed involving these normative dilemmas as they were played out interpersonally within the social organization and culture of house staff training:

One patient, Mr. Forrest, wanted to go home. There was long conference on him as to whether to let him go against medical advice or to discharge him. Intern Wallace suggested discharging him, and JR O'Connell was against it. Attending Marshall was undecided. They continued to discuss the alternatives all throughout the morning. Finally Wallace and Marshall were persuaded by O'Connell to keep him for a few more days and certainly not to sign his discharge papers. (Field notes, GH)

On another occasion:

> Intern Newman told one of his new patients when asked, "Yes, you can go home on a pass. I'll check with the JR." Junior Resident Zimmerman was not willing to let the patient go on a pass until Newman convinced him that there was nothing else that had to be done. Zimmerman was very thorough in checking out systematically the things that had been found with him and the tests that were still outstanding. (Field notes, VAH)

Still another time:

> Intern Elan came down from the ICU and tried to discourage SR Kots from taking the woman patient because obviously he'd have the major patient management responsibility. . . . A little later there was a telephone call to the ER, and SR Shube reported that an ambulance was bringing in a woman with leg pains radiating to her stomach. Shube sarcastically remarked, "Oh, I can't wait to see her." But when the intern suggested that maybe she could go to the obstetric ER, Shube said, "Well, maybe she has other disorders." (Field notes, ER)

In each case, the residents were less inclined to GROP than the interns.

In other situations, however, the opposite might occur; that is, the resident would promote GROP under the guise of "efficiency" while the interns seemed more insecure about when and whom they should GROP. Because they were unsure about the toleration level and flexibility of the system, and much less secure in their own knowledge of medicine and the course and outcome of diseases, interns might err in the direction of holding on to patients. Hence the norm of compulsion in the sense of the fear of missing something could take precedence over the norm of efficiency when it was translated into how much they should do for the patient:

> INTERN PATTY:
> I've already had one of those [decisions where I was right and the resident was wrong]. I wanted to keep a patient in the hospital for longer than he did, and he said, "Send him out, send him out." I said, "No, we're keeping him in," and so he stayed in.

> An elderly black woman hobbled in on a cane complaining of fullness in her chest. There was a debate between Intern Newman and SR Shube as to where she would go. Shube said, "It doesn't sound like heart trouble. She could go to the routine ER. Newman responded, . . . "If it's okay with you, I'd just as soon keep her here." Shube shrugged his shoulders, indicating he did not understand why he'd want to keep her. . . . Newman said he would feel more comfortable with her having an EKG. (Field notes, ER)

Such acquiescence by the SR was not always the result. In numerous cases, GROP action by SRs was more typical of the following example:

Senior Resident Fable told Intern Noch, "My philosophy is that if they don't need to be here, get them out. . . . We've got to get them worked up fast." Noch came in after examining a patient and suggested several blood tests and x-rays. Fable discouraged it all, saying, "Don't do any unnecessary test because, one, it keeps them here too long, and two, we find out things we don't want to know. . . . [Later on] Fable was still complaining that his interns were slow. He saw Intern Kots taking a history from a male patient and said, "You don't need the whole medical history; just find out what's wrong now." . . . And later on Fable still questioned Intern Kots: "Why the work-up?" Fable said to him, "Let's get the 'turkey' out of here." (Field notes, ER)

The SR was more readily able to GROP because he had both the confidence and the authority to do so.

Some house officers admitted that the potential for misjudgment and subsequent errors was omnipresent, and hence they were cautious about precipitous, premature, or prejudicial GROP behavior. Continual recounting of others' mistakes revealed how stressful and tenuous their decision making was, for if they GROPed precipitously or inappropriately, they might indeed be responsible for someone's premature death or the exacerbation and complication of an illness and its treatment. Hence, as in the following two occurrences, the house staff was sometimes forced not to GROP:

Junior Resident Archer consulted with SR Rind. She asked, "If you were me, would you admit an alcoholic man having withdrawal, possibly beginning dt's who is tremulous? He wants help. There's no history of a 'psyche' consult, and I keep thinking of keeping him overnight until he can get admitted. Is it malpractice to send someone like him home?" Rind nodded affirmatively. Archer said, "Well, this is one 'garbage' admission we may have to take," and left. (Field notes, ER)

Junior Resident Kots said at one point to his peers, "Look at him [looking over to a patient who was obviously in the dt's]. What a piece of shit!" Then in response to one of the intern's questions with regard to administering a drug for such patients, Kots replied, "You have to watch him. His dt's are subtle. I know some house staff send them out like that. I don't have the heart to. They could jump out a window. You're really looking for trouble." (Field notes, ER)

The resolution of these conflicting norms included attempting to maintain a balance between them, since each of these norms of professional conduct is in itself a positive goal. Because these goals call for differing and potentially conflicting sets of behavior toward patients or peers, however, they exist in a state of dialectic tension. It appears difficult to achieve the quintessence of one norm without the possibility of violating its contending norm. Consequently, these positive counternorms can produce vacillation and ambivalence rather than the gradually acquired ability to maintain a reasonable balance between them.

The ambivalent orientation toward patients that resulted from being informed by these norms did not go unnoticed by most house staff. In the following comment Intern McGee identified the two norms:

> I think an intern is usually evaluated by how he gets his work done and mostly how conscientious he is in working [compulsiveness]. The evaluation of his knowledge is a secondary component, at least this year. If you can manage to get your patients organized and get the work that needs to be done, done, that's what's valued [efficiency].

One year later JR McGee identified the dilemma in the actual day-to-day work and the no-win dynamics of the two norms in contention:

> As an intern your admitting days are based on the patients you have coming in. You can either get your work done in a hurry and see your other patients, which means you do a poor job on the admissions and see your other patients. Or you can do a good, conscientious, complusive full work-up on your admissions and tend to ignore your patients, except for the acutely ill, for that one day you're admitting. I always tried to do a good job, but that meant my patients on the ward suffered.

CONCLUSION

The normative structure of the house staff subculture is a response to immediate circumstances as well as to exhortations of idealized conduct by the profession. The norms of compulsiveness and efficiency are applied in everyday interaction as the house staff adjusts to the conditions of its labor. Those work conditions include patient overload and attendant shortages of beds, poor and malfunctioning facilities, understaffed ancillary facilities, and bureaucratic politics and waste. The house staff is attempting to learn competence and confidence in the practice of medical techniques that are highly technical. The trade-off for learning such practice is the assumption of the task of primary health care delivery in a public system. Because of the inadequacies in public health care, the house staff finds itself at the end of a system of patient disposal that requires long and hard work. Provision of primary medical care can be a learning situation, but it soon becomes routinized because of the commonness of many of the illnesses and the fact that there is little that can be done for many patients. Moreover, there is an inherent conflict between providing such routine care and learning the practice of internal medicine.

The emphasis in internal medicine is on making the diagnosis. Because of its self-image as the most intellectual of the medical arts, the sign of the competent internist is the ability to know what to look for in the history and laboratory tests and, on that basis, solve the puzzle of the symptoms with a correct diagnosis. Therefore, many patients become, for the internist, little more than the manifestation of their symptoms.

The sheer bulk of patients with their uninteresting or incurable diseases and the chronic bed shortage force the house staff to dispose of patients as quickly as possible. While the increasing census on the service demands that *something* be done, the two norms pull the house officers in contradictory directions. The result for the doctors is that they must GROP their patients as quickly as possible while making sure simultaneously that they do not make serious mistakes. The difficulty of this task creates tension within the house staff and constitutes a potential source of interpersonal conflict on the floor.

Since the house staff exists to provide proper medical care to patients, a key component of professional teaching, then, is appropriate GROP behavior. The contending norms of compulsiveness and efficiency are generalizations that must be applied on a case-by-case basis. In such application the house staff continually refines and redefines GROP behavior. Because it is the deviant act that defines the boundaries of normality, interns often have rude experiences of being yelled at by their superiors for being too slow, or they observe neglect on the part of other house staff members that teaches them proper GROP behavior. Learning when, how, and whom to GROP was defined by new members of the house staff as essential for survival in the system.

Chapter 4

GROP Criteria
Calculating the Worth of Patients

In this chapter the process of determining *whom* to GROP is more fully explored. The system of social categorization of patients used by the house staff, that is, the criteria by which they evaluate various characteristics of patients and calculate their worth, is scrutinized. This process takes place between the realizations that create and compel the GROP perspective and the actual implementation of GROP behavior.

Although they may wish to get rid of most patients and may reach a point during training when they believe that no patient is an ideal or interesting one, house officers cannot successfully evade patients. They are, after all, doctors being paid to provide patient care. They also need some patients in order to learn both the intellectual and technical dimensions of internal medicine. They must make quick decisions on the disposition of each patient, and to make them, they engage in a process whereby they establish the value of each patient. This valuing process involves a complicated system of classification.

It should not be surprising that physicians engage in the process of evaluating patients socially as well as medically and that the results of their calculations affect both their attitude and their behavior toward those patients at all stages of training and beyond. In the two classic studies of medical education, both Martin and Fox (in Merton, Reader, and Kendall 1957) and Becker et al. (1961) found continuous categorizing of patients by medical students.[1] What few studies of physicians in practice exist (e.g., Ford Ort, and Denton 1967; Groves 1978; Papper 1970; Ries et al. 1981; Stimson 1976) demonstrate that social evaluations of patients do indeed continue after training and that the categories of undesirable patient types are extensive.

Jeffery (1979), Sudnow (1970), and J. Roth (1972, 1974b) have studied the behavior of physicians in emergency rooms and have noted that their moral evaluations of patients were based primarily on external systems of social categorization. For example, patients whose afflictions were the consequence of self-abuse were evaluated as less "worthy" of care than those whose pathology was perceived as no fault of their own. Thus derelicts, drunks, and drug overdosers were assessed by the ER doctors as morally inferior to "innocent" accident or illness victims and were generally given perfunctory care or else not resuscitated with any vigor. Crane (1975) found that social functioning or social capacity rather than social value was the basis upon which physicians evaluated the chronically and terminally ill. What is clear from my study is that social categorization and, at times, discriminatory practices occurred regardless of which standard was used and that the two were inextricably intertwined. For example, in determining a patient's social potential, some prior subjective standard had to be defined as to what constituted a "productive" or "viable" lifestyle, and this usually had a moral basis.[2]

Within the house staff culture there were two major systems of social classification. The first depended on the disease of the patient—"interesting" versus "uninteresting"—with the latter category predominating during the house staff's graduate medical training. This system of categorization is basically devoid of reference to the external social structure and to some degree independent of the personal and social characteristics of the patient. It is almost solely determined by professional criteria related to diagnosis; that is, the symptoms are the primary basis of valuation, and outcome of the disease—whether it is curable—is the secondary basis.

The second system of social classification begins with the ideal patient and ends with the despised patient. The ideal patient is described in terms such as "clean," "articulate," "cooperative," and so forth—most of which closely conform to external systems of social status. Despised patients are defined as abusers—of themselves, the system, house staff—and as such are subject to counterabuse.

While the interesting–uninteresting system is for the most part independent of personal characteristics, it does correlate with the ideal–despised system in that often included in the ideal patient category is the trait of having an "interesting" disease. Also, despised patients can have interesting symptoms, so that it is quite possible for a detested patient to be highly valued for his or her symptoms. As the senior house officer cited in the previous chapter stated, "I don't like alcoholics, but I like their diseases."

The stratification system of the house staff creates variations on the mode of classification. Patients who are interesting to attendings and residents may mean even more work for the interns since they will be the ones making sure that the tests are done, the forms are filled out, the patients are wheeled from service to service, and so forth:

JR EDWARDS:
As an intern if you get a patient that your JR says is interesting—all that does is tell you in your mind the pile of hassles you have to go through to get anything done with them. If he has a thyroid problem all you think is how long he's going to be on your service. . . . More interesting problems are harder or more complicated to get done, and you just can't be excited about anything that's halfway interesting.

THE INTERESTING–UNINTERESTING
PATIENT DICHOTOMY:
THE LIMITS OF INTERNAL MEDICINE

Internists pride themselves on making the diagnosis. The emphasis on uncovering disease processes and the esteem in which those who are excellent diagnosticians are held often caused the interests of the house staff to diverge from those of the patients. Though patients certainly need a proper diagnosis, the motivation to diagnose becomes achieving status irrespective of the needs of the patient or the outcome:

SR ROGERS:
[With respect to the skills valued by the faculty and house staff], everyone put a lot of emphasis on diagnostic skill. [It is communicated] when you are an intern. You're constantly talking differential diagnosis when you present cases. . . . It's reinforced all the way along. If you make a tough diagnosis from an x-ray or EKG . . . that's when you do get some positive reinforcement—so it's built into the system.

House staff readily acknowledged how much their desire for diagnostic challenges affected how easily and quickly they became bored or frustrated with many patients and wished to GROP them. House officers characterized most patients' problems as routine and uninteresting because they knew what was wrong—regardless of whether they were able to treat or manage them easily.[3] There were, in addition, groups of patients whom they devalued and even blamed because (according to the house staff) either they had nothing physical or detectable wrong with them, so there was no diagnosis to be made, or else these patients were not able to describe their symptoms so that they could be "diagnosable."

One of the prospective chief residents outlined the range of patients whom the house staff found frustrating:

SR FABLE:
One, patients you take care of even though you can't make better; two, people you can make better but who won't follow your instructions; three, patients who resist your attempts at diagnosing; four, those who you can do the right thing for and the patient doesn't get better; and five, making a good diagnosis but not being able to do

71

anything for the patient. *Diagnosis used to be interesting as an intern, but not as much now if you can't do anything about it* [emphasis added].

The house staff members repeatedly lamented about how little impact they had on many of their patients and how little they and the internal medicine discipline knew about the course and cure of most diseases. The feelings emerged early in their experience, as evidenced by two interns' reactions:

> Another patient was presented who, the medical student said, was doing better. Intern Welles responded: "I'd like to think we cured her but I suspect we didn't have too much to do with it." Attending Moser added, "Well, supportive care sometimes is the best care." (Field notes, PH)

> Intern Berger told me: "I like to cogitate, so I like internal medicine. You know 85 percent of disease is self-limiting. Of 15 percent, maybe 3 percent can be helped by surgical intervention. There's very little [internal] medicine can do outside of infectious disease, and the things we can do something for are usually related to self-inflicted diseases. You tune them up and they go right back out and do it again." (Field notes, VAH)

They were describing the discrepancy that existed in their discipline between making the diagnosis and curing the disease.

Because they were powerless to reverse most disease processes, their feelings of frustration at times seemed to contribute to their emotional and physical distancing from most incurable or terminally ill patients. Given an increasingly narrow professional perspective on the internist's role, most house staff have little awareness of or desire to play other rewarding roles with patients on such occasions. Constantly reinforced in the culture is the overriding orientation: "There is nothing you can do for them [patients], so naturally you wish to GROP."

The extent to which they comprehended their limited effectiveness with many patients was further demonstrated by the significance they attached to opposite situations: those exceptional circumstances in which they had successfully intervened in a patient's disease, as noted in this typical observation:

> Upon visiting two of Intern Garney's patients who seemed to be doing much better or were going as planned, there was some joking around that he had the magic cure because his patients were getting "cured." (Field notes, PH)

Their spontaneous responses to my open-ended question, "What were some of your most memorable experiences during training?" included anecdotes about a few patients on whom they felt they had a positive impact, in addition to several unhappy experiences with patients on whom they persevered without positive effect. In particular, house officers highlighted the unusual occurrences at both extremes—patients who, in their estimation, died but should have lived and patients they thought were going to die but who instead recovered or were stabilized. In discussing unexpected "happy endings," they often attempted to identify the ways in which they may have contributed to the successful outcome. At the same time, attendings and house staff repeatedly acknowledged to each other that many diseases were self-limiting (e.g., "The patient cured himself," etc.) and that many patients would have gotten better in spite of their intervention. In the following interview a former house officer who became an attending physician at SAMs discussed those aspects of professional development and contributed these insights:

> As an intern you're still starry-eyed and idealistic. You try to learn everything. You try to know everything and to some degree believe you can. As a JR you've gained some measure of competence. . . . You can do anything. *But by the time you are an SR you're much more philosophical. You know that you can't do much and that medicine can't do much.* It's like the old saying by Mark Twain, "The doctor's job is to keep the patient entertained while nature heals him." It's really true. . . . *You really see the limitations in medicine.* The adage, "We really treat ourselves," is also true. . . . The one thing you're scared to death of is that the patient will deteriorate in front of you and you won't know what to do; that's always a fear. . . . As an SR when it happens in the ICU you realize you know as much medicine if not more than any other doctor including the attendings. And if you don't know it the chances are it's not knowable or known [emphasis added]. (Field notes, ICU)

In addition, the fact that public hospitals function as dumping grounds for unwanted people expands the number of uninteresting patients. Many patients who had been rejected by others were especially disliked by the house staff for one or more of the following reasons: first, they were often terminally ill patients in the final stage of disease, sometimes awaiting unavailable nursing home placement; second, they frequently were sent from nursing homes, having become incontinent, partially or completely comatose, or incoherent; third, when they did not die immediately, they often got worse or acquired iatrogenic complications; fourth, when they were not-so-sick, they were most often poor and were characterized as negligent or recalcitrant; or fifth, they were middle-class patients whose private insurance had terminated or who otherwise were identified as difficult or demanding patients. Overall, these "dumped" patients constituted the majority of the patient load. The following conversation details house staff feelings about these patients:

> The interns began discussing nursing home patients in general and how, on one service, fellow intern Thatcher got "stuck" with five of "them" on his service. Intern Nach referred to them as "dehydrated UTI's" [urinary tract infections]. I asked them why they're so difficult. Nach said, "Look," [and pointed to an old patient from whom they had difficulty drawing blood]. "There's not much you can do. They make no progress. If there's ever going to be 'disaster,' you'll have it with them." The other intern added, "They never get better. There's no satisfaction. There's no reward. Their IVs run out, and it takes a half hour to stick them again. Then just

as you're ready to discharge them, they develop bedsores [iatrogenesis]." (Field notes, ER)

Their reactions to these medically unsuitable patients of course affected their relationships with those patients:

INTERN GARY:
There are drawbacks [in internal medicine] . . . . I have come to realize more acutely since I started my internship that internists deal with old people and chronic illness, which can be quite depressing, and I'm sure this is a view felt by many in the field. You never know how much to do, how far to work on a patient with a terminal illness, and that's grounds for depression.

This perceptive comment by an intern of seven weeks illustrated that disease and demographic factors intrinsic to the practice of internal medicine contributed heavily to shaping the house staff perspective on large groups of preferred or devalued patients. Ironically, the largest groups of patients for internists in training and practice are those least medically interesting to most of them.

THE IDEAL–DESPISED PATIENT DICHOTOMY: SELF-, SYSTEM, AND HOUSE STAFF ABUSERS

From the day they entered house staff training in internal medicine, new interns as a group already had almost as highly developed a sense of both the ideal and the nonideal patient as did ending residents three years later. Often included in the interns' description of the ideal patient was susceptibility to being GROPed, and conversely, the frustration at not being able to GROP was a feature of their complaints about their typical patient load:

JR MENDEL:
There are times when you feel overworked and you are willing to take less interesting patients that require the least work and I think everyone is guilty of that at times. [The ideal patient] . . . is a patient with something interesting. You'd like someone with some salvageability, someone who is cooperative. . . . *You need to have some sort of "dispo" for the patient, and that can be a real problem [emphasis added].* . . . When you find a patient who is ideal, you're interested in getting them in your clinic because they're so rare.

JR FEIN:
There are different kinds of ideal patients. When you're an intern *the ideal patient is someone you can get out and get out quickly* and who has a place to go [emphasis added]. I think I was more idealistic when I started. I tend to be more fatalistic [now] with a lot of patients. I think part of it is just the frustration of having to deal with problems day in and day out. You feel you're not getting anywhere and maybe

you can't get anywhere. . . . As far as frustrating patients, I think there is a degree of frustration with every patient.

Ideal patient characteristics included patient attributes, attitudes and actions. There were three basic constellations; the first was the "interesting" category just discussed. Second, and universally identified as the most essential traits of the ideal patient, were intelligence, cooperation, and compliance, all of which related to external systems of social categorization. A patient had to be "intelligent" for the purposes of both understanding and communicating with doctors.[4] Almost always mentioned was a patient who could articulate and communicate an accurate medical and related history. A patient had to demonstrate concern about his or her own health and a willingness to take some responsibility for it. A patient had to be willing to accept the judgment and advice of the house staff and follow their instructions. While many house officers asserted a desire to care for a patient who would question them (as opposed to a patient who passively accepted everything), the purpose and substance of the questions desired from patients was usually quite relative and restricted: it was to demonstrate to the house staff that the patient took an interest in his or her disease. Therefore, questions could not reflect disrespect for, or suspicion about, the doctor's knowledge or authority.[5]

The third grouping of ideal patient characteristics included moral evaluations such as cleanliness that bore direct references to personality, quality of life, and lifestyle.[6] Other crucial attitudinal factors such as the demonstration of appreciation or gratitude for care were identified as well. The following are the typical combinations of characteristics cited by virtually all of the house staff:

SR SILVERMAN:
An ideal patient is a patient who is sick with a disease that you can cure, who could give you a good history, who you know that once they were discharged would take the medicine you gave them, would come to your clinic for the follow-up, would cooperate with whatever therapy you wanted to do, and who would understand something about their disease process and avoid any risk factors which would make it worse, and would get better and would appreciate your service.

INTERN LIGHT:
The ideal patient is . . . one who's clean, who has a concise idea of what's happened to him. He's not wordy, comes straight to the point, tells you what's the matter with him, is cooperative and follows your instructions, and allows you to perform whatever procedures you need to.

INTERN FABLE:
[The ideal patient] would be somebody who would walk into the hospital and give you a perfect history, which almost no one can do, could answer every question with accurate information . . . . They are compliant plus they have an interesting disease, but that patient doesn't exist.

Two years later the same house officer responded more succinctly:

SR FABLE:
The ideal patient is . . . sick as shit and get[s] better.

There was a generalized bias toward middle-class patients in that, in the eyes of the house staff, they were more intelligent, cleaner, and more cooperative, but the endorsement of social status was equivocal. They understood there was a trade-off involved in working with middle-class versus lower-class patients (although most of their patients were of the latter group). Middle-class patients, being generally more intelligent and articulate, could give better histories, but they also took up more house staff time in explanation of processes and outcomes of disease, at times even requiring house staff to justify their behavior. Hence, middle-class patients were frequently viewed as demanding and skeptical. Lower-class patients, on the other hand, were usually considered poor historians requiring more initial time but often more passive and acquiescent. They required less time in explanations about procedures but were also considered passive-aggressive (and occasionally suspicious).

Asked directly how frequently they encountered ideal patients during training, many house officers responded with sarcasm, cynicism, or sardonic humor:

INTERN CHAREN:
I would say one one hundred thousandth of 1 percent [are ideal patients], and that's being liberal! It certainly will be a negative factor and maybe draw me away from general internal medicine and make me hit a subspecialty where I won't have to deal with the depressed eighty-year-old woman.

INTERN FERST:
I'd say one-fourth to one-third [are ideal patients] . . . well, that's not true—probably 20 percent as far as following instructions. . . . If people don't take care of themselves and are not showing much interest in their problems, then you can't show as much either. You just can't get involved with someone who really doesn't care about what's going on.

These perceptions were fairly typical as early as beginning internship, for disillusion set in quickly. After one year of internship, there was general, even more despair, resignation, and occasional anger at how few patients met their ideal and how difficult it was to deal with the typical patient they encountered:

JR McGEE:
As an intern whenever a resident told me, "I got a really good case," my immediate response was, "There's no such thing as a great case. It's just another patient I have to work up." Almost every intern comes to view the patient as only more work and it certainly interferes with your doctor–patient relationship.

Most significant, these negative valuations did not automatically subside or lessen at the end of residency training, especially since the vast majority of patients fell into the despised and overlapping categories of chronic abusers and members of the lower classes:

SR BINDER:
They [patients] tend to be uneducated, have led an abusive lifestyle, and aren't intelligent enough to even explain what's wrong with them.

Family practice interns corroborated my overall impressions of the internal medicine house staff and sympathized with house staff actions to get rid of troublesome or frustrating patients. They, too, pointed to a variety of patient-related as well as structural and professional reasons for GROP conduct. In the following two commentaries, the interplay between the medically uninteresting and the socially despised categorizations can be seen.

FAMILY PRACTICE INTERN WOLF:
In the ER no one is interested in [patients]. The [internal] medicine people are only interested in patients who've got exciting diagnostic possibilities. Anyone with a long-standing chronic problem like diabetes or hypertension . . . are [sic] not interesting, and they are not "good patients." And even worse than them are the patients that the internist doesn't think he can do anything for . . . like the alcoholic or the real borderline personality . . . and those people are shoved out of the emergency room as fast as they can be sent out and often with no follow-up. . . . At VAH the patients are viewed with even more disdain. They are not even given minimal courtesy as people. . . . I overheard one female resident tell another, "Oh, I'm upstairs watering the plants." I saw that in a lot of people.

FAMILY PRACTICE INTERN PIKE:
The biggest things . . . [disliked by internal medicine house staff] are patients who come from nursing homes, debilitated and senile, and are called "dumps." They're patients nobody wants, and they're just pushed off to SAMs from the nursing home, and those are the kinds of patients that everyone hates to take care of because they have a lot of problems and weren't [sic] an easy "dispo" so that it meant that they were going to be on the service a long time. . . . [Also] drunks and "sicklers" [sickle cell anemia patients]. . . . The ones that cause the most anger as far as admissions are the ones that are really debilitated. . . . Maybe it's also kind of disappointing too, when a patient is very sick . . . dying and not going to get better and it's a lot of wasted energy, a waste of time and money to keep someone alive.

In summary, there were many categories of disparaged patients who were actively and visibly shunned by the house staff. First, there were the *self-abusers*: those with so-called self-induced diseases, especially those brought on by alcohol, cigarettes, drug usage, and overeating. Second, there were the *system abusers*: those assessed as manipulators, malingerers, psychosomatic complainers ("crocks"), and demanders. Third, there were *house staff abusers*: troublesome patients who are difficult, demanding, suspicious, disrespectful, hostile, or ungrateful and who are also often included in either or both of the first two categories. Because so many patients fall into these categories, house staff continuously raised questions about the costs of caring for these undesirable types.

THE COST FACTOR: THE BOTTOM LINE IN PATIENT CALCULATION

Sooner or later, house staff evaluation of patients interacted with cost considerations. The bottom line of patient evaluation quite literally *was* the bottom line, since house staff had to decide on what resources would be made available to a given patient. In other words, the house staff had to calculate, in general terms, how much a patient was worth.

Indeed, the cost involved in a hospitalization was frequently mentioned by attendings and occasionally raised by the house staff, both formally and informally—although the motivation of each cohort for doing so seemed somewhat different. Many faculty seemed concerned with raising the cost consciousness of the house staff. On several occasions I noted attendings' attempts to shape house staff behavior during didactic and clinical rounds. Here, an attending talked about a particular syndrome with respect to risks:

> We should look at the total cost—the money—since the procedure costs more than one thousand dollars, including the skills of the physician and emotional factors. (Field notes, VAH)

Another time, the topic during residents' rounds was the rather esoteric one of nuclear antibodies. The presenting physician said:

> All these costly tests are not necessary, but labs will try to convince house staff that they can't diagnose an illness without them. Lupis is a benign disease if it's not overtreated [an example of where costs and iatrogenesis were related]. (Field notes, VAH)

Faculty, much more than house staff, were aware of the total cost of patient hospitalization, which included psychological, social, and physical as well as financial costs. Some of this awareness was linked to their awareness of the likelihood of iatrogenesis. Faculty concern for costs was demonstrated in the following interaction:

> A case was presented by Intern Glock. A question arose as to whether or not to CAT scan a patient. Attending Marshall said, "It's the VA and they [the patients] are not paying. If it was at SAMs and the patient was paying, we would add that into the the decision-making equation." (Field notes, VAH)

Both resistance to being limited by cost and ignorance of cost are evident in house staff responses to faculty queries in the following exchanges:

Attending Brown asked, "What if it's pancreatitis? How far should we go?" The interns and residents tried to justify their probing on the basis of just "knowing." Junior Resident Tony said, "Knowledge is power." Brown questioned, "Is it worth doing? We're running up one hell of a bill." (Field notes, GH)

Attending Kirk continued his discussion of drugs, noting the cost of one dose of a certain steroid was $120. He asked them [the house staff] if they knew how costly a week's treatment of the other kinds of drugs were. They shook their heads no. He answered, "$1,000." Senior Resident Farmer responded, "So what, if it's worth it." (Field notes, ICU)

When house staff did raise the issue of costs, it was almost always in regard to patients who were wasting taxpayers' money by inappropriate use of the medical or hospital facilities. This assessment of patients who "abused" the system clearly supported their desire to GROP those who, in their estimation, were costing the taxpaying public millions of dollars for unwarranted care. Rarely did a member of the house staff ask about the broader cost considerations such as whether a patient had to bear the financial costs of the diagnostic or therapeutic procedures they ordered.

Occasionally faculty members would concur with the house staff, likewise displaying a questioning, if not negative, attitude toward the cost of diagnostic or treatment procedures for certain patients:

Junior Resident Stokes asked Attending Dites, "How aggressive should we be?" Dites said, "This patient already got a fifty-thousand-dollar work-up. Neurology thought he was salvageable, but if this was a cancer patient . . . he clearly would be a 'do not resuscitate.' He has a long-term history of ETOH [alcohol abuse]." (Field notes, GH)

The house staff frequently discussed the cost of a visit to the ER or OPC and expressed contempt for people who continued to use those facilities in spite of the cost. They usually blamed the patients for not seeking alternatives or not treating themselves. The following not-atypical examples illustrate the intensity of their feelings toward patients they thought abused the system:

SR PAUL (who became a chief resident):
I remember when I was junior resident on call. This girl came in from Mercy College with a sore throat, and she came by ambulance, and that costs twenty-five dollars a visit. . . . It was just like the straw that broke my back . . . I went out in the waiting room. It was totally inappropriate; I just yelled at her in front of a whole room of people for taking an ambulance in for a sore throat.

SR SILVERMAN:
When I was in the critical ER a junior resident in the routine ER was fed up with the population that was coming in. A lot of people didn't want to stay outside because it was one hundred degrees outside, and the hospital was air conditioned. People would come in and tell me they were having a cold and they wanted to be seen by a

doctor. . . . The resident put up a sign which said, "If you have a cold, aspirin and fluids are the best thing for it. It doesn't need to cost you fifty dollars to walk into the ER and be seen by the doctor." The administration found out about it, and the sign was pulled down.

While the house staff was not in a position to refuse care to most patients, it clearly regarded a significant number as unworthy of the time and cost invested and conveyed that sentiment to peers and to me:

SR Kots:
We get tired of it . . . if it's the fifty-seventh [hospital] admission for somebody who is diabetic who gets drunk and doesn't take insulin and then has to be intubated in the intensive care unit. . . . Everybody says along the way, "Why are we spending all this money on this guy who's trying to kill himself?"

SR Ari:
And the other thing that bothers you is that society is putting so much money into what we do to save some of these people. I mean, you've seen it, in the units, they're in and out over there with self-abusive diseases which kind of wear you down after a while.

THE EXCEPTIONAL PATIENT: "DO NOT GROP"

In certain exceptional circumstances house staff (and sometimes attendings) expressed a desire to continue to care for patients already in their charge or a willingness to admit a patient to their service without reservation. That this orientation was atypical was evident in their need to justify such deviant behavior to colleagues, superiors, and subordinates and in the amount of negotiation often entailed in achieving that end. A clearly articulated rationale was frequently necessary to counter the GROP orientation. For example:

There was a long discussion between SRs Burton and Kots, both of whom had come down from the ICU to the ER, on what to do with a woman in the code room—where to put her and whether to take her in the ICU. Kots offered to take her even though there was some argument about whether her presenting problem was stroke or heart trouble. If it was stroke, she would go to neurology. Kots's dislike of the neurology service was evident. He said, "I'd hate her to be in their hands. The patient would just lie at the bottom [of the neurology rehabilitation service] and not have her heart problem worked up at all." Burton seemed to resent the whole affair and said, "You don't have to take her and you really shouldn't be pushed around." Kots added, "It's not that much trouble." After another half hour of discussion, Burton again asked, "Why the hell are we taking her?" Later on, Intern Elan came down from the ICU. He was trying to discourage Kots from taking the woman because he'd have the major management responsibility. (Field notes, ER)

Social characteristics and disease processes, together with the house staff's perception of their role and responsibility as internists, all influenced patient evaluation and anti-GROP inclinations. Demographic factors such as sex, class, and age, along with their assessment of a patient's social value and the patient's attitude toward them, sometimes militated against the overriding desire to GROP, or at least allowed them to justify to themselves and to others their continued caring for a patient. This is exemplified in the testimony of Intern Zimmerman:

> In my clinic today there was an eighty-two-year-old man who was as cute as a button. He had bad medical problems but didn't want to come into the hospital. I wanted to take care of him so bad because I thought he'd be a great patient—give me a good history, interesting physical findings, problems that would be interesting to manage, and he was a nice guy. I would enjoy watching him get better as opposed to a drunk, all smelly, with dt's, vomiting, seizures—all I could think of is, "You did it to yourself, you 'gomer.'" I really can't get empathetic with [the latter].

and in another instance of positive patient evaluation and anti-GROP behavior:

> [With regard to a patient with a swollen hand], after several consultations, JR Grots said [to his team], "Hand surgery has looked at him." The intern responded, "I don't want to get rid of him. He's a nice guy." Grots answered, "Yes, we're learning a lot from him. We shouldn't cancel him too hastily." (Field notes, GH)

If a patient had an interesting disease or if a house officer believed there was a strong possibility of having some positive impact on the course of his or her illness—both rare occurrences—those factors also affected his or her desire to keep that patient.

Another reason not to GROP was that the patient could be used for house staff instruction; if they could practice or learn something clinically about diagnostic or therapeutic procedures, they would sometimes retain a patient. These occasional interesting patients were kept because they either presented diagnostic dilemmas or manifested some remarkable variation of a disease, thereby capturing the attention, fascination, and time of the house staff and faculty. The compensatory factor for the time and energy and interest in these cases was clearly educational benefit; that is, the individual, the house staff, or the discipline as a whole might benefit from studying that patient.

The social assessment of patients entered into the decision to hold on to them. If a patient was liked (because he or she approximated an ideal or was interesting or some combination), a decision might be reached not to put him or her through additional psychological and financial costs for questionable or unlikely ends. On the other hand, a procedure might be recommended for a preferred patient because a house officer strongly believed it would benefit the patient, even if the house officer did not need the practice. A less worthy or socially devalued patient was apt to be sent home with a rather perfunctory diagnosis and therapeutic regimen (i.e., GROPed as soon as possible) unless the need for practice indicated otherwise.

At times, too, detested patients became interesting cases because they had complex symptoms or were identified as multisystem failures (in their slang, as "trainwrecks"). Moreover, these were often the types of patients the staff could not GROP easily because they were seriously ill and required aggressive and prolonged therapy regardless of the contempt the house staff may have felt for them. In short, there was a great deal of latitude and complexity in the decision-making process, but the bottom line was unmistakable: there was almost always a quid pro quo for a non-GROP action. For example:

> With regard to a recently diagnosed cancer patient, Attending Baumgarten said, "We should keep him here for a learning experience and also to develop a relationship with him. After all, he has a right to participate in what's going on with him. . . . Don't tell them [the ears, nose, and throat department] that that's our motivation for keeping him. They won't like it." (Field notes, GH)

Occasionally a house officer saw him or herself as a savior of his or her patients, as in the following instance:

> An old black man with apparent renal problems, whom SR Farmer and the others called "George," was referred to as a "neat old man" whom they wanted to keep for a while. Junior Resident Grasso presented all the things that were done to him last night. This patient was diagnosed as having prostate cancer, and there was joking about the kinds of surgical procedures the urology department would do [if they transferred him], including cutting off his testicles—which they thought was too aggressive. (Field notes, ICU)

A patient might thus be kept to protect him or her from the larger system, which often included other specialties or departments within the hospital complex. This kind of behavior, which would occasionally prevent a GROP action, was cited as well by other house officers:

> JR Grots:
> [With regard to memorable experiences] . . . I can remember a particular guy that I saved from chemotherapy. I experimented with a variety of drugs—he was riddled with cancer—for six weeks. Afterwards, he was more peppy or alert than he had been for a year. He was delighted and the family was delighted. I think it's a bitter irony that what I had really done was keep him out of the clutches of medical therapy and that was in reality one of my greatest medical triumphs.

The exceptional patient was a rare but important phenomenon. He or she had educational value or provided the opportunity for meaningful intervention in the disease process, in the latter case, helping to bolster flagging feelings of potency, sometimes even causing house staff elation at actually having helped someone. The house staff, aware at some level that they were potentially the patient's worst enemy, could also take pleasure in sometimes helping a "nice" patient evade the clutches of others who might induce iatrogenesis.

CONCLUSION

While this research confirms the existence of the moral evaluations revealed in the pejorative slang of the house staff (e.g., vet, gomer, shpos, solid citizen, turkey, garbage, and so forth), it also reveals that the system of social classification of patients was exceedingly subtle and complex, taking into account the many structural and professional factors discussed in the previous chapter. Hence, before a novice doctor can decide to GROP, he or she must be able, upon cursory observation, to categorize the patient in terms conforming to the coordinates of the house staff subculture. The house staff must learn to social-type patients; indeed, mistyping was a common error among interns and medical students, often leading their more experienced peers to criticize them.

So extensive and contradictory was the range of uninteresting and despised patients described by so many house officers that one wonders whether there is a truly welcome patient. What appears to exist for patients is a double-bind or no-win situation: they may be regarded as system abusers (labeled as demanding, with trivial or vague complaints) who seek care too soon and hence inappropriately or as self-abusers (labeled as neglectful) who seek care too late and hence also inappropriately. Moreover, every patient is a potential house staff abuser. In essence, patients are damned if and when they seek medical care as well as when they do not.

Since these house officers are public hospital providers, they come into daily contact with what they perceive as the lowest level of society. Many resent the presence of these poor wretches. From their position of relative social privilege, the house staff devalue many of their clientele. Because they are interested in learning from the diseases of these patients, and the patients, for the most part, are there to get well, there can be a conflict of interests between the doctors, who want to diagnose and learn procedures, and the patients, who want help but become instruments on which doctors train. If they are unable or unwilling to be such instruments, they are often devalued and GROPed by the doctors, whose orientation is reinforced by the normative standards of the profession and the house staff culture.

Chapter 5

GROP Strategies
Implementing the GROP Perspective

Responsible as they were for large numbers of patients at various stages of illness and requiring varying degrees of medical intervention and being under the strain of experiencing, simultaneously, a desire to GROP—to let go—and the necessity of, or occasionally the desire to, hold on to patients, the house staff continuously resorted to a variety of patient-related coping mechanisms in order to survive in this frustrating environment.[1] This chapter examines *how* the house staff GROP. They learned a set of techniques that distanced them from patients physically and psychologically. House officers got rid of patients physically by transferring, discharging, and at times refusing to receive them and by passing many responsibilities toward them down the medical hierarchy or across to social workers and other nonmedical staff. They distanced themselves from patients psychologically by adopting the mechanisms of omission, avoidance, and objectification.[2] Though I discuss these techniques separately, in reality they often overlapped or merged in the course of house staff's daily activity, which fell into four basic areas of involvement: with colleagues, with diagnostic or therapeutic procedures, with patients' medical records, and finally, with patients and their families.

The house staff's coping strategies could be interpreted as having the quality of defense mechanisms in that there were maladaptive consequences. They did not seem to shield them from guilt or keep doubts from surfacing even though the house officers were not always fully cognizant of their adverse effects.

NEGOTIATION AND EXCHANGE

The concepts of collective definition of a situation, shared perspectives, and negotiated order (Maines 1982; A. Strauss 1963, 1978) can be applied to the processes by which the house staff both attempted to (and frequently could) translate the GROP orientation into action.[3] The house staff learned how to justify its GROP behavior to those to whom it felt accountable and to those to whom it owed allegiance. It was often necessary to convince any or all of a number of constituencies: peers, supervising house staff, subordinates, fellows, attendings, the department of medicine, occasionally the hospital administration, and rarely, patients and their families. House officers also had to satisfy to some degree their own felt need for consonance between their actions and their professional pride, morality, and ethics.

What passed as tolerable and appropriate GROP behavior varied within wide, flexible, and shifting parameters. Further, the definition of acceptable GROP conduct depended on who was reviewing their behavior. How they responded to others' assessments of their conduct was based on the importance they attributed to those assessments and on the anticipated repercussions, should there be a clash of perspectives.

Fostering Cooperation

The house staff seemed to be constantly preoccupied with ways to GROP. Within the legitimate system it could either transfer or discharge the patients or, less frequently, resist their admission. Both Bucher and Stelling (1977) and Mumford (1970) have identified these processes in university hospital environments they studied. Given the autonomous nature of private institutions, house staff physicians in those settings have even more support from the system and the profession for their GROP actions than do house staff training in public settings.

The house staff's ongoing assessment of the quality of its training experience was based in part on how much it was able to control the patient flow on and off its service.[4] For example, most of the house staff preferred the ICUs. Senior residents could control who was admitted to them. There were only a small number of patients to care for at any one time, and there was a high turnover. Patients died or were quickly transferred out, so there was a built-in GROP mechanism. Because patients were in critical condition, staff were not expected to form any relationship with them and therefore they could practice high-technology medicine with a great deal of efficiency.

The house staff jargon reflecting the intense dynamic of negotiated GROP processes included the terms "dispo-ing" (for discharging) and "dumping" or "turfing" (for transferring) as well as the slang labels "rock" and "sieve" for house staffers engaged in those processes. As Mumford (1970) also notes, a "rock" resists patient admissions, and a "sieve" lets them through, the implication being that a rock may be too hard-nosed, a sieve too lenient. In the house staff culture, it was generally better to err on the side of being a rock, as noted by SR Kots:

> I think the things we value as a group are sort of strange but typical of a house staff. We value proficiency in "house staffmanship," which include[s], you know, not admitting those who don't need to be admitted, and all the slang things you probably run across, you know, "turfing" people, "dumping" people, "dispo's," all the sort of tacky side of the whole business.

The connotations of these pervasive, value-laden house staff expressions are significant because they go beyond the technical or administrative aspects of their patient management function. They reflect an endemic ideology—a mutually shared GROP perspective in everyday operation. This one of the countless manifestations of this ideology occurred in the ER, but by no means was GROP behavior limited to this service:

> Senior Resident Walters saw an old man who had an infected foot in the emergency room with an oxygen mask on. He turned to ER Fable and said [with obvious sarcasm], "You've got a great 'turf' there for surgery. They can try and save his foot!" (Field notes, ER)

The tendency to resist taking patients was demonstrated by exceptions to the rule of GROP conduct that actually highlighted its salience. In one case,

> a physician's assistant came in to the ER describing a patient's complaint: "There's a woman with a clot in her eye." This caused the house staff to look at each other with skeptical amazement. Senior Resident Clyde finally said to the patient, "You know where the 'psych' clinic is. . . ." Senior Resident Archer offered to see her since the patient was already on the examining table. The nurse said to Archer out loud, "You're nice, but with some [house staff], *you take your life in your hands if you bring in someone like her* [emphasis added]. I make sure they [the patients] are hanging by a thread before I do that." (Field notes, VAH)

The more typical interaction was one in which the house staff employed one strategy after another to avoid taking patients. Repeatedly the house staff attempted to manipulate and control the situation, sometimes jokingly but almost always with impunity. The following are a few illustrations of the many negotiations I observed:

> Attending Faculty Yanet received a call over the loudspeaker. When he hung up, he told the group that a patient was supposed to be readmitted to their oncology service because of a fever. (No one thought it was an emergency.) Senior Resident Johnson

smiled and said, "Send her to the 'private' service," after he heard it was a patient with metastatic breast cancer. (Field notes, GH)

Senior Resident Flips asked a question about whether or not to bring another sick alcoholic patient back to the ICU. Senior Resident Woody said to Filps, "You'd be in disfavor with all of us if you did." Attending Carl reaffirmed this by saying, "The other units are more appropriate for that kind of 'train wreck' [very sick patient]." (Field notes, ICU)

Social factors continuously influenced decisions such as whether and how to transfer or discharge specific patients, and conversely (for those on the receiving end) when to accept or admit a patient. Commenting positively on the social status or situation of the patient was one way that house officers tried to persuade or cajole other house staffers to accept a patient they wished to GROP, as in this case of a man categorized as a derelict:

There was some negotiation between SR Fable and Resident Miller as to whether or not Fable would take Miller's patient to "clean him out." Miller was very tactfully trying to work the presentation up in a way so that Fable would be so inclined. Finally, Fable said, "No way. I have a 'quad' [quadriplegic] here and I'm trying to knock his fever down so he can go home. There are no beds." (Field notes, ER)

Conversely, moderate or high status as well as complicated or unusual medical problems became a bargaining chip in the negotiating process:

Junior Resident Gard was observed telling JR Jover, "I have a patient for you. He's someone who's a 'solid citizen'! No drinking, many things wrong with him— "interesting" patient. (Field notes, ER)

The internal medicine house staff became a community of mutual interest, support, and collaboration when it came to transferring patients to non–internal medical services within the hospital or to other institutions. When, however, they had to GROP to each other, they generally approached that task sensitively, with empathy, respect, and commiseration for their peers. By and large, the house officers were apologetic to each other and (with a few exceptions) attempted to justify their actions in a conciliatory manner, as in the following exchanges:

Junior Resident McGee had been to see the x-ray of a psychotic woman patient who was sent from the state mental hospital [to the OPC]. He commented to himself out loud, "God knows why she was sent here." McGee telephoned a fellow JR and told him about the patient he had to admit to him [on the inpatient service]. He said sympathetically, "She doesn't talk, only to the birds. I tried to wish 'it' away, but I couldn't. Sure enough, the mass in the belly was there as big as day." (Field notes, OPC)

Senior Resident Smith spoke to Intern Richards, who was on call, about the fact that he had another admission for her. He said, "The patient has crazy chest pains which he developed when his wife said she didn't want him back." Richard replied that she already had two other admissions, so Smith said, apologetically, "There's no hurry to come and get him." (Field notes, VAH)

The patients, then, became, quite literally, a medium of exchange between house staff members. They were, however, usually valued negatively; therefore, in the interests of collegiality and for the maintenance of group cohesion, each member was expected to maintain his or her fair share of patients. Articulated rules specified the conditions under which patients might be "dispo'ed," "turfed," "dumped," or otherwise GROPed. Negotiation over the disposition of patients was carried on in terms of these rules, to the point that, when a physician did not GROP when the opportunity presented itself, he had to make the house staff aware that this was the rare exception to a rule. The GROPing of a patient to a peer incurred a "favor" owed, an unspecified obligation (Gouldner, 1960).

Splits in the Seams of Collegiality

In spite of the camaraderie and compassion among house staff, there still were many instances of potential strain and conflict rather than cooperation and consensus. Attempts to GROP to colleagues were often resisted because the intended recipients were operating from the same principle. Efforts could be thwarted by others who were behaving as "rocks" or who structurally (given the nature of the service) could more easily "dispo" or "turf." The following comment illustrates the frequent and complex dynamics involved in heated daily GROP negotiations:

INTERN MINEY:
There's not too much "dumping" within [internal] medicine. We really feel like we're all in the same boat. We sort of developed together, and we really don't dump on each other too much. . . . [However], you may run into a situation where a patient on GH is a "vet" and they send him out to the VAH. . . . That means another resident has to work him up . . . and to me, that's "dumping."

The disposition of patients was a critical determinant of house staff relations. Intense struggles between staff members occasionally occurred over the issue of dumping. While a certain amount of frustration was taken out on the patients, it sometimes adversely affected collegial relations as well, as indicated in the following interview:

SR RIND:
I hated my patients, and most interns do. I mean you call them scumbags," "dirtbags," "gomers," you know, all kinds of disrespectful names. . . . Everybody wants

to dump on everyone else [here]. It's trying to avoid as much work as you can by dumping on someone else.

Animosity between house staff members was observed on numerous occasions when doctors felt they had been unfairly "dumped on" by their colleagues:

Junior Resident Lovell had an argument on the telephone with JR Leads. He complained that Leads always gave him a hard time. "When I'm at the VAH he sends me all his patients," Lovell said to a fellow JR. . . . Soon Leads called back, apparently refusing to take the patient. Lovell said to the others, "Well, we'll have to load the guy up here; they won't take him over there." (Field notes, ER)

Intern Shu was on the phone with the ER resident. He said, "But this is my fourth or fifth 'hit' [hospital admission]. Please talk to my resident." Junior Resident Cape rubbed his hands in a mock combative style and said to Shu, "I'm looking forward to a good fight. I hate this 'dumping.'" (Field notes, VAH)

These natural antagonisms were at times exacerbated by deviant peer behavior. A certain small group of house officers acquired a bad reputation for being particularly difficult (for example, for exhibiting extreme "rock-like" behavior to their peers), and for not playing the game cooperatively. Most contemptible in the eyes of the house staff was sloughing behavior,[5] that is, sloppy or lazy management of patients that could not be GROPed. This might entail ignoring problems or avoiding important tasks so that it became the responsibility of another fellow house officer to complete or rectify the incomplete or inadequate work left behind. Sloughing was an infringement or imposition on a colleague and, as such, an unforgivable social sin:

SR STELLA:
The reasons I say two out of thirty [of my peers] I would not refer patients to is due to the fact that they are unethical, greedy, lazy sloughs. As an intern, you can't slough, but there's an opportunity to slough as a JR and SR.

SR DEREN:
There are some residents I don't like. There are thirty of us, and there are a few people that are sloughs — they don't pull their share of the work, and it's very disappointing to find out there are people like that. . . . These are the people who will send an unassigned patient to the clinic for someone else to work up after they have already dumped the patient. They try to get out of as much work as possible and make more work for other people. There are some residents who will not take someone who should really go into intensive care and will sort of dump him on the ward. It definitely happens. It's hard to hold them accountable. There is a lot of peer pressure against it, and some people just continue to do it. . . . They are well known as sloughs and they become quite disliked.

Inappropriate GROP conduct was contained by peer pressure (i.e., informal social control). House officers guilty of such behavior were ostracized within the limitations of the structure and occasionally retaliated against, as suggested in this discussion:

> The story was retold about how Intern Newman and JR Belton got a particular [patient] admission from one of their peers. Jones, a former chief resident, said, "That's ridiculous. I wouldn't stand for it. . . . " And when JR Beech was told about another SR who was admitting patients who wouldn't listen to reason, Jones again commented, "I'd tell him to shove it up his ass." Junior Resident Beech said, "*Wait till I'm on the outside admitting patients. I'll really sock it to him*" [emphasis added]. (Field notes, VAH)

In general, house officers favorably evaluated their peers and commended the training program precisely because it encouraged collegial rather than competitive relationships. Not only did most of them feel a camaraderie with their peers, but as noted in Chapter Two, there was evidence that both the peers and the program clearly encouraged collective, self-protecting, mutual assistance behavior typical of the socially insulated individual toward the collective. Support of fellow house officers was not only necessary for individual survival but for the collective survival of the autonomous house staff culture.

Most of the negotiation, manipulation, and exchange occurred informally within the house staff culture, but occasionally, when a chronic conflict persisted or negotiations reached a stalemate, or when too many house staff—a critical mass—began to exploit the game (i.e., to abuse their power and position), more formal structural resolutions were threatened or imposed from above. When outside intervention did occur, regardless of the problem that caused it, the house staff generally resented and resisted it. Overall, they considered many of these dilemmas inevitable and ultimately unresolvable.

As a result, there were limits to the amount and kind of manipulation that could be done in order to GROP. It was acceptable to target the external environment (defined as almost any service outside of internal medicine), but they had to be much more cautious when negotiating internally because acceptable GROP behavior was much more narrowly defined when dealing with colleagues. When they could not GROP to peers, there were two other strategies they could use within the hospital system: they could unload patients (or at least unwanted patient tasks) on their organizational inferiors, that is, GROP down the status system; alternatively, they could GROP laterally to functionally subordinate staff personnel such as social workers.

PASSING THE PATIENT DOWN THE HIERARCHY

In the vertical GROP process, the house staff took advantage of the formal training hierarchy within the medical center. Authority began with the attending faculty passing down suggestions (with varying degrees of firmness) to the residents; the residents then passed them along to interns and sometimes to medical students; and then, on occasion, the interns instructed the medical students.

A variety of patient-related responsibilities, especially those that fell within the realm of the caring function (Mauksch 1973) or the humanistic aspects of patient care (Howard and Strauss 1975), were frequently given directly to the least experienced person on the team—the third-year medical student—or to the busiest and most harassed person—the intern. While it is true that the educational goal of training is to provide novice physicians with a variety of patient care experiences, decisions to apportion patient interaction tasks seemed seldom to have been made on that basis alone. Rather, they seemed, for the most part, to be made on the basis of privilege and preference. For example:

An elderly black male patient who was sitting rather passively was discussed. Junior Resident Jovers asked the intern if the patient could be trusted to take certain medication. Intern Chu said he wasn't sure but he had a sister and he would talk to her. Chu then mentioned to the patient that the *medical student* would give him full instructions. (Field notes, VAH) [emphasis added]

Attending Kirk suggested an EEG [a test of brain functioning] to determine whether they should be aggressive on a patient. He asked, "What does the family know?" and SR Farmer responded, "Unfortunately, we have not been able to speak to his wife yet, but *Intern Krist is hoping to do that today*" [emphasis added]. (Field notes, ICU)

On another occasion,

the wife of a patient had apparently given her husband the wrong drug. . . . Attending Quog then turned to the medical student and told him he's going to have to instruct the wife better.

The overall message was that the house staff had neither the time, inclination, nor responsibility (in the case of the residents) for carrying out these patient or family-related contacts:

Junior Resident Cape responded sarcastically to a medical student's questions with regard to talking to a family. "I don't talk to the family anymore. Tell Intern Cory. He'd love to talk to the family." (Field notes, VAH)

Junior Resident Patty told me, "sometimes it's better when they don't have a family. . . . Because of the time, it's almost a relief not to have to sit down and explain to a family what the patient had. It takes a lot of time. . . . After Mr. V. died, the intern handled it". (Field notes, VAH)

Most interns considered these contacts an imposition on their time and energy and looked forward to the time when they could GROP down the hierarchy:

Intern Zorez commented, "One thing I'm looking forward to as a JR—not having to deal with families." (Field notes, VAH)

Instructing patients on medical dosage, advising or comforting a family, and otherwise personalizing patient care was regarded as "fluff" to be palmed off on others. The narrow definition of what constituted internal medicine, together with the stress and the inundation of work in internship, resulted in such tasks receiving low priority. When they could not assign a task to medical subordinates and the need was great, they would GROP to ancillary staff.

PASSING THE PATIENT ACROSS THE SYSTEM

The most commonly acknowledged way to GROP horizontally was to use social workers, for they had an accepted and formal role in the discharge process. The house staff evaluated social workers on how efficiently and expeditiously they helped the house staff GROP by completing chores or overcoming obstacles to GROP behavior:

INTERN MCGEE:
I was somewhat impressed [initially] with the social workers at the VAH because there were long social work resumes about patients on the charts. [After a consult] . . . I said, "Oh my God this is a real hotshot unit. They're going to start turning my patients out" . . . and then I realized that there was . . . no action and my patients just sat and sat and sat and I'd call the social worker and I'd get the run around.

Social workers were frequently blamed when patients remained on a service longer than deemed appropriate by the house staff:

FAMILY PRACTICE INTERN PIKE:
I think there's an attitude that they're the ones [social workers] that you went to as far as dispositional matters . . . and there was criticism about them because they weren't able to get them [patients] out fast enough.

JR SAUL:
[My relationship with social workers is] poor. I think we feel that they sort of get what they deserve. . . because they don't help us when we ask for help. . . .We say place a patient, and they don't work that hard. That's pretty much the consensus. . . . An intern is desperate to get people to help you, and you get irritated when they don't.

Only rarely did the house staff acknowledge the serious structural problems involved in disposition, especially when residential placement was needed. Very few ever showed an awareness of the professional component of discharge planning: the skill involved in making complex and sensitive social, psychological, and financial arrangements with patients, families, and community or institutional resources (Mizrahi and Abramson 1985). To them, so-cial workers and other ancillary medical staff were important only in so far as they were useful in the GROP process. Hence, relationships were often strained, as ancillary professional staff reacted to the narrow, often one-sided communication. Ironically, by not sharing patient care management decisions with nonphysicians, many house officers subverted their ability to GROP efficiently.

OMISSION: NARROWING THE FOCUS OF INTERACTION

There were times when house officers, particularly interns, could not, for medical or social reasons, unload patients or patient-related responsibilities on others. Then they attempted instead to cope with the heavy demands on their time and energy by controlling the scope and substance of their interaction with patients and their families.

Limiting the Patient's History

The emphasis on efficient data collection became a coping mechanism that distanced the doctor from the patient even though at times it conflicted with the norm of compulsiveness. In an attempt to treat efficiently the overwhelm-ing numbers of patients, the house staff narrowed both the scope and the sub-stance of interaction, eliminating all but the "essential," while continuously condensing the definition of essential. For example:

FAMILY PRACTICE INTERN DANET:
I used to get frustrated with people because patients rambled. Now I just don't give them a chance to ramble. People might be offended because I do that, but on the other hand, it is much more efficient than to have somebody take a half hour or forty-five minutes of your time and really not be able to get everything that you want. You need to be able to get the gist—what's important. . . . You know what you're trying to find out, and a lot of times they do have a lot of important things to tell you, so you have to watch out. You could become so objective that you don't get what you want out of it.

A thorough history and physical can take as long as two hours. The interns reported that one of their goals (which was reinforced and promoted by super-vising house staff) was to learn how to complete the process in substantially less time without sacrificing thoroughness. To accomplish this, they sought to learn, through constant negotiation and redefinition, what to include and what to leave out. For the history to be considered complete and "textbook" cor-rect, the house staff learned they were to focus the history taking on current medical problems, past medical history, family history, and social history.

Being able to elicit a good history from the patient is the essence of internal medicine, as house staff were reminded by attendings and fellow house officers. Yet the ideal of the centrality of the patient history in internal medicine practice came into conflict with the reality of the demands on staff time. As a result, the house staff frequently blamed the patient when the history was incomplete or incorrect. I repeatedly heard in formal and informal interactions among colleagues and supervisors such comments as "The patient is a poor historian"; "She may not be telling you the whole story"; "The patient is an unreliable or unbelievable historian"; "That's a bizarre story." On rounds

> a patient clearly indicated that he wasn't drinking anymore. Everyone on the team snickered, believing it probably wasn't true. (Field notes, GH)

The house staff learned the technique of omission. House officers learned that it was acceptable to short cut the patient history and omit information if it did not seem directly pertinent to the medical diagnosis. Simultaneously, they learned that to spend extensive time engaged in the doctor–patient relationship went unrewarded and indeed might even lead to sanctions from their mentors if activities more important in the latter's eyes were ignored or postponed.

As they progressed through each level of training, the definition of the information to be obtained from the patient as part of the initial history was defined in increasingly narrow terms. While new interns had been socialized in medical school to accept the importance of a thorough patient history, many quickly learned through extensive contact with supervising residents which data were essential and which could routinely be ignored. A junior resident summed up the dynamics:

> You know I'd love to sit and hold their hand for half an hour and more but you also want to get home sometime before midnight and you have other things to do. If you don't sit and talk with the cancer patient for a half hour, in terms of your job description and what's expected, nobody will be upset with you. But if you don't know what the hemoglobin is on that patient, they [the resident, chief, and chief of medicine] are going to be very upset.

The house staff's perception of the importance of their involvement in the broader social dimensions of patient care was limited in spite of the growing body of literature on this subject. While pragmatic considerations governed the attention they paid to these factors, level of training was clearly also a determinant. For many, the belief that social factors were irrelevant to medical treatment of their patients deepened as they progressed through training:

INTERN PATTY:
I'm not a very psychiatric-minded person. I'm not one of those people who says a patient need[s] to go into therapy. . . . It's sadly true; their psychiatric problems are

94

probably last on my list. . . . I don't have time to sit there and discuss this guy's future with him. . . . There are certain patients who are sociopaths. . . . You can't do anything for those people. . . . In theory these factors are always important in a patient's care. In practice, you're always so busy taking care of their actual medical problems that you don't have time to sit there.

JR ZIMMERMAN:
The amount of time spent on social factors depends on the situation. Sometimes I probably did a lot and sometimes I probably did little. . . . If it affect[ed] them either going home or coming back and was medically appropriate, I dealt with it. Otherwise, I didn't get into it. I don't see myself being their private physician. I don't feel that I have the time or the energy or really the desire to get into their personal lives.

Regardless of the role orientation with which they may have begun internship, there was continuous mutual reinforcement for a less comprehensive approach to patient care during training. Senior Resident Beech epitomizes the result:

I guess I could use the excuse that I don't have the time to do that [deal with social problems]. . . . It would be nice to bullshit with your patients for an hour or so and get a feel for their social situation. . . . It may affect the complaints they present with. . . . If I was Marcus Welby [a former TV physician] and saw one patient per week, maybe I would be more concerned.[6] I doubt it though, because it's really not appealing to me. If I really wanted to do it, I would have majored in social work or psychiatry. What appeals to me is treatment of sick people by diagnosing their diseases and giving medications. *I like good hard facts and physical findings*—things I can deal with on a tangible basis—not some intangible nebulous feeling of what their social situation is [emphasis added].

Learning the Omission Technique

From their own experieces, several of the house officers and all of the family practice informants described how they learned the omission technique, that is, how they learned to narrow the focus of their interest in patients:

FAMILY PRACTICE INTERN DANET:
I started the first year [presenting the social history] . . . where they live . . . how many children, etc. No one cares about that on rounds . . . so you end up just putting the minimum—that's all they care about. . . . *You'd be making a presentation as an intern and you'd realize that that bored them* [emphasis added]. They'd say, "Get to something important." You learn pretty quickly from what the residents and interns consider important that they don't want to hear all this other stuff.

FAMILY PRACTICE INTERN WOLF, summed up the process:
We were taught that the social history is supposed to be anything that pertains to a patient's life outside the hospital. . . . But the only thing that ever gets asked is smoking and drinking habits. I think a lot of people start out with the attitude, "These factors are important, but I don't have time." . . . As your training goes on,

you ignore them more and more; eventually *there comes a time when those things don't even enter your consciousness anymore—you become more and more narrow in your approach* . . . a lot of it is not intentional. . . . *It's what's rewarded* [emphasis added].

The more experienced residents thus clearly signified to new interns and medical students what was and was not valued. Whenever the novices presented anything defined as nonessential, the more experienced residents, and occasionally the attendings, gestured for them to "get to the point" or exhorted them to "give only the pertinent facts." Sometimes a house officer would snap his fingers impatiently. Other times they would fall asleep, yawn, and otherwise communicate boredom and restlessness. Little in the organization or culture contradicted this narrow and detached view of the doctor–patient relationship. The directive "Obtain just the [medical] facts" was thus elevated to the status of an unofficial but sanctioned norm of house staff–patient encounters.

The technique of omission was part of a larger behavioral repertoire that distanced physicians from their patients. Omission was part of a process of instrumentalization; that is, the doctor–patient relationship was defined as if it belonged at the extreme end of the instrumental–affectivity continuum. This instrumentalization process may have been functional in getting work done, but it only reinforced already existing social–structural differences between doctors and patients. Moreover, many of the house staff at SAMs expressed antipathy toward many types of patients and used avoidance techniques.

AVOIDANCE

The actual time spent in direct patient interaction was, with a few exceptions, brief, and the purpose was almost exclusively the acquisition of necessary information directly related to the disease. I found myself staying on site late into the evening in the hope of getting to observe individual house staff–patient and family encounters beyond the taking of the initial history. My assumption was that such interaction would be necessary to help the patient and the family understand and properly manage the disease, to allay their fears, and for the house staff to be able to assess the psychosocial and emotional factors that directly and indirectly affect healing and compliance. Such interaction almost never materialized, as Duff and Hollingshead (1968) and Williamson, Beitman, and Katon (1981) also observed.

The Procedural Orientation

The house staff was constantly busy filling out forms; ordering laboratory tests; consulting with others; reading voluminous medical records; preparing for, conducting, or following up on various rounds; doing or teaching myriad procedures; transporting patients and records; writing on charts; and more. Interacting with patients was but a minor activity, as indicated by the testimony of Family Practice Intern Richards:

> The amount of time the [internal medicine] house staff spends with a patient after initial history and physical depends. It may be as little as five minutes a day, three to five minutes on morning rounds. . . . Sometimes if the family can catch you, you may spend more time [answering their questions]—if they actually grab you and drag you into the room.

The house staff's own perceptions of the small amount of time given to direct interaction with patients and their families was indicated by these typical comments:

> JR McGee:
> If I was really busy, I was avoiding patients. I wouldn't avoid those who were critically ill. It would be the patients who were just on "automatic pilot" where the family would want to know—say—"Would she ever play the violin again?"

> In an afternoon spent with Intern Cory, the question was posed: "How much time do you spend with each of your patients?" He responded . . . "That's a good question. Because I wonder sometimes what I'm doing—not more than fifteen minutes at the bedside, then a half hour or more writing notes, entering orders, checking on labs, etc." (Field notes, GH)

Regardless of whether the house officers felt procedures were necessary or justified, they felt compelled to learn about and directly experience as many of them as possible. The house staff labeled extremes of this behavior as "shotgunning"—ordering everything to avoid a small chance of being wrong or "rubber banding"—stretching the diagnostic indications for a procedure for educational rather than patient care purposes. At times, focusing on the instrumentalities of medicine seemed to be a strategy for psychologically avoiding the patient as a human being. Others have labeled this type of coping mechanism as "escape into work" (Coombs and Goldman 1973) or "turning to technique" (Light 1980). House staff especially avoided patients and their families during those times when they could not justify a particular test or when the procedure produced no positive, or else negative, findings. The list of tests for which they felt obligated to obtain the patient's or a family member's written permission also shrank as they learned how lenient the system was toward the ordering of most procedures, and the instances of mandated patient interaction shrank accordingly.

Involvement with procedures occupied house staff time and took precedence over patient interaction. Patients' feelings and opinions were often disregarded or not sought in the first place. So intent were the staff on doing everything *to* the patient, there appeared to be little time or awareness devoted to doing anything *with* or *for* the patient, for example, just comforting him or her:

> Prior to attending rounds Intern Zorez told me that it was okay to follow him around. "You'll see. You have to spend so much of your time doing these things (he points to the computer) such as entering lab data, scheduling tests, labeling lab data, etc., instead of being a doctor. *I have no time to think about my patients' problems.*" (Field notes, VAH)

The Personification of the Medical Record

When they were not involved in the preparation, implementation, or evaluation of diagnostic or therapeutic procedures, the most significant portion of the house officers' time was spent with the patient's medical record. Indeed, it appeared that as much, if not more, of their actual time and energy each day was devoted to patients' charts than to any other activity. Hours each day were occupied with requesting, waiting for, reading, reviewing, discussing, and writing in medical records. While the importance of accurate record keeping cannot be denied, it also became clear that, as the staff read and discussed its contents, the chart became the focal point around which all else revolved, the very personification of the patient.

Action ceased when there was no chart. Being forced to act or decide without a chart made house officers notably tense. The chart became the basis of patient management. This preoccupation with and ultimate reification of the medical record reinforced both attitudes of mistrust toward many patients and the predominant professional inclination to focus on diagnosis. To diagnose without missing anything, the house staff needed to know "everything" about the patient—past and present—and the chart was the vehicle for becoming informed. Not only did they commonly believe that, in many cases, they could learn more from the chart than from the patient but that often they would learn more accurately. For example:

> In the (ICU) Intern Zorez consulted with a surgeon with a patient who had become a surgical emergency. . . . When the surgeon asked Zorez about the patient's pulses, he said, "Actually, I never checked them, but in the chart it said. . . ." (Field notes, PH)

When there was a discrepancy between what they learned from the chart and what they learned from the patient or family, they frequently believed the medical record, as in this example:

> A patient was presented by a medical student. . . . It was mentioned in her social history that she had a forty-five year history of smoking and occasional drinking. The medical student added emphatically, "But her chart says she was a heavy user." (Field notes, GH)

Given the cultural and class barriers between the house staff and the typical patient population, together with its lack of time to communicate extensively with patients, the chart often became an easier and surer source of information. The chart actually seemed to replace the patient at times, as when the staff talked about a patient while pointing to and looking at the chart—in the patient's presence as well as absence.[7] The preoccupation with the chart allowed the staff to avoid patients and contributed to the related coping technique of objectification.

OBJECTIFICATION: THE PATIENT AS A "NONPERSON"

Goffman (1959:151) has described the role of being neither audience nor actor as the status of "nonperson." He points out that it is a discrepant role and that the "classic" nonperson is the servant. Treating patients as absent when they are physically present denies the existence of the human subject. By treating most patients as subjectless objects, the house staff eliminated them as active participants in patient care in spite of increasing data on the importance of patient involvement (Howard and Strauss, 1975; Sorenson 1974). Techniques of objectification were applied in collegial and patient interaction and appeared to be grounded in the basic process and structure of graduate medical training, such as doctors' behavior on rounds (also identified by Mumford [1970] and Roberts [1977], among others). They also seem basic to the professional orientation of medicine, for they help doctors to separate the patient from the disease; to deny pain and suffering, especially if it is not, in their estimation, organically based (Coombs and Goldman 1973); and to discredit or dismiss commonplace or uncomplicated illness.

Objectification during Rounds

Rounds often included a visit to the bedside, with or without attendings, and, in the case of a new patient, a brief physical exam and history taking. During these bedside visits the house staff talked about the patients in the third person, used medical terminology incomprehensible to most patients, and often looked past them, failing to establish eye contact. It frequently appeared as if the patients and especially the family members were invisible to them. (Roberts [1977] describes the encounter between patient and physician in a medical center as a clash of two different world perspectives.) For example:

> There was a lot of discussion on rounds about the kinds of procedures to do on a black male patient. Intern Old was in a quandary about how to treat the UTI [urinary tract infection]. All this time the patient was trying to eat. They went on talking. Intern Cory said something to the group about the patient's hand. The patient looked

up and said, "I sprained it," showing that he did hear and understand what was being discussed, although he had been ignored. (Field notes, GH)

Clearly, ignoring the patient was intended to expedite the patient care goal while emphasizing the teaching–learning goal. The passivity of the patient role was also impressed upon both the novice internist and the patient. If time were taken after rounds for more extensive patient contact, then rounds behavior could simply be viewed as functional, but house staff rarely returned to the bedside.

Sometimes the use of objectification techniques confused, frightened, even hurt patients. While there was no evidence that these consequences were intentional, this house staff behavior seemed to affect a patient's mental, if not physical, status adversely, at least temporarily. For example:

> Ms. Gim was visited by the team. While they talked to her she had to tell the house officers several times that her hand hurt terribly and asked them not to touch it. Both Chief Resident Ryder and JR Massey continued to touch it several times (without explaining to her or anyone why it may have been necessary to ignore her wishes). They were preoccupied with the discussion of symptoms and the physical exam. This seemed to prevent them from actually hearing the patient, who tried to talk. (Field notes, GH).

When patients or family members tried to interject themselves into a conversation for social or medical purposes, they rarely received a full response. Sometimes they were teased, occasionally given a curt or patronizing answer:

> The room of an eighty-year-old patient was entered. She immediately said she was feeling worse. Junior Resident Cape joked with her. She commented, "I didn't sleep well last night because I've been worried about what's going to happen." No one responded to her. Instead Cape asked the medical student to formally present her case to the assembled physicians. (Field notes, PH)

> Someone mentioned the patient's blood gases by the patient's bed. The patient asked what those were. The medical student responded they were to measure oxygen. The patient persisted: "Is that good or bad?" The medical student smiled and said, "Oh you're doing fine," and continued talking to his senior colleagues. (Field notes, VAH)

Objectification during Collegial Interaction

Much of the doctor's time spent away from patients was occupied in discussions with peers and superiors (and occasionally with students) on a specific patient's medical status or on general aspects of the diagnosis or treatment. During these informal conferences, consultations, and conversations, the patient was often objectified by being presented as a thing. This type of objectification during interaction with junior and senior colleagues was continually reinforced by faculty as well as by senior residents and occurred under almost every circumstance. I heard comments by both faculty and house staff such as "The stroke is over there," "Look at the nice little fits," "Look at those 'sicklers' [people with sickle cell anemia]," "A great case is rolling in," and so forth.[8]

In the novice internist's interaction with attending faculty and other house staff, this process of objectification underlined the all-important goal in internal medicine: to understand and detect disease. This everyday orientation and its vocabulary created and reinforced a view of the patient as object, as in these typical observations:

> Junior Resident Lovell was observed commenting loudly, "You can see some great 'pathology' coming in the ER and then there are the patients!" which led to laughter and more joking among his peers. (Field notes, VAH)

> Senior Resident Walters said to his fellow house officers and the attending in the ICU, "I'd like a 'triple-lobe pneumonia' to come in tonight with a touch of edema, just enough to put the 'wire' (a Swan-Ganz catheter) in." (Field notes, ICU)

Much of the language used by the house staff went beyond the affectively bland process of objectification to become an evaluative language of disparagement and, at times, intimidation.

INTIMIDATION AND DEATH FANTASIES

The house staff's negative feelings about many of their patients and their diseases provided further impetus to objectify patients. At times the expressions house staff used demonstrated annoyance and impatience and conveyed to the patient or family a sense of contempt that went beyond inclination to separate the person from the disease for efficiency. If the objectification of patients as nonpersons were merely consequences of the constraints of the performance of labor, the patients would hardly be subjected to a climate of social disparagement. Although house officers only infrequently verbally abused their patients to their faces, they often let their attitudes have free reign, when they were in the protected company of their peers, especially on those services where there was less faculty or administrative supervision: ER, certain VAH rotations, the OPC, and ward services.

A "patient-as-object-of-ricidule" orientation was often justified by the house staff:

SR DEREN:
Everyone has jokes about the VAH. The typical "vet" is an alcoholic. One doctor once told me that God created veterans as the closest experimental model to man. That's not nice but at the same time, it relieves a lot of tension. . . . You don't

know why you're helping this person because they are making no contribution to society—and yet you're working your ass off to save that person. It leaves you with a dichotomy in your feelings towards that patient.

Some of the house staff did acknowledge that such slang was probably overheard by outsiders including patients and their families:

SR LEEDS:
It's the way the doctor keeps his sanity . . . calling people "turkeys," "gomers," "Shpos," etc. I guess it's sort of sick humor and I probably use it too much. We use it too much. *People say it in the elevators and use it in the streets and places where they shouldn't* [emphasis added].

More important is the extent to which these negative patient assessments affected actual behavior toward patients or otherwise resulted in detrimental medical outcomes for them. Any adverse consequences undermine the functionalist argument that the use of gallows humor is a necessary tension-relieving mechanism to prevent physicans from taking out their frustrations on patients (see Coombs and Powers 1975; Coser 1959, 1960; Emerson 1963; Fox 1959; or Robinson 1977 for that interpretation). Most house staff admitted treating less thoroughly those patients they labeled derogatorily and some admitted to making mistakes because of their attitudes, for instance delaying necessary tests or sending a patient out of the e r prematurely:

JR ZIMMERMAN:
At least 40–50 percent are gomers. Some weeks there is nothing but alcohol-induced diseases. The other night on call I met only three people with "genuine" diseases—having nothing to do with anything they ever did to themselves. I spend hours [with them] and check them everyday, but some guy who comes in with alcoholic pancreatitis—I'll tune him up and fire him out the door, and not give two shakes about him.

INTERN SMALLEY:
A drunk was rolled in to ER. . . . He was intoxicated and complaining of low back pain, having fallen downstairs. . . . X-rays came back negative. . . . The resident covering stopped by. . . . He told me to get rid of him. . . . But I didn't. I kept him around. . . . I couldn't let him out as drunk as he was. . . . He was sleeping away, and I was seeing a lot of other patients. When I went to wake him up, I couldn't rouse him. He probably had a stroke.

Others commented that no one in the system received optimal care. In treating many aged people, women, blacks, and poor derogatorily, the house staff was, of course, mirroring the ageism, sexism, racism, and classism of the larger society.

The dehumanized climate created by the exaggerated use of objectification and intimidation techniques was manifested in house staff attitudes toward death and fantasized destruction. Several house officers referred to death as the ultimate GROP solution. Death was a "relief" in a situation where there were always patients waiting to be cared for; a dead patient was one less patient for whom the staff was responsible:

JR EDWARDS:
At that point [when a patient dies], *you're just interested in your own survival.* Sometimes it's hard to relate to people who die, and it's a *relief* that they die, not only because they're so sick and what you put them through is often worse than death but the fact that you don't have to do that anymore. It saves time and energy, so you think in terms of the overall benefit [emphasis added].

JR PATTY:
[When my first patient died] . . . it was terrible. Now if they die, it's usually, you know, *it's almost a relief* [emphasis added]. Especially if the patient has 101 problems and, you know, should die. Best for him, best for the family, that he should die.

Coombs and Goldman (1973) and Glaser and Strauss (1964) consider such expressions of relief a coping technique, that is, handling death by rationalization.

Death became a subject of black humor when house staff fantasized to each other about ways to GROP by deliberate acts of omission or commission, also at times citing the examples from *The House of God* (Shem 1978):

Junior Resident Jovers came by and talked to Cape about a patient who last night was in the dt's. Cape said, "Apparently, the Haldol [a drug] didn't work." Jovers responded, "I don't like Haldol. I prefer to give Valium until he's sedated and stops breathing, then he'll go into [cardiac] arrest and the i c u will have to take him and I'll get rid of him." Cape smiled. They looked at me as if to acknowledge their humorous intentions. (Field notes, VAH)

Occasionally an attending faculty joined in, as in the following instance:

The team discussed a cancer patient. Junior Resident Olot said . . . If you stop his Synthroid, you'd kill him." Attending Zitz reinforced that by describing how that could actually occur and that the only reason this man was alive was because of the drugs they were giving. There was some discussion (with participation by Attending Zitz) of ways in which they could hasten the death of the patient. (Field notes, VAH)

The line between black humor and more serious discussions of responsibility for a patient's death was sometimes hazy. Countless deliberations took place every day over decisions as to who was to live or die and more specifically on how "aggressive" to be with patients. For example, a family practice informant commented:

It's my feeling that the decision about whether the patient should be a "code" or "no-code" [resuscitated or not] should never be left in the hands of the intern because there's always a subconscious realization that if the patient is a "code" you're going to have to be the one to code it. Also if the patient is a code, it means they'll be alive that much longer for you to take care of. In other words, *the intern really has the motivation for letting someone die, and that can't help but influence you subconsciously in your decision* [emphasis added].

All this notwithstanding, within the house staff subculture the death of a patient, even if seemingly inevitable, was often defined as a failure. Therefore despite the fantasized death wishes, most felt compelled to keep patients alive at all costs. This created two sources of stress: First, the prolongation of life often meant a longer period of suffering for the patient. Second, a patient's death, even when all agreed there was nothing to be done, could reflect on the competency of a house staff member. Thus the house staff were sometimes caught between medical ethics and norms combined with a desire for a good reputation on the one hand and the guilt incurred by inducing or prolonging a patient's suffering on the other. It is the guilt and potential culpability that must be rationalized.

The house staff would constantly complain to each other about the amount of work they had to do with terminally ill patients, especially elderly ones who lingered near death but did not die. Yet, since there was a limit to the number and types of death that could be accepted without self- or peer recrimination, neither house officers nor attendings wanted too many patients to die on their service. Too many deaths, regardless of culpability, resulted in lengthy professional and administrative explanations they wished to avoid. Therefore, the house staff's goal frequently was to get rid of the patient before death occurred, which often entailed dogged negotiation with other physicians or medical services. Here is an example of one typical attempt that failed:

> Attending Paul discussed with Senior Resident Leeds the problems of trying to get the patient upstairs (off their service) before "disaster" came. Senior Resident Mora reported, "The patient was here to 'rule out' chest pain, and then the nurses tried to get him back to [the] PH but were hampered. It seemed that no one wanted him to die on his service." (Field notes, ICU)

Regardless of whether patients were physically harmed or neglected as a result of black humor or fantasized destruction, the result was a dehumanizing climate inconducive to a harmonious doctor–patient relationship.

CONCLUSION

The system-perpetuating GROP mechanisms of negotiation, passing the patient along vertically or horizontally, omission, avoidance, objectification, and intimidation cannot but impair house staff–patient relationships and limit the quality and frequency of the interaction.[9] The house staff generally believed that there was limited benefit to be obtained from direct encounters with patients, so they maintained an apartness from patients physically and psychologically and substituted instead encounters with colleagues, procedures, and charts. First, the small amount of time invested in interacting with patients was subject limited and almost wholly oriented toward instrumental ends. Second, most time was spent away from patients. Third, even in the presence of patients, patients were often excluded from discussion and certainly from decision making. Thus patients were objectified and discounted, and those whose diseases or social situations were assessed negatively were especially ignored or intimidated.

Patients are relatively powerless, especially when they are lower and working class, black, female, or aged. Given the level of status and prestige of the house staff, both in origins and destination, it is not surprising that their attitudes toward the patient population are basically negative. In one sense, the coping mechanisms of the house staff represent a form of struggle between dominant and subordinate status groups. Such a confrontation can dehumanize social relationships for both participants. The working conditions, normative structure of the profession, and priorities of training seem to make such a consequence inevitable.

Chapter 6

Barriers to Doctor–Patient Relationships: No Time Is the Right Time

The house staff, oriented to GROP was unable and unwilling to develop a sustained relationship with patients. The scope of everyday responsibilities, combined with the expectations and values inculcated and rewarded by mentors and colleagues limited doctor–patient interaction. Structural, cultural and professional factors further restricted the time available to acquire interactional skills. While the house staff was socialized to adopt a GROP perspective, they were simultaneously detracted from adopting a caring attitude toward patients.

This chapter will discuss the aspects of medical training particularly detrimental to house staff–patient relationships. These include the intrinsic limitations of the medical rotation system; shared negative attitudes regarding the learning or practice of relationship skills at all levels of training; and the lack of situational and structural time to acquire this competency. Hospital training set aside no time for house officers to directly engage in didactic or experiential learning about the doctor–patient relationship during the entire three-year internship program.

STRUCTURAL BARRIERS: LIMITATIONS OF THE ROTATIONAL SYSTEM

The hallmark of clinical medical education (which is unique to the universe of professional training) has been its rotational system. The practical or experiential learning of physician trainees is structured to ensure that they will experience a series of different medical services and relate to a variety of medical mentors and colleagues—and presumably interact with different types of patients—in order to be exposed to a wide spectrum of medical problems. Whereas, for example, the training of teachers and social workers structures the practicum to ensure the development of a stable, sustained, and intensive relationship with a supervisor and a group of clients, the education of student physicians is constructed to achieve the opposite, namely, the formation of quickly established, time-limited relationships that can and must immediately be severed when the trainee is transferred to a new environment and a new set of structured interactions.

The structure is deliberately designed so that there is constant overlap, movement, and change, with varying intervals. Medical students, interns, residents, and attendings, who make up the patient management team, all rotate on different schedules. Therefore, not only does each member rotate monthly, but even within the month on a particular service each will work with different groups of team members.

Further disrupting the continuity of relationships is the system of *coverage* and *on-call* responsibilities. On a specified number of alternating days, house officers were assigned the responsibility for *all* hospital admissions to their service during a twenty-four hour period. During these on-call nights they were also expected to oversee ("cover") their peers' patients on that same service. For example, in GH the interns and their residents were on call every third night, while in PH the residents and interns worked as a team during the day but during the evening had different patient admission responsibilities. There were even more complicating factors at the VAH, where the interns were on call every third night, while the residents admitted patients to the hospital every fifth night; therefore, a resident could have admitted to his or her care patients on a service to which he or she was not formally assigned that month. The whole rotational system with all its permutations was exceedingly complex, occupying a great deal of the time of the chief residents and administrators who were assigned to designing the system. It also was a major preoccupation of the house staff,[1] as in this intern's comments:

FAMILY PRACTICE INTERN DANET:
As a student and also an intern [I was bothered by the fact that] everybody was always switching. And now with the JRs you switch every two weeks into the schedule. . . . Different JRs handle things different ways, and you have to get used to them. . . . A new JR comes [on the service] and wants to do some things that the other JR didn't want to do. . . . That makes it difficult at times.

Quite often, individual house officers were heavily involved with certain patients, usually because of the nature or seriousness of their diseases. Their investment of time, if not emotion, was considerable. At the end of their monthly rotation (and to a lesser degree on their nights off), however, they would abruptly halt their patient contact, transfer their responsibilities almost immediately, and the next hour or day turn their attention to the new service and almost never look back. Only in exceptional or fortuitous circumstances would they ever see those patients again; I never saw them purposely reinvolve themselves. Clearly, the demands of the new service and the expectations of their colleagues and mentors precluded any continuity of care for former patients, whatever their own personal feelings. That the house staff was able to make those abrupt transitions with very little observable surface disruption to the system as a whole was a continuous source of amazement to me. Almost instantaneously they had to pick up where someone else had left off, literally the minute or hour before.

While these abrupt rotational changes could be a source of anxiety for the patient and family, for a house officer coming on to a service and inheriting a set of sick patients and having to deal (however reluctantly) with the emotional and human dimensions of patient care, it also was often a disconcerting experience. Many times, while still complete strangers to the patients and their families, they had to convey to them serious and sometimes tragic information, with no time to adjust to the situation. Yet, the system was taken for granted; its repercussions on them and on patients rarely discussed. These complex arrangements created confusion for patients and families already in stressful situations, since the mere presence of so many different people in white coats could by itself be bewildering:

INTERN MARTA:
I think the biggest things that the patients complain about, the thing that really stands out in my mind, is lack of continuity of care. What I mean by that is that [as a medical student] we were on the service and so were the interns, and the residents were there for only [two weeks]. If you get involved with the patient, you have to leave the patient, and a number of the patients that I worked with were upset by that. Now they would really rather see the same doctor consistently but they never do.

While never looking back was the norm, on occasion one house officer might pass along to a colleague some information about the latter's former patient. Rarely, however, did I encounter a house officer initiating an attempt to find out about a former patient, and never did any of the house staff return to a previous service to see a former patient. While that behavior may have occurred on occasion, it was not a norm of conduct, and more important, it was structurally difficult to carry out.[2]

Another important factor, which the house staff itself considered an organizational barrier to the continuity of patient care, was the dichotomy between the inpatient and outpatient services. Presumably having responsibility for the same patients on the outside as on the inside would be the first step in establishing quality doctor–patient relationships. Under the SAMs system, however, it was extremely difficult to follow a patient on the outside after hospitalization or to admit and follow a clinic patient in the hospital. Although some house officers stated that they built up part of their clinic population from a select group of their inpatients, this required initiative and persistence and was neither expected nor the norm. Neither was it easily possible to monitor any clinic patients who needed hospitalization. Some house officers complained that, while they often wished to be apprised when someone else hospitalized their clinic patient, they were rarely even given that professional courtesy:

SR DEREN:
One of the most frustrating things for me is having the patient that I've followed for a year or two in clinic come to the ER and get admitted to the hospital, be discharged, and I never knew the patient was in the hospital. . . . I really feel a responsibility for the patients I take care of. . . . That's a lack of courtesy among the house staff that has never been talked about before. It has never been stressed that if someone is taking care of someone else's patient, you ought to let him [the clinic doctor] know. . . . I think the patients would like to at least have you come by and say, "I've discussed your case with doctor so and so and he's doing a real good job."

The structural limitations of the rotational system clearly had their effect on house staff–patient relationships. Knowing in advance that they had limited time in which to develop quality relationships with patients and that to all intents and purposes any relationship established would soon end, house officers withheld any major investment of energy in trying to establish one in the first place:

JR SAUL:
I can't have the OPC and have responsibility on the wards and still have time to be myself and be calling people at home and checking on them to see if they're okay. I'm just not capable.

JR EDWARDS:
It's such a mess [here] as far as any follow-up and who's the primary physician. It's really hard to see how that one patient contact [on the inside] fits into the wider spectrum of a patient's life. As an intern all you care about with that one patient is to get them [sic] in and out of the hospital where you have responsibility for them [sic].

Since there were no extrinisic rewards for developing relationships and since the norms of professional conduct within the house staff culture militated against such behavior, it is not surprising that relationships rarely developed.

ATTITUDINAL BARRIERS: "YOU EITHER HAVE IT OR YOU DON'T"

The house staff as a whole almost totally discounted the value, appropriateness, or usefulness of teaching about the doctor–patient relationship, which included rapport building and communication skills as well as psychosocial and environmental (PSE) factors. They recalled little exposure to any such material in medical school[3] and even less at SAMs. More important, what they did remember (irrespective of whether the teaching was didactic or experiential and where it was taught) they viewed as largely irrelevant:

> Junior Resident Weiss observed: "When you're a medical student, it [instruction on PSE factors] is too general. [It's] sociological 'bullshit.' Now as a house staff it would be more appropriate but there aren't any formal discussions." (Field notes, GH)

> INTERN TONY:
> A lot of time was devoted in medical school [here at SAMs] to PSE factors, although a lot of my peers tended not to take it seriously. . . . [Also] there's a lot of jargon in social and behavioral sciences so that [those] things are more vague. . . . They want to have things concrete. . . . I think the attitudes toward behavioral science basically reflects the uncertainty of a lot of [those] things.

> JR McGEE:
> I think there's a baseline cynicism especially in medical school where we're all scientists. . . . You're trying to learn all this incredible fund of information, and it can't be wasted on the "fluff"—the psychosocial aspects of medicine.

Hence attitudinal barriers to acquiring competency in doctor–patient relationships also existed. For the most part, the house staff believed that the components of the doctor–patient relationship could not be taught in any formalized or consciously designed way:

> SR DEREN:
> A lot of [PSE factors] can't be taught. . . . If you had a lecture on it, most of the people [house staff] would just turn off. They wouldn't pick up on it. They are really oblivious. They're walking through life on a cloud.

Over and over they reiterated the singular importance of personality or intuition: "You either have it or you don't!"

> SR SILVERMAN:
> I think it's something you're born with or not born with. . . . Coping with social and emotional factors is a reflection of your own psyche and your own upbringing or background. Either you can do it or you can't. I don't think there's any residency program in the country that can teach you that.

Despite this mutually shared defense, some house officers spoke of methods by which they learned their doctor–patient skills, namely, through their own experience, or less frequently, by example:

> INTERN FERST:
> I unconsciously adapted I guess what I saw others do.

They emphasized that they had to learn them on their own, by trial and error, and many asserted that to be the only way one can acquire such skills:

INTERN FONER:
You have to learn through your own experience.

The impact of the positive faculty role model, while occasionally cited, was difficult to evaluate. Many house officers noted how infrequently they actually observed more than fleeting attending–patient interaction. Those members of the house staff who identified a few faculty members as having a humanistic attitude toward patients discounted the impact of those attendings on themselves. Thus, when humanistic behavior was manifested by a few attending physicians, it was perceived as either the exception to the rule or an artifact of the attendings' privileged removal from everyday patient care. Furthermore, the instructors' teaching in these areas during medical school, who often were noninternists and even nonphysicians, were discounted as being too patronizing or too unrealistic:

INTERN McGEE:
[In medical school] we had two courses in social medicine—basic psychiatry, environmental care of dying patients, interviewing techniques. . . . [They were all] generally a waste of time, mainly not taught by people that medical students respect. [The teachers are] people who seem to think that everybody is a bed of roses and is a wonderful person . . . and after a while you just stop listening. . . . Everybody thought they [the teachers] were off the wall and wished they'd just go away and stop bothering them.

Hence, while most house staff recalled little about the formal process of acquisition of doctor–patient relationships skills in medical school, the few house officers who did remember some didactic or experiential teaching discounted its usefulness for one or more of several reasons:

It was too simplistic (i.e., "It's just common sense").
It was too idealistic (i.e., "It's irrelevant").
It was too didactic (i.e., "It's impractical").
It was too general (i.e., "It's not applicable").

Moreover, what role modeling did occur consisted, rather, of mimicking house staff, who demonstrated in large measure a GROP orientation toward patients. Senior Resident Filps summed up the cumulative effect of negative role models:

When I was a brand new third-year student I saw residents and interns joking about patients, and I said, "I'll never do that. . . . " I'm more cynical now. . . . I've definitely changed. . . . It's common for us to sit around clinic at the end of the day and ask, "Well how many pounds did you see today?" You talk about a two-ton and four-ton clinic because I have at least two dozen women that weigh over three hundred pounds apiece.

THE INCOMPATIBILITY OF
SITUATION AND STRUCTURE:
NO RIGHT TIME AND CIRCUMSTANCE

The right circumstances and structured set of responsibilities needed to develop competent doctor–patient skill never occurred during the seven years of formal medical training (Table 6.1). From the time the doctors-in-training began medical school to the time they left the internal medicine residency program, barriers prevented the assignment of priority to the acquisition of this competence.

Medical School: "It's Too Early"

The views of the house officers with regard to teaching or learning about relationship skills in medical school were virtually unanimous in spite of the fact that they attended two dozen or so different medical schools. Most house staff asserted that there was little exposure to any significant teaching on any aspect of the doctor–patient relationship.

The most critical reason for the absence of learning of doctor–patient skills by medical students was, however, structural: the learning and practicing clearly came too soon. When role playing did take place, its importance and relevance were missing because, according to the house staff, medical stu-

TABLE 6.1. The Incompatibility of Structure and Situation

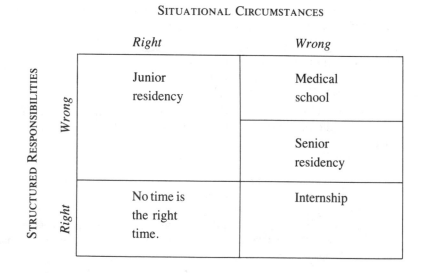

		SITUATIONAL CIRCUMSTANCES	
		Right	*Wrong*
STRUCTURED RESPONSIBILITIES	*Wrong*	Junior residency	Medical school
			Senior residency
	Right	No time is the right time.	Internship

dents do not have real responsibility for patient care. Hence, all other factors discarded, this area remained ultimately unlearnable because it was untimely:

JR SAUL:
I think it [teaching about psychosocial factors, communication, terminal illness, etc.] is a prominent part of most medical schools' curricula, but during the first and second year, when it seems perfectly logical to you, you ask, "Why are they teaching me this? . . . It's logical to do this," and you may disregard it. . . . And certainly by the time you get to be a third and fourth year medical student and you're actually dealing clinically, these points are no longer emphasized. . . . You think [the PSE factors] are there, but I will get to them later, but you never quite get to them.

JR McGEE:
I don't think you're ready to learn it [PSE factors] until you realize its importance. And I don't think you can see the forest for the trees in medical school.

Internship: "No Time for Patients"

Interns considered themselves to exist in an oppressive environment where they had barely time to do what was essential to survive. Yet, by virtue of role definition and responsibility for patient management, they were in the ideal position to develop a primary relationship with their patients. Interns recognized and experienced this paradox profoundly. They realized quickly that there really was no other physician in the system with whom the patients had any significant relationship; the buck stopped with them (see Jonas 1978; Lowenstein 1979), and they had no time.

Senior residents and even the attendings often got rid of major doctor–patient responsibilities by passing them down to the interns. These tasks included family or patient education; patient support, especially during critical and terminal phases of illness; patient placement; and patient advocacy. All the PSE factors of patient care, when identified as important at all, were supposed to be addressed by the interns. Because of the priorities established by themselves and the system, however, interns had little time or energy left for attending to these matters. The goal of internship was to survive intact, so the immediate needs of these new house officers came first:

SR RYDER:
Internship is the worst time to change the clinical approach to patients. Patients are numbers to you and they're work. . . . Later on, when the patient load lessens and you have more time to devote to them as people . . . if you still don't have that approach [then], you'll never have it. . . . Some will learn it [in residency], but if they do it's simply because the foundation was laid long ago.

SR MINEY:
I don't know whether my attitudes [toward patients] have changed. It's not as much fun and there's not as much appreciation [from patients] as you imagine in medical

school. . . . Out of necessity you couldn't waste a lot of time talking to people when you're an intern.

According to many interns, a profound *deterioration* in the doctor–patient relationship actually occurred that year—a decline from which many house officers believed they would never fully recover. By the end of internship most patients had become objects to GROP. Feelings of cynicism and frustration were paramount for many ending interns, countered only by the relief at having finished the grueling year. A minority expected to have a more positive patient outlook as junior residents:

FAMILY PRACTICE INTERN WOLF:
The JRs have a good deal more time to know all the patients and to study them—to read—because once they've made their initial assessment—they don't have the nitty-gritty scut work. Most JRs don't even write a progress note once they put their impressions down.

At the internship level of training the responsibility was right but the circumstances were wrong for learning patient relationship skills.

Junior Residency: "It's Not My Job"

By the time they completed internship, house officers were fatigued and indifferent and in some cases embittered by their experience. While, theoretically, they had more time as JRs, they no longer had the structured responsibility to develop patient relationship skills:

JR McGEE:
The doctor–patient interaction suffers during internship. . . . Internship is the most devastating thing to the doctor–patient relationship. [As a JR] you have more time and can treat your patients better, and if you have that possibility you can establish a better doctor–patient relationship, but you're no longer the primary physician. . . . You're a consultant, and to get too involved in [it] is to usurp your intern's job. You're in a bind in that you now have more time [as a JR], but it's not your place.

Since they had two or three times the number of patients under their direct supervision, they could not get to know the patients as well as their interns did, even if they so desired:

JR SING:
It will be a nicer way to look at patients now as a JR without being lost in all the things that have to be done, but it will be difficult to know each one [patient] with twice as many patients.

JR WHITE:
[The JR year], I think it's going to be almost as hard as far as hours go early in the year. . . . I'm going to be responsible for more patients but less intensely. I'm going to be indirectly responsible. I won't know them [patients] as completely.

The JRs common definition of their responsibilities together with their structured set of relationships with attendings and interns precluded any meaningful involvement with patients:

FAMILY PRACTICE INTERN WOLF:
Junior residents are in a kind of consultant role. He [sic] sees them [patients] once in the morning . . . but the JR doesn't really develop as close a relationship with the patients as the interns do.

Their assignments through most of the year were to oversee the work of interns and to teach medical students on the wards about the diagnostic and therapeutic decision-making processes, imparting to them medical knowledge in a generally didactic context.[4] While they might assist the new interns with their assigned work—depending upon the needs of the interns and the service—they were quite careful to cite protocol with regard to usurping the intern's responsibility for direct patient management. Most had no interest in doing more than absolutely necessary to keep their service running smoothly. They kept reminding themselves and others, including patients, that the intern was the patient's primary physician:

SR MAHONEY:
When you're the intern, you're the patient's primary doctor. . . . I remember talking to my patients as a JR, and then I realized that by my doing it, I was interfering with the relationship between the intern and the patient. The further you advance, the more "supervisory" role you take as opposed to primary patient care, and the more distant you are from the patient necessarily.

Having just completed the frustrating and tension-filled internship, their desire to acquire doctor–patient skills or learn about the broader dimensions of patient care was minimal. Given both the educational and social deprivation that almost all acknowledged, most JRs had no desire to concentrate on these areas even though the circumstances now seemed appropriate:

FAMILY PRACTICE INTERN WOLF:
In internal medicine many times during the year my resident signed out at 2:00 p.m., left me to do everything, and came in the next morning and said, "Why isn't that done?" . . . Once you finish your internship in medicine, you never want to work that hard again, and as a JR and SR you leave progessively earlier.

Many junior residents left the hospital early and justified this behavior as appropriate to their job description or by recalling how hard life was as an intern. Many house officers claimed that just compensation was now owed them for the previous year: "I've paid my dues. Now it's their turn." Most JRs desired to pursue personal goals, including finding more time for reading and attending conferences, in order to learn more about the whys of the science of disease and medicine; more personal time outside of medicine to spend with family, friends, or alone; and more time to earn extra money through moon-lighting activity:

FAMILY PRACTICE INTERN DANET:
I was told by an SR when I wanted to spend more time with a patient, "Well, as an intern you can't afford it." That really should be something the JRs and SRs do more. . . . Well what happens is, you know what you went through as an intern and you have a family and outside interests and you have reading you need to do—it ends up not a high priority.

Those few house staff who did identify the JR year as one in which they could focus more on patients thought primarily in terms of now having more time to *think* about the patient's medical problems. For almost all the JR, this meant more time to focus on the diagnostic and therapeutic aspects of disease processes, not on the broader patient care dimension. Moreover, there was no structured teaching built into the system and no tangible incentives for devoting time or energy to patients' relationships. Relieved from the pressures of internship, the JR year could have been devoted to regaining and strengthening doctor–patient skills, and even teaching them to the novices, but their structured responsibilities together with their personal interests and culturally shared negative attitudes toward patients, precluded it. The JR year hypothetically represented the right circumstances but the wrong time.

Senior Residency: "It's Too Late"

By the time they reached senior residency year, the house staff were not unlike students in their final year of any educational endeavor. They had one foot out the door. For the most part, SRs were divorced from mandatory patient care responsibilities and hence distanced from any possibility of improving or developing doctor–patient relationships. Once again, as in medical school, it was a case of the wrong time and the wrong circumstances, though, by contrast, at this final level of training, it was too late rather than too early:

SR WALTERS:
By this time [March] of your SR year, you sort of get philosophical. You're a "lame duck." You don't complain much. Nothing phases you.

SR BROWNING:
As you get further along you get separated from your peers. . . . As you become an SR everybody gets a little skeptical of everybody else. . . . You're no longer spending all your waking hours thinking about the same things [as you were as an intern].

With the exception of ER, ICU, and ongoing clinic experiences, the entire year was devoted to subspecialty electives where their primary focus was educational. On those rotations, their role was to advise and to assist the primary physician involved with a "case." Structurally, this consulting role precluded any opportunity for meaningful doctor–patient interaction; indeed, professional protocol prohibited the formation of any expanded patient relationship:

SR AYRES:
As an SR [you're not called to put PSE knowledge into practice] simply because you don't actually have primary patient care that much. . . . The further removed you get from patient care, sometimes the easier [it becomes] to "slough off" [patients'] problems because you're not as intimately associated with them.

SR SILLS:
As an SR what I'm doing now is like a consult. You're sort of dealing with them [patients] more as interesting problems, and I guess the compassion isn't there, because you just come in at one point in time, see the pathology, and leave.

The vast majority of the SRs welcomed the opportunity to become advanced students again, especially since in hindsight most defined their JR year as more strenuous than they had anticipated. With heavy supervisory patient management responsibilities, most had spent less time during the previous year in educational and personal pursuits than they had desired. They likened their SR experience to being a fourth-year medical student, where, after a hard third year of clinical medicine, they could once again become detached from major responsibilities:

SR CONLEY:
The experience of the SR compared to that of a JR is such that there is some distinction. . . . The JR is responsible for teaching the interns. The SR does that [only] when he supervises the interns in the ICUs and ER situations. So the JR has more contact with the interns, and therefore the SR has more time and responsibility for teaching himself and refining his knowledge before he goes into practice.

Furthermore, personal concerns intervened to keep the SRs structurally separated from their peers and from patients even if they wished to devote more time to practicing—or instructing subordinates in—doctor–patient skills. As a group, they were engaged in preparation for the next phase of their professional careers, for example, visiting fellowship programs or prospective job settings. Many (approximately three-quarters) were also engaged in moonlighting activities at various hospitals in the area. The house officers' responsibilities on their moonlighting jobs, as on the elective rotations, were primarily crisis-oriented or consultative. The structured expectations were such that they left any important patient (or family) interaction to the primary physician in charge. They considered it a breach of professional etiquette and possibly even unethical to interact or intervene with a patient or family in any meaningful manner, especially with respect to a sensitive or serious patient management issue.

Further, the required SR rotations (the ICUs and ER), considered to be the most difficult and strenuous services, were so structured as to preclude the development of meaningful doctor–patient relationships. The crisis nature of those services, the patterned expectations, and SR's experiences all assured little time or opportunity for sustained patient or family contact.

SR PAUL:
The most valuable experience was the medical ICU. . . . It's pure medicine with the most exciting problems. You get an acute problem and you manage it and you send the patient out to someone else, so you don't get bogged down with cultural problems.

Of necessity, transactions had to be quick, and in those circumstances the physician believed actions more effective than words. In addition, the patients were usually too ill to be capable of communicating with the physician, and the families were generally ignored or addressed for pragmatic purposes alone.

Because of the limited amount of sustained interaction with patients during the final year, most of the ending residents referred to their clinic patients in any discussions I initiated about doctor–patient relationships. Since the OPC was the one place in the system where, theoretically, there was the right opportunity and circumstance for practicing those interactional skills, it is important to examine. From both observation and questioning, I determined that it was an unwanted and devalued experience for most of the house staff, including SRs, in spite of the fact that several of them admitted to forming attachments to some of their patients.[5] Nor did the volume of patients and organizational arrangements allow them to devote any time to learning about or practicing a different relationship style with most patients. (Mizrahi 1984b). Hence, the structured set of expectations prevented senior house officers from forming or improving their relationships with a large proportion of patients. As a result, patients' psychosocial and cultural world (and in general, the human aspect of patients and their families) continued to be ignored.

CONCLUSION

Within the sams environment there was little formal attempt to socialize house staff in the ways of effective doctor–patient relationships. First, within the profession, there is an ideological bias that considers and rewards only that learning which is technical. When they are taught at all, PSE dimensions of patient care apparently are relegated to the least respected members of the faculty. The level of professional contempt for PSE factors was revealed when they were termed "sociological bullshit" to me, although I was publicly known as a sociologist.

Second, the educational experience is structured to militate against the development of humanistic doctor–patient relationships. If, as the house staff says, PSE factors cannot be taught but have to be learned by doing, then the intern year is critical in the development of such relationships. It is, however, a period when the novices themselves are being systematically dehumanized, which only fosters the deterioriation of the doctor–patient relationship rather than allowing it to develop as something positive. Medical school is too early while the junior and senior residency are too late because the attitudes have been inculcated; apathy, if not alienation, has generally set in; and residents have structured sets of responsibilities that effectively remove them from primary patient care. Since many patients are generally undesirable, and relief from them is a badge of social privilege, most residents accept that opportunity for relief as payment for their prior degradation and turn to more professionally, rewarding, lucrative, or status-building pursuits.

Chapter 7

Outcomes of Internal Medicine Training

The three-year program had profound effects on the ending residents. All were affected by the antipatient socialization experience. The GROP perspective permeated their attitudes toward patients and influenced their career choices, which, in many instances, seemed to be reactions to the negative aspects of their training.

PROFESSIONAL COMPETENCE AND COMMITMENT

Despite all the struggles and fatigue, the house staff believed that they had acquired competence and confidence in their ability to practice internal medicine. As Bucher and Stelling (1977) also found, residents assessed their development and mastery retrospectively, usually in contrast to their earlier performances. They ended their training believing that they were an elite group in which almost everyone had acquired basic knowledge and skill in internal medicine. Upon being questioned, most house officers asserted that they were "one of the pack" or as good as most. They were not denegrating their achievements when they said that there were few or no "stars." To be average among the best was still to be at the top.

SR WALTERS:
SAMs teaches you how to take care of sick patients. As an intern the differential diagnosis is not complicated [for most patients]. Lots of things aren't esoteric—they're the "bread and butter". . . . You come out of internship feeling really confident with keeping the patient going and stabilizing problems that are reversible. . . . It's a retrospective satisfaction.

In basic patient management skills, the house staff included the more esoteric areas of knowledge they had acquired during the residency years. During internship, they had learned the "hows," and in the final two years they had learned the "whys" and the "fine tuning":

SR ARI:
I like the pathophysiology of all those disease states, and we've learned them. It really makes [internal medicine] challenging.

Most were satisfied overall with the training they had received. They felt they had learned the basic clinical and technical skills needed to practice internal medicine. Two cautions must be noted, however. First, for the most part, they defined internal medicine in narrow technical terms divorced from total patient care. Second, most of them discussed the outcome in terms of trade-offs or compensatory factors like the collegial relationships formed with peers and the temporary or time-limited nature of their difficult training, which for some was the only compensation:

JR KOTS:
Being a physician interfered with your learning during internship. You had a lot of junk to do, but that's what the year is for. Everyone expects that. . . . *You're never an intern again. It's your rite de passage* [emphasis added]. Who does all these things? There's an eternal class of people. It's perpetuated. It's a one shot deal.

Some considered the effects of the resentment harbored from their internship year permanent:

SR ZOREZ:
I felt during internship that service far outweighed learning. I believe it dehumanized me somewhat and has left me with a cynicism I will probably never lose.

Many house staff members, like SR Filps, in discussing the trade-offs, asserted that they had paid a price to learn internal medicine:

SR FILPS:
What I wanted was to be a good doctor and comfortable practicing medicine. I feel I got those things. . . . I can practice and do as good a job as 60–80 percent of people in practice. *But I got some things I didn't want to—like cynicism. . . . I think almost everyone gets it.* . . . It's part of process. . . . We see a lot of people who did it to themselves. . . . And that's really disgusting [Emphasis added.]

Senior Resident Conley conveyed the intensity of the disillusionment felt by a sizeable minority:

[When I began] I didn't think I was going to be an idol, but I'm sure everyone is more idealistic before they go into it [medicine]. A lot of people are out after doctors. I think the government is. . . . You see it every day in the press—all the deficiencies in doctors and medical care. . . . You see it in the patients' attitudes,

121

and you run into hassles . . . and people threaten you with this or that lawsuit. . . . You know it's a pain in the butt. I'd just as soon go fishing and enjoy myself.

For some house officers, the costs outweighed the benefits. They appeared to be turned off or burned out. Having made such investments of time and energy, at a great personal sacrifice, however, their rejection of the system was not total.

PERSPECTIVES ON PATIENTS

Most of the house staff completed the SAMS internal medicine training program with attitudes toward patients ranging from apathy to antipathy. The only major differences I could discern in attitudes toward patients were: first, whether or not they had a need to justify their negative attitudes and actions to each other or to outsiders; second, whether they wholly blamed the patient or blamed, as well, the system or themselves; and third, whether they believed that ideal and interesting patients were a complete myth or were only absent in the present environment. Particularly telling were responses to a question concerning the effect of the presence of so few patients who in their estimation were ideal. Some thought the types of patients they treated prevented them from developing good skills in patient rapport. For that small group of house officers, establishing rapport was still an idealized value—even given their narrow definition of that skill. The alientation in doctor–patient relationships led to what they saw as a deficiency in their training, namely, as SR Weisel commented, "We never learn to discuss illnesses in detail with intelligent, articulate patients."

> JR TONY:
> I don't think [the SAMs patients] will be much like [those in private practice]. In fact I'm a little bit worried about being able to deal with them in the same way. They will be more demanding, requiring more explanation. . . . *Most here are pretty passive. They practically let you do anything to them* without much explanation. . . . It's a trade-off [emphasis added].

Ironically, during the three years of training, most house staff disliked their time in PH, in part because the patients were generally not as passive as those in GH.

For those who answered that the existence of so few ideal patients was positive, it was clear that the most important part of their training was learning to identify and handle illness, to make diagnoses and manage patients medically. In their view the more "pathology" presented, the better the results for their learning. Their view was that the SAMs patients were sicker (often because they abused or neglected their bodies) so the staff could learn about and practice a wide variety of diagnostic and therapeutic skills. They learned the "bread and butter" of medical practice from the sheer volume and types of patients seen. For this large group of house staff, most patients were little more than manifestations of symptoms and disease. Because they believed these patients were less than ideal, they could more easily, with less guilt and remorse, distance themselves with a variety of GROP strategies. Further, there were a few house officers who delighted at not having to establish relationships with patients precisely because it was not something they either desired or felt was necessary. This group included those who chose critical care and emergency medicine as their specialty. There was support within the house staff culture for the perspective expressed in this house officer's view of the ideal patient:

JR PATTY:
I like someone who is sick and can't talk! [Laughter]. No, I'm serious—critically ill . . . that is. I like dealing with physiology, and it just may be the fact of the frustration of the internship year. I like people more "gorked out" so I can almost play with their "numbers." It sounds terrible, but that's the kind of patient I like dealing with, and I like dealing with people who are salvageable physically.

The house staff, moreover, disliked the OPC experience even though they knew it resembled private practice more than any other service. While they believed that improvements could be made in the organization and delivery of SAMs clinic care, they denied the need for more or better outpatient training. Many viewed patient management skills as automatically transferable from inpatient to outpatient settings. They also blamed the patients and their diseases in addition to the system for the defects in clinic training:

SR JONES:
[House staff don't value the OPC experience because], one, it takes away from other things you really want to learn; two, you don't have the clinical teaching that you have elsewhere, [and] the diseases on the outside are not as severe as the ones on the inside. *If you learn how to treat the hardest ones, it's easier to treat the ones on the outside* . . . plus the hassles of the clinic are unreal [emphasis added].

SR BATT:
Everybody hates the clinics. It's an intrusion into their time and on the wards. . . . If there were fewer patients and better attending coverage it could be much better. . . . The main problem is the patient load. . . . I tend to agree with those who think that the best way to be an outpatient doctor is to be a very good inpatient doctor. That the more you are exposed to in the way of acute care and sick patients, the more you appreciate when someone is, as opposed to when someone is not, sick.

What many learned from treating patients in the OPC (and to some degree in the ER) was what they did *not* want to do professionally for the rest of their lives. They disliked routine, chronic, and social illnesses. At best, most were bored, and at worst, the training experience confirmed for some that having to consider the social dimensions of patient care was something they detested:

JR BEECH:
I hate [the clinic]. It's supposed to be a learning experience but it isn't. All you see are mundane, routine cases, nothing exciting or unusual. . . . It's supposed to be for the purpose of giving us some exposure to what it's like in real private practice but it's not. We're overbooked and very busy. It's a zoo. The clinic is a real dump for LMDs [local medical doctors] who don't want to see patients or the patients run out of money or they're undesirable in some way. (Field notes, OPC)

SR LEADS:
The clinic is routine, elementary, not much of a learning experience. That's why I'm not going into private practice. It's probably just like this. You treat hypertension and diabetes and obesity. That's why I chose a subspecialty like g i [gastroenterology]. You can do all kinds of procedures to keep it interesting. (Field notes, OPC)

While the house staff generally discounted positive patient feedback and deprecated any emotional commitment to patients in its shared public posture, there were a few exceptional situations that served to corroborate how little positive reinforcement they received from anyone. There was a small group of patients with whom the ending residents apparently had interacted intermittently in their clinics for as long as three years and to whom they had become attached. A few house officers admitted privately to the acquisition of personal attachments in specialized instances.

They affirmed their surprise or delight at receiving any kind of caring sentiment from patients. This unanticipated reaction not only confirmed how few personal rewards from patients they received, but it demonstrated the guilt many felt when they received this occasional response because by their own standards they knew that they had been delivering less than optimal care. As a result, a process of cognitive dissonance seemed to occur for some house officers as they left the program. Ironically, this led to further discounting of the value of patient feedback. The question What do they know? took on a double meaning, for their shared responses to these ending encounters with some clinic patients also indicated how very little the patients really did know about them and how little meaningful communication there had been. The positive contact was too little, too late. Senior Resident Kots discussed this sentiment poignantly:

I've been more satisfied this year because I've gotten to know people [patients] this year. People [in the clinic] really start to remember your name for the first time, and that's nice because I think we can do a better job if they know who we are. . . . They are asking [as I say goodbye], "What are you going to do?" They *realize that I'm a person* [emphasis added]. . . . A lot will feel bad when I leave that they're going to have to go through this thing again. . . . I feel sorry for them. . . . Now that I'm toward the end and I'm getting some feedback from the patients about what they thought about the care and a lot are spontaneously offering their comments, what they valued most was they felt that I had some concern for them and would do what was best for them, although in many cases, I haven't achieved anything as far as whatever disease process—I've hardly done anything anyway. . . . Most of medicine doesn't do anything anyway. . . . I was surprised because I know where all the kinks are, incompleteness, weakspots. . . . They don't know . . . but everybody likes to be liked and it's happening to the few [house staff] I've talked to. . . . They realize that maybe they had some impact on some of these patients. . . . And now the feedback comes that they [patients] really appreciate what it was. . . . It's something that would have been nicer earlier. It might have put a different shade on the relationship.

Whether it really would have made a difference or not is a moot point, since the staff experienced little to counter the GROP perspective. It is notable that, while displaying sympathy for patients, SR Kots subtly blames the patients—who are subordinates in a hierarchical relationship—for the poor quality of that relationship. A public system of ambulatory medicine that relies solely or principally on provision of adult general medical care by novice internists who characterize themselves as harassed, oppressed, overworked, and underpaid and whose personal goals and professional orientation to medicine are often opposed to the needs of the basic outpatient population, is programmed to produce profound deficiencies in the doctor–patient relationship in that setting (Mizrahi, 1984b).

The question that remains is How did the adverse experiences of the last three years [and for some, the last seven] affect their career choices and anticipated relationships with future patients? This question is significant because it addresses the differences between situational and internalization theories of socialization.

ANTICIPATORY SOCIALIZATION AND CAREER CHOICE

Experience with the patients at SAMs was crucial in many house officers' selection of future practice settings and types of careers within internal medicine. Social as well as medical characteristics of patients loomed large as criteria in their selection of fields of practice and of setting in (and, for a few, outside of) internal medicine. Patients, however, were combined with other considerations, including the nature and limits of internal medicine and their own personal plans apart from their medical careers. Senior Resident Silverman's explanation for his choice of a GI subspecialty in an academic setting was typical of about one-third of the house staff:

I'm going into a GI fellowship. I like academics, tertiary referral institutions, and doing procedures. You see the best cases—the challenging variety—the sickest people come here, plus there are always people around to bounce things off, people you can go to for help, if you need it. . . . There's an economic disadvantage—it's not as lucrative, but compared with academics you have less free time in private practice, and there's more prestige in academia. I don't want to sit behind the desk and see patients every fifteen minutes; that would be as boring as I possibly could imagine since 99 percent of what you see in office practice is psychosomatic.

Their house staff experiences often altered their expectations:

SR PAUL:
I used to think that I would go to a small town and have a private practice or partner-ship. And I would stay there for one hundred years and watch a whole population grow up, have kids, etc. Now I think that would be very boring.

Hence, a large number of house staff opted for intensive care, emergency, or hospital-based medicine. It was dramatic: they could play an occasional medical-macho role on "exceptional" critically ill patients. There were no ex-pectations of sustained doctor–patient relationships. Responsibility, while in-tensive, would be time limited. Many were also repelled by private (i.e., middle-class) medicine:

SR FABLE:
I could never stand a private hospital. It's too boring. I know it sounds terrible, but I am a much better doctor the sicker the patients are. I do better with people who are "going down the tubes." . . . It sounds crazy, but I much prefer indigent black pa-tients. Private ones are boring. I would go out of my mind taking care of little old la-dies with diarrhea and headaches.

For three years or more, these house officers had viewed private practice through a skewed lens. First, they saw all the "rejects" and mistakes (to use their words) from the private sector. Second, in moonlighting roles they were often in a position to, and frequently did, assess both the medical and social skills of the LMDs. Quite often they related horror stories and otherwise gos-siped about community-based private medicine. They frequently regaled each other with their "rescue" experiences—how they saved a patient from some horrible fate at the hands of an LMD or negligent nursing home administrator. For some house officers these observations served to reinforce their fears of and discomfort with the private practice of medicine:

Junior residents Lovell and Weiss exchanged stories about the bad management of patients at local community hospitals and by LMDs. All of these doctors did things that in their estimation were inappropriate. Someone asked, "How do they get away with it?" All kinds of comments continued about how inadequate coverage is and how poor records are. . . . Someone added, "At T. M. Hospital the doctors don't even come in." (Field notes, VAH)

126

Simultaneously, then, they were in a position to defend—or at least find some compensatory justification for—the narrow intellectual practice of academic internal medicine, although many conceded that it also deviated from their image of the ideal doctor–patient relationship. Local medical doctors became negative role models (Bucher and Stelling, 1977) for many. Even the few who chose community practice found themselves hoping they would have the ability or willingness to "keep up." Senior Resident Sills expressed that sentiment aptly:

> I'm looking forward to trying to put together all that I've accomplished in these seven years and go out and practice. . . . I hope I can improve the quality of care of my group [medical practice] and not be an LMD that funnels patients to a hospital.

In addition, the knowledge explosion contributed to their desire to subspecialize:

> SR FILPS:
> Internal medicine is a broad field. It's very intimidating and humbling, and you'll find out over half to three-quarters of my peers are going into fellowships to subspecialize. The reason is there is so much to know, and they don't feel like they can know it all . . . and they want to be expert in something.

Senior residents Silverman and Fable above identified further reasons for opting out of community based practice, at least at the level of general medicine. They did not want sustained responsibility for patients. Time for themselves and for nonmedical pursuits—or "the ability to live a more balanced life" as one resident put it—loomed large in their choice of career setting. Many house officers came to believe that there was little reward for taking full responsibility for patients, while they could be blamed when things went wrong:

> SR FILPS:
> As an intern . . . I wanted out of internal medicine. . . . I wanted to go into radiology, dermatology, anesthesiology—to never touch patients, to never stay up all night with people who smoked or drank too much, to never deal with someone really sick. I wanted to balance their "numbers" . . . and not take responsibility for them after that. . . . I realize that in a way becoming a pulmonary fellow is an attempt to narrow my responsibility.

> SR RIND:
> I wanted to go into nephrology and be a "real doc" when I started. Now my expectations are more within reality. I've seen the kind of lifestyle that would be demanded of me. For my own personal happiness I'm going into dermatology. I don't want to be worried about seeing patients in the middle of the night, because I see what happens to doctors who don't see their patients. They practice bad medicine and I don't want to fall into that trap.

127

The minority who chose community practice did so in part as a reaction against academic-type medicine:

SR MAHONEY:
I'm looking forward to getting out from under the wing of mother institution. When you're married and twenty-nine and have essentially been going to school 30 percent of your life, people are telling you what to do. I'm looking forward to getting away from the state and federal government for a while . . . and a little more free time to do other interests.

Examining the reasons for the career choices made by the house staff in this study raises questions about the concepts of commitment and internalization that Hadden and Long (1978) identify as problematic in understanding socialization.[1] For many, regardless of the type of setting chosen, the choice came out of dissatisfaction or disillusionment with aspects of internal medicine or desire to get away from the problems of either academic or community practice:

INTERN CHAREN:
After finishing three years . . . depending on how frustrated I get with general internal medicine I may go and subspecialize. And I think it's going to be more of being pushed away from general medicine as opposed to really finding some specialty that really turns me on.

These outcomes counter the idealized image of the young doctor—one who is a humane, committed professional with integrity. After seven years of training, many emerged ambivalent or disillusioned about the pursuit of internal medicine.

ADAPTATION TO INTERNAL MEDICINE

In attempting to develop a systematic understanding of the social fact that the career choices of many of the house staff were in some ways a response to the negative or alienating aspects of their training, I developed a framework based on their relationship to their health care delivery system. Table 7.1 depicts the interaction between career choices and relationships to patients as well as the repercussion of those choices in the medical profession and in society. Ultimately, what emerges is that regardless of the career choice an internist makes, the whole patient is likely to continue to be ignored or denigrated—mentally, if not physically, GROPed.

There were, basically, four adaptive responses to the system of organized medicine and the careers within it: system perpetuators, system rejectors, system defenders, and system distorters.[2] Each of these types had a corresponding work setting and mode of internal medical practice informed by different

TABLE 7.1. Modes of Career Choice

	System perpetuators	System distorters	System defenders	System rejectors
Work settings and mode of practice	Academic medicine (research and teaching)	Large referral community practice	Mainstream academic and/or community practice	Within internal medicine: ICU; outside internal medicine: radiology, pathology, emergency
Motivational factors	Status (from peers), power, knowledge	Status (from public), money	Combination of extrinsic and intrinsic	Personal lifestyle
Relationship to patients	Distant	Discounted	Indifferent	Divorced
Repercussions	Aloof from everyday needs of patient Perpetuation of system of medical training	Aggressive activist Exploitation of patients and public medical system	Bread and Butter medicine Performs basic services while supporting the present system	Time-limited, technologically oriented practice No responsibility for or direct contact with patients

motivational factors, perspectives on patients, and effects on the larger system of medical training and service delivery.

System Perpetuators

The system perpetuators, usually based in an academic setting, become the acknowledged leaders in the specialty. This is the group that engages in research and in the teaching of novice physicians, thus perpetuating the system of house staff training in their roles as attendings and administrative heads of departments. They are similar to the group of physicians described by Miller (1970) as the "medical elite" and by Alford (1975) as "bureaucratic/corporate reformers." In seeking to "rationalize" the system, they at the same time consolidate power in the hands of institutional health providers or "health empires," the large teaching hospitals and medical centers (Ehrenreich and Ehrenreich 1970). Hence they are motivated principally by the extrinsic rewards of status and power and by intellectual interests:

> JR SAUL:
> Who gets to be a chief of medicine? . . . What qualities are looked at? . . . Well a surgeon made a comment the other day, "You know I really used to love to play racquet ball . . . but I had to give it up." Or "I really liked to play the piano. I was really good and then I got into medicine and I had to give it up." They are the real go-getters and do medicine to the exclusion of everything else and get rewarded here. "Oh you went to the library after you haven't had a day off for three weeks. That's good," and so it perpetuates itself, and that's how you go on to be a big academic type.

Probably more than any other group, they internalize the goals—if not the means—of academic medicine as those goals thus continue to exist in the world of medical socialization as well as the world of academic-based medical practice.

As attending faculty, they are quite distant from patients and from direct patient management, although they usually carry a small private general or specialty clinic practice (distinct from the public clinic system operated by the house staff). Many of the house staff recognized the irony that SR Trump noted:

> Attendings view patients pretty indifferently. I'm not saying that's good or bad. Most people would not be in an academic setting if they were interested principally in patient care.

Senior (soon to be Chief) Resident Ryder put it thus:

> I think there's no real work incentive here for anybody [faculty or house staff] to increase their work load or see patients. They [faculty] view patients . . . as a detri-

ment to their normal daily routine. And it's a side track. . . . Nobody wants to see patients. It's blamed on the house staff, but I don't think that's the real reason. . . . By and large no faculty [member] wants to see patients [either].

Attending and department heads who are aloof and apart from both the world of the house staff and the world of the patient cannot easily impart a humanistic approach to the doctor–patient relationship to novices. Their views are discounted by most house officers. What is more, they are, for the most part, more interested in and rewarded for teaching and research in their area of subspecialization.

System Rejectors

The system rejectors reject internal medicine, not usually the profession as a whole. They do so by giving up the definition of internal medicine as including care for the whole adult person and by pursuing instead a career either in critical care medicine (intensive care or emergency medicine) or in those specialties that have little or no patient responsibility, such as radiology, pathology, dermatology, or opthamology, as noted by senior residents Filps and Rind quoted earlier. One resident aptly describes the rejectors:

JR SAUL:
There's another group of people at the other extreme [from the perpetuators], who really see [internal medicine] for what it probably is. . . . They can't look down the road and see that it's bad now but it'll be better [like the system defenders can]. . . . They say, "No, these hours are just impossible. They're inhuman. I'm not going to stand for it and I'm going into some other field." . . . And they leave and go into the nonpatient contract field of radiology, as they say in *The House of God* . . . predominantly because internal medicine is the most intellectual of the fields, and radiology is really a lot of intellectual games . . . especially in differential diagnosis. . . . So it's appealing to internal medicine types . . . not to mention the money and the good hours. . . . So instead of influencing the nature or structure of internal medicine, they're gone.

As Saul indicates, these physicians are influenced by personal lifestyle and intellectual factors. Those leaving (i.e., retreating from) the high-status specialty of internal medicine need, more than any other group, to justify their actions to colleagues and often do so as Saul indicates. The system rejectors are divorced from patients. They have opted for the easy out. They have traded a wholistic for a narrow and technical view of patient care and have delimited their patient relationships to almost nil.

System Defenders

The system defenders find their niche in basic mainstream academic or community medicine. Likewise motivated by considerations such as prestige and

131

money, they carry on the basic traditions and practice of internal medicine. What distinguishes them from the system perpetuators is their orientation to the socialization process. The system perpetuators may prefer some modest reform but "realistically" accept the necessity for the process as it is. System defenders are less concerned about the outcomes and defend the form of socialization as a necessary rite of passage.[3] This is the group that maintains, "I did it—so can you," or "Now it's your turn," as noted in this comment:

SR ARI:
Your experience here depends upon how wet you get your feet. . . . It's kind of like the Marine coming out of Paris Island saying, "I loved it!" The only way you can survive [medical] training is to come up with a defense mechanism that's going to tell him that he liked it.

Junior Resident Saul put it this way:

Then there are the people . . . who have really forgotten how terrible it is to be an intern. I mean there are JRs who've forgotten already. And they treat the interns, saying, "That's so bad . . . without any feeling of, "Gee, that's really hard for them." I mean, it's easier to do—if you have something bad and don't want to remember it—to just phase it out, and in the same sort of way you're not as keyed in to the patient's needs. They say [to the patients], "I stayed up all night and was feeling terrible and I made it. What are you complaining about? . . . They veer toward the other end and want to deal with more factual sorts of things.

In describing this constellation of denial mechanisms, Saul was intimating that the defenders have not internalized the ideals of internal medicine so that, depending on the setting, they may end up apathetic and neglectful of their careers. Hence some are potential LMDs. Defenders are indifferent to patients. Medicine is not the dominant force in their lives any more. They accept it essentially for what it is—a good job with lots of compensations for all the difficulties they had to go through.

System Distorters

The system distorters, because they have not internalized the expressed goals of the profession but use its means, exploit the system for their own ends. They are motivated by monetary rewards and community status, in contrast to the system perpetuators, who seek status predominantly from their peers. This group finds its niche in the growing network of community-based subspecialty and referral practices. They work hard, are technologically sophisticated, and are sometimes in the business end of medical delivery, such as owner-operated nursing homes, proprietary hospitals, corporate group practices, and so forth. They overuse the system and are thought of by the house staff as a second major type of LMD—those who dump unprofitable patients on the public system:

JR SAUL:
On the other end of the scale are those who sort of see it for what it is, and they're just really teed off. . . . This person has had eight years of training; imagine taking a professor of mathematics, a doctoral candidate in mathematics, and making him an intern and doing the equivalent . . . or a biochemist . . . it's not imaginable. I just can't see it. And to be treated as such a low, really nonhuman being essentially— they're irritated and they want something back in return for that. And those are the people who rip off the system and are out to make as much money as they can and usually at the expense of patient care. The majority of time they probably do a pretty good job, but there are definite instances where they are out to make money and pa- tient care suffers.

System distorters feel they have been abused by the system and are now in a position to take full advantage. They project their aggressiveness onto pa- tients, placating only those patients whose demands for medical diagnosis or treatment are profitable. In the process, they discount patients' basic human needs. Distorters are the ones who view the medical profession as a means of capital accumulation leading to early retirement, wherein they live a life of leisure and voluntary activity. Within the house staff, this type was a small but distinct group who were identified as having violated norms of professional conduct. While this group had acquired the requisite medical knowledge and skill, they had limited commitment.

ANTICIPATORY SOCIALIZATION TO PATIENTS

This adaptation model suggests imperfect or inadequate career socialization for many if not most of the house staff, an outcome even more evident in their own projected future relationships with patients. One might have expected SRs to exhibit a more muted, less negative evaluation of their experience by the time they completed formal training. Since they were removed from any sustained responsibility for patient care, they could choose more freely the amount and scope of their work. I, therefore, expected that they would ex- press less dissatisfaction with their doctor−patient relationships, but this was not the case. Many who were ending the program disappointed indicated they would carry some of those feelings with them to affect their orientations to- ward patients in the next phase of professional development:

SR STRELKO:
I don't know about [medical practice]. If it's anything like the experience we've had at SAMs, I don't have anything to look forward to. As far as the frustration of clin-

ics, labs, and hospitalized patients; families trying to get rid of old people and you get stuck with disposition problems; a lot of alcoholics—that's nothing to look forward to. I know these frustrations exist [out there], but you are going to have more independence. . . . Making diagnoses, treating them, and not wasting your time.

Their projection of how different their future patients would be depended on their career choices. There were two typical responses. As Strelko commented above, most were relieved to be leaving the SAMs environment, or at least leaving the direct care of so many of less than ideal patients to a new generation of house staff:

SR HARPER:
SAMs patients are probably unique. . . . You don't follow these people in the same way. I don't think it's a matter of SES [socio-economic status], but these people aren't accustomed to the kind of relationship you'd like to have with your patients. . . . You don't really develop much of a rapport with your patients here, and their concern about you is very little.

There were also those who no longer believed that an ideal patient existed anywhere:

SR MELON:
The fact that half the people here [don't meet my ideal] is negative. I'm very much aware that I'm not going to be dealing when I'm in practice with these same people. Not to say that the people I will be dealing with are any easier because they have their own difficult problems.

SR MINEY:
I don't really anticipate encountering as many people who can't talk, who don't know what's going on. [Yet] in private practice . . . there's always a lot of pressure from patients. . . . It will be a bit different. . . . You can sit down and talk with middle-class patients easier, but then again they may be more demanding.

No doubt these perspectives will be tempered or reinforced, depending on the norms and organization of the chosen practice setting and their own continuing professional activities (Freidson 1970b, 1975).

Depending on actual choice of career setting, one can also speculate about the prospective opportunities to broaden and deepen doctor–patient skills in their future professional pursuits. For those who choose fellowships for further subspecialty training (almost two-thirds of each of the recent graduating cohorts of residents), the emphasis will be on further refining diagnostic and therapeutic skills and on learning the content of the medical subspecialty. Much of the fellowship years resemble the elective component of the SR year.

For those projecting a permanent career in academia (almost one-third of each senior cohort in recent years), there will be little primary patient care responsibility. While they may carry a small subspecialty private clinic practice, they will mostly be involved in teaching medical students and house staff about their expertise in medicine, in research, and in other administrative and supervisory responsibilities.

For those few going directly into the general practice of internal medicine (fewer and fewer each year), during the first few years at the very least they will be preoccupied with organizational, managerial, and financial concerns. Even though many house officers recognized that they would have to treat their private patients better than they had treated SAMs and VAH patients if they wanted these fee-for-service patients to return, two factors make it unlikely that they will do more than the minimum. First, the more patients they see and the more procedures they do, the more money they will make, so in their view, they might not be able to afford time for extensive interaction. Second, given their training-engendered expectation that many patients in private practice will also be demanding and difficult, they will be apt to blame the patients for problematic interactions rather than focus on their own deficiencies.

CONCLUSION

Career choices are often a reaction against the conditions experienced in the training context. Doctors have learned to view patients most benignly as boring and intrusive, at worst, as candidates for avoidance. At the end of training, doctors desire to recapture what remains of a personal life, acquire the social status and concomitant social privilege that is the reward for their service and sacrifice, control the conditions of their labor, and regulate their relationships with patients, for in their training, patients have come to embody a recalcitrant and exploitive system.

Chapter 8

A Retrospective View
Professional Practice and
Patient Perspectives

Five years after the original study, I selected a random sample of twenty-six former senior house staff members (one in three from the original study) to participate in a follow-up. Depending on the cohort, they were five or six years beyond their graduate medical education. The purpose of the follow-up study was to ascertain the nature and quality of their medical practice; collect their retrospective views on their medical education and its influence on their careers; assess changes in their careers; identify changes in their relationships with patients following residency; and gather data on their plans for future career development. (See Appendix A for a detailed description of research method.) Each respondent was interviewed personally or by phone. Conversations were tape recorded with the consent of the interviewees. The tapes were transcribed and the responses coded and compiled under each topic. This chapter presents the data of that follow-up interlaced with analysis in light of the original data.

Of the twenty-six subjects, twenty-one (88 percent) went on to postresidency fellowships in internal medicine subspecialties; nineteen completed them and thus are certified in both internal medicine and an additional subspecialty. Only two of the twenty-six went directly into general internal medicine private practice. Twelve of the twenty did their fellowships at SAMs, and of those twelve, five had been at SAMs for all their medical training.

Tables 8.1 and 8.2 provide the breakdown of their current professional settings and practice arrangements. Nationally, the SAMs physicians are probably slightly underrepresented in the general or primary care internal medicine practice. (The figures usually given are that approximately one-third are in general internal medicine exclusively or primarily.) Only one former SAMs house officer has left internal medicine to practice full-time emergency medi-

TABLE 8.1. Current Professional Settings

	Number	Percentage
Private practice:	14	53.9
Full-time specialty[a]	(8)	(30.8)
Part subspecialty, part general internal medicine[b]	(4)	(15.4)
Full-time general internal medicine	(2)	(7.7)
Academic medicine:	10	38.5
Subspecialty	(6)	(23.1)
General internal medicine	(4)	(15.4)
Other:	2	7.6
Emergency medicine	(1)	(3.8)
Hospital staff	(1[c])	(3.8)
Total	26	100.0

[a]Includes oncology, nephrology, cardiology, pulmonary medicine, gastroenterology, and rheumotology.
[b]The data here includes the one physician who refused to be interviewed.
[c]This physician is completing his military obligation and is going to join a group practice in cardiology.

cine. The group reflects the national trend away from individual practice and into partnerships and group practices. All of the physicians currently in individual practice (and two of the four subspecialists in multispecialty group practice) are actively looking for partners.

All except three of the SAMs physicians remained near where they did their last level of formal training (whether residency or fellowship). Almost two-thirds (sixteen of twenty-six) of the sample established their practice at SAMs or in the SAMs vicinity (see Table 8.3). Thus, if one could imagine SAMs at the center of several concentric rings and the cohorts as dots located in relative proximity to the center, the further the distance from SAMs, the lower the likelihood of a SAMs physician establishing a practice there. This suggests that SAMs is primarily a regional supplier of physicians and that within that region, relationships among doctors may be based on a network radiating out from SAMs. Corroborating evidence for this conclusion came from the three physicians who lived furthest away from SAMs. All three relocated near their *undergraduate* medical school.

TABLE 8.2. Current Practice Arrangements

	Number	Percentage
Institutional:	12	48.0
Academic medicine	(10)	(40.0)
Emergency medicine	(1)	(4.0)
Military hospital staff	(1)	(4.0)
Group practice:	10	40.0
Single specialty	(4)	(16.0)
Multispecialty	(6)	(24.0)
Solo practice	3	12.0
Total	25[a]	100.0

[a]Unknown for the one uninterviewed physician.

Throughout this chapter I refer to the former SAMs house staff as the SAMs physicians (rather than the SAMs internists) because the professional identity of almost all of those practicing in a subspecialty (or outside of the discipline) is *not* internist. They identify themselves primarily by their subspecialty title (e.g., cardiologist, nephrologist), secondarily as a physician, and rarely as an internist unless they are practicing general internal medicine. Moreover, many of those in full-time subspecializations regardless of whether in academic practice or community-based private practice have consciously divorced themselves from internal medicine:

TABLE 8.3. Current Practice Location

	Number	Percentage
At SAMS	6	23.1
In SAMS city	3	11.5
In SAMS state	7	26.9
In southern region	5	19.2
In Northeast	2	7.7
In north-central region	2	7.7
In West	1	3.8
Total	26	99.9

Gastroenterologist Silverman said, "I never wanted to be an internist." Gastroenterologist Browning, in separating himself from the specialty, commented: "It's hard to be a general internist keeping up with everything—to call for help when you're in over your head."

REEXAMINING THE SAMS EXPERIENCE

In looking back on their training at SAMs, almost everyone was more satisfied than they were upon completion. Hindsight, experience, additional training, and maturation seemed to increase their positive evaluation. All felt they had learned how to manage patients, and most considered the amount of responsibility they had as interns and residents extremely positive. They expressed dissatisfactions less frequently and less intensely five years later. They remembered patients at SAMs as the primary negative factor in their training, the SAMs system as the secondary one. Several former SAMs house officers specifically recalled patients they defined as abusers. They thus blamed certain sectors of the patient population for interfering with their training. Few questioned other conditions of the job such as poor facilities or staff.

Although many disliked the social characteristics of many patients (and to a lesser degree, their medical characteristics), they had learned their trade on them. Most had viewed the SAMs patients *only* as a training ground for doing things better later on with a "better class" of patients:

EMERGENCY MEDICINE (EM) MAHONEY:
I think [working] with the indigent is the best situation to do graduate medical training in that if you can get histories from them, figure out the diagnosis and treatment—then when you get in private practice with middle-class clientele it's going to be a cinch.

Only twice did former house officers spontaneously comment about their dissatisfaction with the way SAMs patients were treated as in this instance:

PRIVATE PRACTITIONER (PP) NOLAND:
I was dissatisfied when patients were not treated on a more humanistic personal level. The fact that there are constantly different doctors taking care of one patient, the patient does not get enough emotional support. . . . It's a fault in the way the system is organized.

Bond with Peers

Virtually all the physicians identified their peers as the most important cohort for them during training. This included residents above them and, as they progressed, residents at their own level. Almost all of them felt they had learned the most from their colleagues; only a few even mentioned attendings.

139

Moreover, it was the evaluation of the peers that carried the most—and for many, the only—weight:

PP CURREN:

As an intern all you have time to do is keep people from dying. . . . The ward resident explains to you why you're doing what you're doing. . . . As a JR or SR it became more important to be talking to the guys on your own level. . . . If I thought the attending was a clod, I could give a damn whether he thought I was doing my job right or not. There are a number of times when you're positive you know more medicine than your attending does, and it's usually true. . . . If I thought an attending was very good, it made a difference to me.

PP NOLAND:

The residents really make or break a program. If you have bad residents and good attendings, you're still not going to get a good educational experience. If you have good residents and bad attendings, you still get a pretty good educational experience.

These physicians five and six years later valued the peer culture about as much as they had at the end of training. They rarely mentioned attendings unless I asked. The reasons they gave were similar: attendings were not around during the critical times; peers shared similar experiences, knew each other personally, and perceived themselves as at least as knowledgeable about internal medicine as most attending physicians.

Impact of Training on Themselves

Upon completing training, the SAMs house staff had identified the stresses and strains as the cause of their ambivalence about, if not disillusionment with, the practice of internal medicine. Unquestionably, the SAMs physicians had put their training experiences into perspective. When I asked them to reflect on their overall professional development from the beginning of medical school to their current position, emphasizing house staff training, almost all of them looked back on training through the lens of their present practice.

I asked them to identify at which points they were happiest, least happy, most and least challenged (see Table 8.4), and most and least stressed. Only nine (36 percent) identified internship as their *least* happy time (while another three identified other aspects of the residency period). Almost half (twelve) viewed internship as the most challenging time, while an additional seven included other years of residency. Thus, overall, almost half were most unhappy during their house staff training, while approximately three-quarters were most challenged during that period. For the rest of the cohorts, other periods in their professional development were more significant to them: medi-

TABLE 8.4 Evaluation of Career Phases

	Most happy		Least happy		Most challenged		Least challenged	
	Number	Percentage	Number	Percentage	Number	Percentage	Number	Percentage
Medical School	7	28	6	24	2	8	5	20
Internship	2	8	9	36	12	48	0	0
Residency	5	20	3	12	7	28	5	20
Fellowship	2	8	2	8	5	20	1	4
Practice	13	52	3[a]	12	6	24	2[b]	8
Total[c]	29	116	23[d]	92	32	128	13[e]	52

[a]All three indicated they were least happy during the first year of private practice, but *none* was least happy at the time of the follow-up survey.

[b]One of the two limited the "least challenged" designation to the first year of private practice.

[c]Totals sometimes add up to more than twenty-five or 100 percent because some physicians designated more than one career phase for a given category.

[d]Two physicians did not respond.

[e]Four physicians indicated they were always challenged; eight did not respond.

cal school (almost one-quarter were least happy then) and postresidency times (seven were least happy or least challenged during their fellowship phase).

On the positive side, the period of house staff training was the happiest time for 28 percent (including two who said they were happiest during internship), while medical school (usually the fourth year) was the happiest period for another 28 percent. Slightly more than one-half said they were happiest in their present situation (sometimes in combination with another period during which they were just as happy). No one indicated being least happy currently, and only one physician (in academic practice) was least challenged currently.

Of those who were asked the question about stress, more than half said they were presently most stressed, while only about 20 percent stated that internship was the most stressful period in their careers. Significantly, almost two-thirds indicated that they anticipated being more stressed in the future, while the rest indicated the level of stress would remain the same. (Future stress was usually related to anticipation of government encroachment into their medical practice.)

Hence there was a wider range of responses than one would have anticipated at the time the SAMs physicians completed training. The fact that, for more than half, the tenure as SAMs house staff was *not* the most dissatisfying time is an important and somewhat unexpected finding. It becomes even more significant when viewed in combination with their responses to the following questions:

Many physicians discuss the stresses and pressures they were under during house staff training. What kind did you experience? How did you cope with the stresses? What kind of toll, if any, do you think training had on you? and Do you think the present system of internal medicine training establishes unrealistic expectations or makes unrealistic demands on trainees?

The problems of sleep deprivation, too little time for outside interests, and the fear of making mistakes while handling people's lives during internship and residency were the stresses they recalled, usually in that order of importance, but many downplayed their impact on themselves: 35 percent (nine) stated that the training program did not take any toll, while 28 percent (seven) responded that it had taken a great or serious toll on them, the rest (with two not responding) stating that it had taken some toll (see Table 8.5). Some typical responses:

PP BROWNING:
The biggest stress was sleep deprivation. I coped with it by acting crazy a lot. I think it took its toll. It shortened my life by five years I'm sure. I had very little personal life, and I'm sure it had a negative effect on my marriage. My sex life suffered.

TABLE 8.5. Evaluation of Internship and Residency

	Number	*Percentage*
Toll taken:		
None	9	36
Some	7	28
Serious	7	28
No answer	2	8
Total	25	100
Demands unrealistic:		
Agree	3	15
Disagree	17	85
Total	20[a]	100

[a]Five did not answer the question.

AP (Academic Practitioner) DEREN:
I coped with the stresses by losing my temper a few times. I wasn't totally appropriate; I partied a lot; I had close friends [peers], which made a big difference. . . . At this point I don't feel a toll. I'm sure that it's aged me . . . a little more quickly though.

Ironically, although more than 50 percent stated that the program had taken some or a great toll on them personally, only a small minority (three) felt that the training program made unrealistic demands on its trainees; the rest disagreed, many emphatically so:

PP BATT:
I didn't appreciate the amount of time and fatigue. . . . Otherwise, I thought it was a reasonable trade off for my goal and therefore not much of a toll was taken. House staff training is a necessary indoctrination. You've been a student all your life, and you've got to get shoved into doing this—making decisions, getting up and doing things. It's not pleasant, but probably it's as efficient a way as there is.

PP NOLAND:
[Unrealistic demands?] . . . It's like the old boy who's gone through fraternity initiation and says, "I did it, everybody ought to do it." I feel like it's being cast in that light. I think the hours you put in in your internship are only long in retrospect. . . . I was on call every third night in internship; now I'm on call every third night. I'm my own intern now. So what do those guys think they're going to do out there in practice when they get called at 3 a.m.? Are they going to say, "Clutch your chest until 8 a.m. and then come into my office?"

The impact of the program on its house officers has to be analyzed at three levels: First, is the perceived amount and type of stress induced? Second, is the stress perceived to have had any permanent repercussions? Third (by implication), in spite of possible negative consequences, would they change the program or do they think it should be changed? While most former SAMs house officers admitted to some physical, psychological, or social stress themselves during training, very few retrospectively saw a need to have the system changed in any signicant way. Those who mentioned systems changes at most included changing some of the patient care experiences or extending the program a year to make it less intensive. This response was typical:

AP LOMBARD:

I don't think [it established unrealistic demands] except sleep deprivation. . . . One of the real keys to the teaching and learning process is to take care of patients being there alone. . . . Practically speaking, that occurs at night when no one else is around . . . to formulate a plan . . . making decisions in your mind at least. . . . Nighttime is a fairly important time.

Most of the SAMs physicians, like Batt and Lombard, saw the training as a necessary, if not ideal, way of learning internal medicine. Others, like Noland, felt that the stresses were exaggerated or else good preparation for the "real world" of private practice.

Views of the stresses of residency training were linked to the way the SAMs physicians perceived theirs or their colleagues' present professional circumstances. Of the fourteen physicians in community-based private practice, nine discussed the fact they were presently more stressed than they were in training, usually comparing themselves to academic colleagues, as Noland does:

People in academia don't work as hard. I've talked to several people. . . . They usually admit it. They also don't get as well paid—it's a trade-off. They don't have primary care responsibility. They don't have to get up in the middle of the night. They have residents, interns, and fellows, and they can say, "Sic 'em boy. Call me in the morning."

Several of those in academic settings also cited the pressures of their colleagues in private practice in addition to a host of different kinds of pressures on themselves (to be discussed below). Their professional practice had begun to put their training in perspective.

Relationships with SAMS Patients

Upon looking back on their relationships with patients during training, only a small minority of the physicians were unconditionally satisfied with the care that was given to the SAMs patients by the house staff or with the care that they delivered personally. The most prevalent responses were to qualify the care they delivered by distinguishing between the social or attitudinal component of patient care and the technical or medical treatment they provided. For example:

AP STRELKO
Medically, the patients were treated very well, but emotionally they weren't. The treatment of va patients was the worst.

AP DEREN:
Most of the time I was satisfied, but I think some house officers were abusive at times, were not nice to people. In general, the house staff is more respectful to patients than other people in our society. . . . There's certainly no doubt that our patients have always had excellent medical treatment. At times attitudinally there are problems. There will always be problems when you have middle-upper-class young whites taking care of poor blacks. There are always some house officers . . . who are angry and who take it out on the patients. I think it's more a societal problem than a system problem.

Everyone corroborated the collective opinion during training that very few of the SAMs patients approximated the ideal. The physician's estimates of the percentage of SAMs patients who were ideal ranged from less than 1 to 25 percent (with one physician stating that 40 percent of his *clinic* patients approximated his ideal patient). This same group of physicians in almost every instance indicated that most of their current patients—ranging from 60 to 95 percent—approximated their ideal patient. Almost *all* the SAMs physicians felt they engaged in better relations with patients currently than they did while in training.

I asked the SAMs physicians who had read *The House of God* (Shem 1978; see Chapter Two) whether they still thought it a valid portrayal of their own experiences. They were more divided about its accuracy than they had been at the end of house staff training. Six (23 percent) felt that it was either not true or grossly exaggerated—a response never appearing five years earlier. A few of the former house officers were even angry or upset by it:

AP DEREN:
It's exactly like any other satire—many exaggerations. . . . It tends to be somewhat one-sided and therefore inaccurate. . . . Someone who is in the system will take it for what it's worth. . . . The only thing that bothers me is people who haven't been in the system, reading it and thinking that's what it is like. It's not really exactly like that.

PP BATT:
The problem with *The House of God* is that it's written by a psychiatrist about his experience in internal medicine, and his experiences were negative. What it does by

145

dwelling on the form is miss the substance of what went on. Most doctors have an innate sense of responsibility.

The rest of the former house staff still considered the portrayal completely or partly true. One physician even felt it was understated. Most of the SAMs physicians thought the psychological trauma expressed by interns in the book was overstated. This makes sense in light of their attenuated responses to the stress of training. The dynamics of the negative doctor–patient relationship and the insular house staff culture, however, they considered accurate and representative:

PP LYNCH:
I enjoyed it and I empathized with it. . . . "The only good admission was a dead admission" expressed probably what most people don't care to express outwardly.

PP NOLAND:
It was great. They used all the right terms and everything that's true. That's what I was talking about. You're just providing a service, and you don't have any personal connection with the patient. They're slabs of meat that you're here to process.

GROP Revisited

All the physicians concurred that patients had been characterized as "hits," and those who still had contact with house staff stated that the practice continues. Five or more years after training virtually all the former house staff could recall and define a wide variety of slang terms used during training for patients and patient-related situations, almost all of which were pejorative. In all but three instances, they readily admitted having used them themselves.

The questions I investigated with respect to the GROP perspective were: first, whether the SAMs physicians considered it an accurate or an exaggerated perception; second, whether they justified its use; third, whether the GROP perspective (which included the acceptance of slang terms and a combat mentality) affected how patient care was delivered; and fourth, whether they still considered it applicable or thought about patients in those terms.

In discussing his training, one former chief resident presently in academic medicine corroborated the seemingly universal conditions of internal medicine training:

I have to admit that I had forgotten the pain. I can now remember some of the instances where colleagues came to me crying. We cried. . . . The internship year is recycled every year. . . . This constant turnover that treats an enormous population of patients, and it affects them. You can't prepare yourself for that tour of duty as a soldier. *There's so many slang terms for the enemy*, which is all around us . . . the foxhole mentality . . . [emphasis added].

Another physician noted the carry-over to the present:

PP AYRES:
During house staff years you look on patients as adversaries sometimes. That goes away at some point. There are still a few I look on as adversaries now.

All but four of the physicians believed the GROP perspective to be an *extremely* accurate reflection of their house staff training. Many offered reasons, explaining, if not justifying, it by pointing to the constraints of the situation, the necessity of relieving tension, and the nature of the patient population:

PP BROWNING:
Patients are called hits. The goal of every single day is for the intern to just finish it—complete it—and go on to the next day. That meant there was one less day of having to do that, that's part of the *trenches mentality* [emphasis added]. . . . Have you ever read *The House of God?*

PP LEEDS:
Using slang terms is a way of blowing off steam. We goofed around. First-year medical students would think residents are horrible, unfeeling people. By the time they get that far they do the same things.

PP BATT:
The term ["hit"] was used a lot in training. . . . But a patient is still a "hit" if the doctor has to get up at 2:30 in the morning.

Four of the twenty-six physicians felt that the GROP perspective was either exaggerated or situational. This small group believed that those attitudes were endemic only to the house staff culture. Some attempted to justify them:

PP CURREN:
Most people wanted as many patients as they could get. The catch was they also wanted to get rid of them all. You wanted to admit raftloads of patients with raftloads of different problems, get them straightened on up, and get them the hell out so that you didn't have to make rounds on four hundred patients.

AP FEINAST:
[You can become humanistic after training.] It might happen automatically. If you get into the habit of calling everyone "hits" because everyone else is—and if you leave a setting where the first question in the morning was "how many hits did you get last night?" you begin to lose that stimulus to consider patients as hits.

As already noted, many SAMs physicians acknowledged that some, if not all, SAMs patients received differential treatment on the basis of social or medical characteristics and that such labeling had negative effects on patient care:

PP SILVERMAN:
No question [using slang terms] affects patient management adversely. It gives an improper view of the patient, who is a human being. . . . It affects care because you

prejudge the situation. . . . With "turkeys" and with "gomers," it's a statement about their social situation. Right away there was a socially embarrassing kind of patient. . . . If the guy was really sick, it lifted him to a new level because it was a challenge to get him better. If he wasn't sick, your object was to "water him up," so to speak, and get him out as quickly as possible.

Most confirmed that it was within the peer culture that the GROP mentality emerged and was maintained, as Feinast noted and as reflected in the remarks of another former SAMS house officer:

PP BEECH:
I tend to treat patients more as real people now than I probably did as a house staff. . . . Everybody else was calling them dumb words, for example, "turkeys," "gomers," etc. There was a lot of peer pressure. Deep down inside you may have called yourself a schmuck for using them—but you kept on doing it. If you sat them down, I don't think my fellow house staff were as separate from our feelings when we were house doctors as books would have you believe.

The GROP perspective appears to be perpetuated both because of the insular nature of the house staff peer culture and because of attendings who, while distancing themselves from it to varying degrees, tolerate, if not condone, it:

AP PAUL:
There's one term I used and still use: "turkey." It's a person who's putting something over on you . . . a dishonest patient. But I won't allow it in a formal setting. When it's used amongst each other, it's one thing, but it shouldn't be used on rounds, particularly if there are students present. . . . I don't want to set that tone in a working relationship. . . . It's like raising kids and not swearing in front of them.

AP SCOTT:
"Hit" is a universal term. Here [at a midwestern medical center] they also use the term "move the meat." Now I have more luxury to choose my patients, so I don't use the term.

Those in academic practice recognized they had more control over the number and type of patients they treated and therefore could "afford" a better attitude. Those in private practice repeatedly stated that they did not view patients as hits because patients mean money, and almost none have a clientele similar to the SAMs patients. Most treat middle-class patients almost exclusively. Many have consciously refused to accept Medicaid patients or to take patients from ERs. Others distinguish, as they did in training, between the poor but deserving patients, whom they will accept, and the undeserving poor, whom they discourage. Nevertheless, about one-third of the SAMs physicians admitted to still using slang terms for some patients:

EM MAHONEY:
I still use slang terms like turkey and gomer, sometimes. It's a protective defense mechanism. I wouldn't stop other people from using them if I heard them.

CHANGING PATIENT PERSPECTIVES

I asked the SAMs physicians a series of questions comparing their present attitudes toward patients with those they held in their training years:

> Looking back since you began medical school, have your attitudes toward patients changed? Since beginning and ending internal medicine training? Overall do you consider yourself more positively or negatively disposed to patients now? Would you say that over the years you have become more cynical or more tolerant of patients and their behavior? More empathetic or more apathetic?

With three exceptions, the sentiment of most physicians was that they have become more favorably inclined toward, trusting, and tolerant of patients. Many of them traced the acquisition of their patient perspectives to maturation in themselves, a shift to a middle-class patient population, the fact that patients paid them for the care received, or a combination of these reasons. Typical of their responses were the following:

AP FEINAST:
Within the last year I've started trying to see more of the patient as a person. It was there to begin with; it disappeared for a while; and then it came back.

PP LEEDS:
I listen more accurately to things I didn't have to worry about at SAMs—their job situation, their social situation. . . . I went from being in awe of patients, to being uncomfortable around them, to calling them "gomers," to seeing them as people. . . . I hope it stays that way.

PP ODOM:
You can't treat people lousy in private practice without losing them. Those who end up in private practice like to take care of patients more. Not everyone in medicine is good at taking care of patients. Also the patients are easier to take care of. We're not choosing the poor, recalcitrant ones, where we get dumped on and we have to take care of them [like in training].

Of the three who expressed some cynicism toward patients, two were still connected with the SAMs environment, and one, ironically, was a physician who never used slang patient terms or characterized patients as "hits." Academic practitioner Paul, on the faculty at SAMs, provided an explanation in terms of the quality of patients:

> If you get into private practice I think it's a matter of whether you are identifying with the patients or not. So if you are in a practice situation where you are caring for your peers or social equals, it's different. . . . Here [at SAMs-VAH] we're dealing with a lot of con men. There's no way around it, and you're going to be looking at them in those terms.

As can be seen by the different perspectives of the academic and private practice physicians, the constraints of the marketplace upon private practice

149

physicians require them to be more considerate of the feelings and concerns of their clientele. Academic physicians tend to be less concerned, since their clientele is not, for the most part, determined by market forces. The generalization that can be made from the testimony of the sample is that the combination of work conditions, patient load, the rotational system, and patient characteristics led to the suppression of humanistic concerns by the house staff. Consequently, relieved of those constraints, relationships seemed to improve across the sample, with private practitioners noting a positive impetus for viewing their patients in more complex, humanistic ways. In general, the academic practitioners were distanced from patients and overall tended to characterize their relationships with patients less humanistically than private practitioners but better than house staff. Hence, the SAMs physicians corroborated the fact that socialization of doctors suppresses positive relationships with patients, while the organizational context affects the socialization process.

REDEFINING COMPETENCY IN MEDICINE

Goldfinger (1977) suggests that residents deny fallibility and have an "it-can't-happen-to-me" attitude. The SAMs cohort, to the contrary, both as ending residents and certainly as physicians five years later, feared failure. Many wondered whether they could and would keep up with advances in the field. All those in subspecialties admitted to losing some knowledge and skill since training in general internal medicine. Several admitted that they would not do as well on (or even pass) their internal medicine boards.

Virtually everyone agreed that the intellectual thrust of internal medicine reigned supreme in the training environment. Sound diagnostic skills, a fund of medical knowledge, and a compulsive nature were, in their view, the most important components of a competent internist. But, as the SAMs physicians examined their own professional practice from the vantage point of academia or the community, a major shift emerged in their perspective on medical care. *Without exception*, their definition of the competent physician changed, first, by giving priority to the patient relationship (and PSE factors) and second, by substituting depth for breadth of knowledge. They all believed using these different evaluation measures that they are better physicians now than they were at the end of training:

PP Silverman:

I think my views of what goes into a competent internist have changed in one respect in that the humanitarian aspect has been emphasized more than the mechanical. In residency, it's how many Swan-Ganz catheters did you put in—or did you get that lumbar puncture on the first or sixth try. That's not as important now as the question Did you hold the patient's hand, stroke her, and make her feel better when you walked to the patient's bedside?

PP LYNCH:
I worry about it all the time. . . . If I were to compare my fund of knowledge to a third-year resident, I suspect I'm out of date—but I feel I've gained other skills which are probably effective—judgment and communication—that gives [*sic*] me an edge. . . . In clinical skills I'm better now.

These community physicians for the most part no longer define themselves as internists. Perhaps that makes it easier to forgive themselves for not remaining current with internal medicine. Those in academic practice also recognize the change but have distanced themselves from needing to know "everything." The academic doctors also admitted to learning from the house staff and welcoming the teaching role precisely because it forces them to keep up:

AP STELLA:
I'm already out of date on the other subspecialties, but s a m s gave me a good sense of disease. I know the right questions to ask the house staff when I don't know the details.

Their definition of physician also included, almost unanimously, the broadening of their concept of patient management:

PP BROWNING:
There are different kinds of knowledge. In terms of factual [knowledge], nobody knows as much as when they finish their training, but they're not the best doctors.

Reassessing PSE Factors

At the same time, the SAMs doctors confirmed almost unanimously that they had little or no training in the PSE dimensions of patient care. There were some differences, however, as to whether the lack of coverage was a deficiency in their graduate medical education, an appropriate omission given the number of other areas to master, or an appropriate omission because PSE awareness could not be taught at all.

While a minority did label it a deficiency when directly asked, almost no one mentioned the lack of PSE training as a reason for dissatisfaction with the SAMs training program. Even though practicing physicians in other studies have identified a need for including these factors in training (Kantor and Giner 1981; McCue 1981; Young 1975) and some of the SAMs cohort stated that much of their practice (even at the subspeciality level) was devoted to handling PSE factors, the ambivalence toward PSE training remained:

PP BEECH:
I see how much social and environmental factors affect patients and illness. I didn't anticipate this during training. It is a deficiency that the program doesn't focus on

nonmedical aspects. *But I don't think you can teach them. I don't think they'll believe it.* [Emphasis added.]

PP Noland:
They didn't really teach you how to deal with patients in the training program. That's something you either knew or didn't know. . . . I think it's important, but I'm not sure you'd do it.

PP Curren:
Not really [any time was devoted to p s e during graduate training]. What happens in medical school is you get lectures on how to take a history, and it touches on the psychological approach to the patient. There's lip service paid to mak[ing] sure you understand what you're talking about when you talk to the patient and mak[ing] sure he knows what you're talking about. There's a lot of emphasis on taking a history . . . and then they put you in the VAH, where nobody can give a history. . . . We knew in an intellectual kind of sense that there were social parameters to disease; that living in this kind of neighborhood made you more likely to have this kind of disease. . . . You're not taught anything about the social surroundings of your patient because they're not important. You never see them. *You see the patient as sick as a goat . . . and as soon as he's not that way you kick him out.* [Emphasis added.]

In five years almost all have come to believe much more forcefully that there is more than one way to practice medicine. In learning that they cannot know or do it all, they have also have come to recognize that other physicians may know something they do not; the gray areas in medicine have become more pronounced. Therefore they are not only more lenient in self-evaluation but have become more understanding and flexible when assessing the care given by colleagues.

The LMD Dilemma

Nowhere are the SAMs physicians' changing perspectives on the practice of medicine more evident than in their concept of the LMD. Within the house staff culture the term LMD was used as a blanket pejorative label for almost all physicians outside of internal medicine or the training institution:

PP Beech:
I used [the term "LMD"], but a lot of house staff don't realize that us poor LMDs take care of 98 percent of the stuff. They see 2 percent of the screw-ups. I was calling them LMDs in the middle of the night—like everybody else who felt dumped on.

PP Sills:
You wind up in a training program, and you think of yourself as at the end point in medicine, and that's not necessarily true. There's a lot of good medicine being practiced on the outside. . . . *Before we would be real hard lined* [emphasis added].

One private practitioner explained how work conditions, in addition to the intellectual orientation of internal medicine, contributed to a skewed view of medical practice:

PP BATT:
At SAMs when you were called, you had to get out of bed and make rounds or work up the patient. *Patients used to be an imposition on you*, rather than the way you made your living, so obviously you felt that some incompetent doctor in town had blown it [emphasis added]. . . . Now I can appreciate what the guys had to deal with. I haven't encountered anyone who's not trying to take care of their patients. When you're a house staff, you think LMDs are touring around in Cadillacs, not answering their phones, etc.

While many admitted that they had seen some incompetent or negligent community physicians, they were more tolerant of the styles of patient management they observed. They could no longer distance themselves from the world of private practice as they could during training. Some could see their own foot slipping already:

PP SILVERMAN:
I don't think I've lost any ground, but if I continue to do this five or six more years—no question, I'd be burned out and I wouldn't be able to keep up.

PP BEECH:
I have some doubts as to what kind of doctor I'll be at sixty, when a bunch of young whippersnappers come into town.

Even those in academic settings identified the trade-offs in providing broader dimensions of patient care:

AP MOSER:
That's why I'm not in private practice. I couldn't keep up. In general they [community doctors] do a good job, and in communicating with their patients they do better than we [academic doctors] do.

AP PAUL:
I'm more forgiving with LMDs because I realize that they tide people over. I think the personal touch counts a lot more in my book than it would have in the past . . . so their medicine may be on the sloppy side, but the interaction with patients is worth a lot.

Almost all the private practitioners recalled instances where they were viewed—sometimes disparagingly so—as "LMDs" by university medical centers or tertiary hospitals to whom they referred a patient. It was both painful and ironic to them as they described the dynamics:

PP HOBART:
I'm an LMD. I went on rounds up at SAMs with a friend, and the house staff was talking about a patient referred from an MD in southern county. Several derogatory

terms were used . . . when the doctor didn't do everything. Boy, it's easy to do that in retrospect! . . . *But I remember doing the same thing when I was there* [emphasis added].

In commenting on their changing relationship with and attitude toward the academic environment, the SAMs physicians were also corroborating the perpetuation of the intellectual, distanced-from-patients, ivory tower view of medicine in medical training.

RELATIONSHIPS WITH PRESENT HOUSE STAFF

Because the SAMs attendings as a group had limited impact on the SAMs house staff, it is important to know how the SAMs physicians perceive their relationships with current house staff. I thus asked, "How do you feel now that the shoe is on the other foot? Do you feel like you have any impact on house staff now?" These physicians are not so far removed from the world of the house staff as to forget it, especially the house staff culture. Of the SAMs doctors, 40 percent are in academic practice full time and therefore have had extensive contact with the house staff, while an additional 36 percent in private practice have had some contact with house staff during or since their fellowship years. These physicians interact with house staff primarily in a teaching role and secondarily in sharing responsibility for managing hospitalized patients. Therefore they are in a structural position to influence future groups of physicians.

In general, the more their own perspectives on competency in internal medicine had changed to encompass the doctor–patient relationship (or as some characterized it, a "reasoned approach to the patient"), the less impact they felt they had on present house staff:

AP FEINAST:

I don't have as much impact in many ways as I would like. I give the residents a lot of opportunity to develop a relationship with patients. I ask them about those relationships. The house staff want to do more procedures more often—it's a different perspective.

The academic physicians admitted to being removed from patient management decisions and, hence, distant from the house staff culture. Those who stressed intellectual, problem-solving, or didactic aspects of internal medicine felt they had some impact. Occasionally, a clash of perspectives surfaced between the SAMs academic physicians and present cohorts of house staff, regardless of training institution:

AP SCOTT:

I don't enjoy the house staff when they're taking care of my patients. It's a lot easier to deal in abstracts than to do battle with them over the specifics of a given patient.

AP STRELKO:
My own peeve is how unreasonable they [house staff] are. They all have knowledge. They can quote the latest literature, but how do they apply it? I wish they would get off [their] ego trip. . . . The house staff are pretty good but some are less willing to accept the humanistic part of medicine—too concerned with medical minutiae which might be important to them but is fairly irrelevant to the patient. I think the style here [at SAMs] is strictly a house staff one. I don't like it. I think once they have to deal with *real* people, they'll have to develop into something different than they were here. Here they don't want to care for patients. It's "this guy's had a stroke. Call 'Neuro.' . . ." They don't want to see the patient anymore.

The SAMs physicians in academic settings corroborated the existence of a strong house staff culture everywhere, and they confirmed the limited effect of the attending faculty on that culture. Those in private practice all felt they did not have much impact on house staff, and most did not care about having any effect.

STRESSES AND SATISFACTIONS OF PROFESSIONAL PRACTICE

The sources of satisfaction received from their medical careers are vastly different for the academic and community physicians. The academics enjoy the challenge of research and discovery, the relative ease of pace, and the intellectual stimulation:

AP STELLA:
I enjoy being on the frontier. I often thought of private practice and doing patient care full time, but I know I'd be frustrated and bored within six months if I were only able to treat patients with currently available treatments. It's fun to try new drugs. I like to be around doctors [for the intellectual stimulation]. . . . My quality of life is better than I anticipated. I don't come into the hospital in the middle of the night. In private practice they're always on call, but they are compensated by an enormous salary—it's a compromise.

Community practice physicians are rewarded by the stimulation afforded by the pathology they see in their practices, the fact that they are building something for themselves, community esteem, financial rewards, and autonomy:

PP LEEDS:
If I had the time to do everything right now, I'd be in heaven. I'm doing exactly the kind of practice I wanted [noninvasive cardiology]. I see lots of sick people, have plenty to do—all the gimmicks, all my own equipment, lots of nurses around, the intellectual stimulation is fine, I'm financially rewarded more than I ever thought. Now if I only had time to spend it . . . I'm looking for a partner—I think that would be my salvation.

155

PP NOLAND:

[As a private practitioner] I like the intellectual stimulation, and a certain amount of innate respect in the community, which is nice. I agree it's not deserved—but it's nice, and I like the financial security and being my own boss.

While no one felt that he had the ideal situation, most of the physicians were satisfied with the choices they had made. Five and six years out of residency training, most of the SAMs physicians were in settings they anticipated would be permanent. Uncertainty as to future career settings was expressed by only three academic physicians, two of whom were overtly dissatisfied with their present situation. In all three instances these academic physicians were in general internal medicine or primary care positions, as was the one community physician who was not fully satisfied with his life as a general internist.

In discussing the dissatisfactions and stresses of their current professional life, the community physicians almost always included aspects of patient care. Almost all those in private practice felt under greater and different kinds of pressure from patients than they did in training. They either referred to a lessening of patient confidence generally or else identified specific attributes of certain groups of patients as causing cynicism or disillusionment in their everyday work. These comments must be put in the context of the fact that they are much more satisfied with their present patient population than when they were in training:

PP CONLEY:

Patients can be very demanding, and the buck stops with you. You can't put them off like you can in a socialized situation—like the army hospital or a teaching institution. . . . You have to be available, you've got to make sure everything gets done. The patients are rightfully very demanding, sometimes more than they should be.

PP BEECH:

My father's a doctor, and I also saw Kildare and Casey [former TV doctors]. . . . People are supposed to respect doctors, and doctors are supposed to have stature in the community, have some influence, and be liked by their patients and by people in general. . . . I think that's what attracts people to being a doctor. . . . But now I really think the feds, Blue Cross/Blue Shield, insurance companies are trying to make people believe doctors are crooks. . . . I think we are being unjustly blamed. . . . Because of this propaganda, physicians enjoy less of a place in society.

PP LYNCH:

You have to put up with a lot of crap. People are not all nice. It's hard not to interject your own personal emotions. . . . It's not a job you can take lightly.

Thus, there were two sources of strain among the community physicians: first, the expectations of the patients; second, the erosion of the medical community's prestige. Because they were in private practice and the patients tended to be middle class and footing the bills directly or indirectly, patients expected more from them. Moreover, the SAMs physicians tended to view the market for their services as competitive and therefore felt a need to keep their customers satisfied. Although doctors still have a great deal of prestige, they view the profession's status against the time when its authority was unquestioned by the laity. This sense of relative status deprivation gives the private practitioner a wistfulness about those old days and pressures him to compensate for the failings of the profession.

The pressures felt by the academic doctors were generated much more by the system and by peers than by patients. Overall, they spend no more than 20–25 percent of their time in direct patient care responsibilities, and some of that time is in supervising residents and fellows. These academicians experience the traditional pressures of academic life—publish or perish—and the more recent funding pressures generated by federal cutbacks. Almost all of the academic physicians expressed cynicism or disillusionment about the politics of academia, which included competing for grants and status within their institution. Academic Practitioner Paul's comment is an extreme version of the views of most of this cohort:

> In academia, it amazes me that these people who grind out one paper after another through research can't teach, can't take care of patients, hate patients. . . . The rewards are greater for those things that are often garbage.

Other academic respondents confirmed that patient care and teaching responsibilities were not rewarded. These academics are constantly being challenged, and most view the diversity of their roles positively. Yet they have a greater fear of failing then do the community physicians, who, once established, have an abundant patient population:

AP JONES:
Sure [I have self doubts]; whether I can do everything on this job and do it well. Be able to keep up with medicine, do research, teach well, take care of patients.

For most of the academic physicians the financial renumeration was satisfactory, and for many, more than adequate to meet their needs. They all acknowledged that the income of those in community practice was higher, but if they were satisfied with the administrative and clinical aspects of their jobs, then they generally felt the trade-off was worth it:

AP SCOTT:
I invite my friend from private practice down, and he drives a new Mercedes. I drive a Honda, but then he's never home. He needs it. He spends more time in his car than he does with his kids.

The community physicians felt the greater financial rewards were justified because of the scope of their patient responsibility and the greater number of hours they worked each week. (The SAMs community physicians worked from sixty to eighty-five hours a week, while the academic physicians worked from fifty to seventy hours a week):

PP CURREN:
Last week, I walked into the doctor's parking lot at [my] hospital and saw a Mercedes 450 next to a Turbo Saab, and I drive a b m w 528. I thought "God Damn, look at the cars we drive!" Then I thought, "It's 3:30 in the morning and everyone of these suckers is in the hospital [seeing patients]."

Almost all of the community physicians had concerns—some serious— about the lack of intellectual stimulation. This was often combined with some expressed fears of not being able or willing to keep up—because of the knowledge explosion or boredeom settling in. Those who were more isolated saw it as a greater problem:

EM MAHONEY:
The intellectual stimulation is a problem when you're not in an academic environment and not directly competing. It's too easy to let things slide. . . . It takes discipline.

The fear of failure for many of those in community practice was deep and almost always linked to the clinical diagnosis and treatment:

PP MELON:
I face [the fear of failure] every time I can't figure out what's been going on— which lately has been frequently—not on treatment but on diagnosis. It's the uncertainty.

These self-doubts concerning patient management continuously surfaced among community physicians:

PP SILVERMAN:
You always have self-doubt when cases are not going the way you want. The more I stay in private practice, the more I realize our capabilities are very limited. It's the good Lord who decides it—independent of what you do. On the other hand, it's fulfilling when people you never thought would get better, get better. But more often the first happens. They don't get better no matter what you do.

Academic physicians, unlike the community physicians, had an out. They could always go into private practive in their specialty if they "failed," and a few were flirting with this possibility:

AP SCOTT:
The fear of failure doesn't bother me. If this whole academic thing fails, I'm fully trained and equipped to practice [cardiology] with the best of them.

Scott was the only academic doctor who asserted that the strains of academic life vis-à-vis the pressure to "public or perish" were grossly exaggerated. From his vantage point, the politics, pressures, and time constraints were far greater in the world of private medicine. In virtually each instance, those academic physicians who were dissatisfied with patient relationships were still in the SAMs environment interacting with the same types of patients so intensely disliked during training. These academic doctors were considering a change of setting to private practice, fantasizing about how much better the relationships with private patients would be. The academics generally did recognize, however, that they were divorced from many of the pressures from patients because they were not dependent on patients for their income. As a result, some sympathized with the private practitioners, while others condemned the unethical practices that resulted from private practitioners doing what the academics believed were unnecessary procedures:

AP DEREN:
I won't do it [give a Valium to patients]. . . . It's easy for me to be ethical because my salary doesn't depend upon whether or not the patients continue coming to me.

AP STELLA:
That's why I'm not practicing oncology. I see too many questionable treatments that are justified by those doctors. I can't help but thinking that there may be a conflict of interest in private practice.

Among the former SAMs physicians there was a sense of trade-offs between academic and community practice. Academic practice was perceived as more stimulating and challenging, allowing for a relatively more relaxed lifestyle and allowing for stronger peer relationships. It was seen as problematic in that bureaucratic politics, pressure to win grants, publish or perish, and the presence of less than ideal patients all had to be coped with. Community practice meant high financial rewards, the possibility of dealing with patients on a more humanistic level, community esteem, and autonomy. The problems were seen as a high work load, isolation with a consequent failure to keep up with the field, and greater patient expectations. Although community practitioners did not fear failure as much as the academics who struggled for research grants and academic tenure, the academics could move into community practice if they failed in academia. The converse was not necessarily true.

VIEWING THE FUTURE

In discussing their current professional life, virtually all the SAMs physicians felt that, while the stresses were heavy, they could not conceive of themselves doing anything else in or outside of medicine. Nevertheless, there were degrees of dissatisfaction and strain, and some were certainly more disillusioned or cynical about the practice of medicine than others. These differences became evident as they responded to certain specific questions about the future — for themselves, for their children, and for the medical profession in general. Even though they were, for the most part, in a career trajectory that was satisfactory and rewarding, they were considerably less sanguine about the future prospects of the profession, as PP Conley noted:

> There's going to be an impingement of the practice of medicine. There's going to be more regulation. You're going to be told what to do and how to do it. The government is going to dictate what to do, how to do it, and how much you can charge. I'm not sure if it is good or bad, but I have a feeling it is going to be negative. Overutilization of resources and reimbursements are going to have to be corrected. . . . Government regulation is not the answer, nor is opening up the forces of the marketplace. Medicine is not just a business. If they are going to treat it like a business, then patients are going to be treated like merchandise. . . . I don't think the public wants to sacrifice the quality for the cost. I'm working to be able to leave medicine fifteen years from now. I won't need medicine to make my living. I don't want to practice if I can't practice the way I want. The loss of freedom isn't worth it.

I queried the SAMs physicians about what the future holds for them: what they are looking and not looking forward to in the next five years or so, what changes in the medical profession over the five to ten years they ancitipate that are of concern to them, and whether they are generally optimistic or pessimistic about the future of medicine. Like the physicians surveyed by the Harris organization (1981), I found that they anticipated many changes in medical practice, only a few of them positive:

AP SCOTT:
The DRGs [diagnostic-related groups] are going to put some financial constraints on things. There is a drying up of research funds. You have all these interests groups — the Catholics on abortion, the antivivisectionists. The DRGs are ill conceived. . . . Somewhere along the line something like that should work, but the flaw in it is you are penalized if the patients live.

One of the most important indications of changing perspectives on medicine was the physicians' response to the question to whether or not they would recommend medicine as a career for their children. In all but three instances this was a real, not hypothetical, question. Of those responding to the question, only five would recommend it more enthusiastically than they would have right after training, while more than half (thirteen) would recommend it less enthusiastically than earlier. This finding correlates, although not perfectly, with the fact that only thirteen of the twenty-five respondents considered themselves happiest in their present position. Even among those who reported that they were the happiest currently, some still had reservations, perhaps based on their perceptions of the future directions of the profession, while others who were not the happiest currently would still recommend a

medical career enthusiastically. The extreme positions were represented negatively by PP Curren, who stated, "There's too much work for what you get out
of it," and positively by PP Browning, who said he would recommend it enthusiastically because "it's a good income with lots of job satisfactions."

The Harris Organization (1981) found that one-half of the 1,430 physicians
they had studied nationwide had sufficient doubts about the future of medical
practice that they would not recommend it as highly as ten years previously.
They found that recent entrants were as pessimistic as those with the longest
practice experience and that salaried physicians (including academics) were
much more positive about the medical profession than those who were self-
employed. Mawardi (1980) found (in her follow-up study of physicians), that
academic physicians dropped from first to fourth place in overall job satisfaction in the late 1970s. In the SAMs study expressions of pessimism were
about equally distributed among academic and community practitioners.

CONCLUSION

Five and six years after their residency, the SAMs physicians have established
themselves as successful physicians. Most are reasonably happy with the
fruits of their education and training. They have ample financial rewards.
They recognize the various trade-offs between academic and private medical
practice and with very few exceptions, are content with the choices they have
made. It would seem, on the face of the evidence, that SAMs physicians are
fairly typical of physicians who have graduated from U.S. medical schools.

One significant finding is the continuing importance of the graduate medical school and, to a lesser degree, the undergraduate medical school for the locations of the SAMs medical practitioners. Even though private practitioners
fear isolation and loss of technical skill because of their separation from
SAMs, the data indicate that the vast majority have located their practices
within close proximity to their final place of study. One might expect that
such location would lead to an interactive network of practitioners who are involved in a system of interlocking referrals. The private practitioners, however, because they are in competition with each other, do not consult with
SAMs or other physicians within their subspecialty for fear that patients will
be stolen. The close proximity of the physicians to their site of last study is
not indicative of a cohesive community of practicing professionals but, rather,
of independent business groups cutting up a market into subsectors, each jeal-
ously guarding his proportional share. Practically speaking, the SAMs research indicates that the medical profession is a nonmonopolistic agglomera-
tion of local and regional markets composed of medical institutions of
regional breadth to which individual and small-group entrepreneurs are at-

tached. These entrepreneurs may or may not continue to be linked to the institutions in which they trained. The graduate medical school is not only important, then, for the inculcation of skills and attitudes in its interns and residents but as a primary resource base for its graduates, who, in most cases, pursue their careers within reasonably close proximity.

The house staff training was compared to fraternal initiation rites by PP Noland, who noted that he now spent long hours as a private practitioner. The consensus was that although the experience was dehumanizing and took serious tolls on their lives, it was necessary and effective. The SAMs doctors, once beyond internship and residency, had concluded that the trade-off of a few years, was for the most part, worth it. The hardship of those years was sublimated—the worst thing they remembered from the experience was their sleep deprivation—and they accepted it as inevitable and necessary. They were now ensconced in academia—where they chose their own diseases—or private practice—where they chose many of their own patients. They were themselves at the upper levels of the upper middle class. At almost no time did any members of the sample consider the effects of the context of training on the treatment of the indigent patients they treated and neglected or abused as house officers. They *were*, however, concerned about the treatment of their own patients by house staff at SAMs or in other teaching institutions.

Thus, there is a bitter irony among the private practitioners who have been accused by the new SAMs and other house staffs of dumping and incompetence. Out of medical training, they have broadened their definitions of good doctoring to include, finally, PSE factors. On their side of the nexus of social privilege, they view house staff as rude, abrupt, uncaring, and, in the words of PP Sheldon, "snotty kids." They recognize that they have lost some of their intellectural and technical virtuosity, but they see themselves as having gained a deeper, more humanistic perspective. They see the dehumanized way in which the house staff treats some of their patients and resent it. To them, it is a moral problem.

It can be said that the SAMs graduates emerged from their training satisfied with it and relatively comfortable with the success they were experiencing as doctors. Their main concerns were restricted to what immediately affected them: the care of their own patients, the vicissitudes of the competitve struggle, their own careers. They had concluded that, for the most part, the sacrifices they had made in internship and residency were worth it. They had developed confidence and competence. Their careers trajectories were satisfactory—with the exception of one or two members of the sample. The medical profession had reproduced itself. All members of the sample noted, however, that it would not always be this easy. There are clouds on the horizon. Medicine is heading for dramatic change, they feel. They perceive the future as one of incipient decline: more regulation from the outside, a surplus of doctors, a decline in income. The SAMs doctors see themselves as one of the last generations of doctors who are "free" professionals. In this perception they are probably correct.

Chapter 9

Conclusion

This study is significant in three ways: first, the focus on the effects of graduate medical training on the doctor–patient relationship has revealed previously unexplored consequences of the socialization process; second, the participant observation method has been able to uncover at the level of social interaction the socializers and their methods of inculcating behavioral norms, and it has also revealed the impact of situational, organizational, and even societal factors that impinge on the socialization process; and third, through a follow-up study, the mutable and permanent consequences of the socialization of internists are identified.

THE SOCIALIZERS

Theorists have emphasized the hierarchical aspects of socialization, stressing the relationship between the members and the neophytes as central to the process (Hadden and Long 1978:118–19). While this may be true in the earlier phases of medical socialization, it is clearly not the case in residency, wherein hierarchical relations between members (i.e., attending faculty) and neophytes are minimized. Socialization activities primarily occur within the house staff, its neophyte officers deferring to its somewhat more experienced officers. Neophytes thus become immersed in a subculture that discounts the socialization activities of the traditional members of the certifying group— the attending faculty. Socialization activities are collegial. Neophytes essentially socialize each other while "members" are relegated to the fringes of the socialization process—and accept that relegation. Contrary to the dominant

164

perspective, which presumes faculty are the primary socializers, they are actually distinctly secondary actors in the residency years.

The empirical reality of the residency years is that house staff provide primary patient care and are, by default, the primary physicians even for patients formally under the supervision of the attending faculty. The house staff develops a subculture that is insular; it constitutes itself as an ingroup, making attendings an outgroup, thus systematically excluding them from important socializing activities, especially at the everyday level of providing health care. House staff view the attending faculty as "above" their concerns and regard them as exemplars only insofar as they can diagnose complex symptoms or teach the finer points of medical knowledge.

Observation and interviews confirmed that the relations between house staff and attendings are limited to these formalized situations and that any attempts by attendings to extend their influence beyond those boundaries are resented by the house staff, who perceived such action as an infringement on their autonomy. They recognize that the labor of the house staff generates the surplus out of which comes to the attendings' salary, privilege, and autonomy.

The house staff had its own normative system and sanctions that arose from the immediacy of the conflict and the tension-ridden situation; this structure was organized around problem-solving activities arising from the job situation. The most important norms of the house staff subculture were those of compulsiveness and efficiency, and these two norms reflected contradictory expectations. The norm of compulsiveness demanded that the novice physicians attend to all possible details of patient care: consider all alternatives, administer all relevant tests, take into consideration all sources of information, and leave no gaps in the process of making a diagnosis. Failure to examine every detail of diagnosis and remediation scrupulously could elicit an accusation of the sin of sloughing. But at the same time, novice physicians were supposed to be efficient because the sheer number of patients and the limited hours available made it impossible to deal with a patient unhurriedly. Thus, if a house officer was too slow or negligent in patient treatment, leaving others to fill in the gap, those others might label him or her a slougher and resent and ostracise him or her. Yet, if the officer was too quick in getting rid of patients, especially by dumping them on other internal medicine services, he or she would also be resented for causing others to do his or her work. The norms of efficiency and compulsiveness were thus in continual tension.

The lowly organizational status, pace of work, lack of adequate facilities, low wages, long hours, bureaucratic politics, tension-inducing situation, and normative conflicts all led to a frustrating experience for internists-in-training. Any organizational or social system must have outlets for the venting of hostilities and frustration. In medicine as in other social service bureaucracies, those with the least power are often the targets. Thus patients, in addition to filling an educative function with their pathologies, became socializers by presenting themselves in such vast numbers.

As socializers, patients were for the most part a source of aggravation and tension for the house staff. Most public hospital patients were poor, and many complicated the doctors' lives by being unable to give proper medical histories, by resisting attempts at treatment, by exhibiting passive-aggressive behavior, by suffering from maladies induced or exacerbated by self-abuse. House officers often became defenders of the system against patients who abused it, even though the house officers were also its victims. Thus, the teaching hospital replicated a fundamental artifact of social stratification: one category of victims—albeit, temporary ones—victimizing a second weaker category.

THE GROP PERSPECTIVE

The idealism and concern for the patient with which house staff may have begun internship were quickly effaced in the trauma of that year. The conditions of labor as an intern, including the overwhelming workload, the degraded status of many of the patients, the necessity of jockeying for beds, the paperwork, the scut work, the fears—the actuality—of making mistakes under what seemed to them like battle conditions, all served to lower the regard of the interns for the subjectivity of the patients and for themselves. Thus, the most important lesson for the interns to learn was how to get rid of patients, to GROP. Not only was this impressed upon them by their more experienced peers, by the attendings, and by the hospital administration, but by the physical necessity of surviving internship. The technical orientation of the profession was reinforced as interns learned to GROP. They tended to become mechanical or procedural in their orientation toward patients, screening out the more subtle, subjective considerations. Diagnosis became a "detective" or "numbers" game. Psychosocial and environmental factors were given over to social workers or, more likely, simply ignored. GROP became an art form within the house staff subculture, and those who were especially good at it were esteemed and called "dispo kings."

Because there were so many patients who had to be treated in a short amount of time, the house staff was obligated to treat and GROP as quickly as possible. To determine the appropriate GROP action, neophytes had to learn to categorize patients according to two complex systems. One was based on the patients' symptoms, classified as either "uninteresting" and "interesting." Easily diagnosed symptoms and garden variety diseases were routine, boring, and uninteresting. Complex symptoms or a form of rare disease were interesting. The residents were constantly on the prowl for interesting patients, necessarily a small minority. When they found one, he or she was used by the attending faculty and house staff as a pedagogical tool or "clinical material," an occasion for further instruction.

The interesting – uninteresting classification was largely independent of the second system of classification, which corresponded more closely to the larger social structure. This second system was not categorical like the first. Rather, it consisted of a continuum from the ideal to the despised. The ideal patient corresponded roughly to the characteristics of the middle class: intelligent without questioning the doctor's judgment, clean, deferential, helpful, cooperative, and so forth. The despised patient was one defined in the subculture as an abuser: a self-abuser, system abuser, house staff abuser or some combination. Such patients were frequently labeled with slang terms reflecting derision and contempt.

House staff learned a variety of GROP strategies. One was to transfer patients to another service, which involved negotiating with other house officers and often meant haggling over the availability of beds. Others included releasing patients as quickly as feasible or transferring them to another hospital. Even death was often perceived as a relief, especially in the case of patients who had long, drawn-out and ultimately fatal diseases. When they could not physically GROP, they used other techniques including passing along unwanted patient management tasks to anyone identified as subordinate to them: social workers, other ancillary staff, or medical students. When they could not get rid of patient-related assignments, they learned to GROP mentally or psychologically by objectifying, intimidating, or avoiding patients.

EXTERNAL SOCIALIZATION FACTORS

The socialization process is also influenced by external conditions, the two major external influences being the structure of the health care delivery system in the United States and the increasing development of medical technology. American health care delivery occurs in a two-tiered system of private and public health care facilities. Public health care has always been understaffed, underfunded, and generally provided with facilities inferior to the so-called private sector, which is not strictly private. It depends on a variety of government subsidies to maintain its delivery system, including reimbursement through Medicaid and Medicare, tax exemptions and abatements, depreciation allowances, research and program funds, and so forth, which come from the various levels of the government and are ultimately paid for by the taxpayer. By subsidizing the private sector and underfunding the public sector, the state has maintained a dual system of health care that roughly corresponds to the larger social structure. The public hospitals not only cater to the needs of the lower-class groups in the population, in facilities that are poorly staffed and funded, but they also provide dumping grounds where the private sector can get rid of unwanted patients with little fear of retribution. This further burdens the public system and provides increased sources of tension and frustration for the house staff in the public sector. Since public facilities are forced by economic necessity to exploit the labor of their house staff to make ends meet, the two-class system has a direct impact on the conditions under which such house staff is forced to work. The effects of this situation were obvious at SAMs, and according to the testimony of the house staff, the situation was not unique.

The second influence, medical technology—expansion of testing, laboratory diagnosis, and patient preparation procedures—actually increases the responsibilities of internists. In addition to providing treatment, they must keep voluminous records, negotiate with a variety of technicians, move patients from one test to the next, and consider the possibilities of all the tests in making a diagnosis. While increasing the internist's ability to diagnose and deal with previously unreachable conditions, expanding technology has also vastly increased the actual work load. In the hurried, impersonal public health care setting, it has also dramatically increased the risk of iatrogenesis.

Technology has also put the internist in a double bind. Internal medicine is the largest branch of the profession concerned with the "whole adult patient," and technological advancements have multiplied the fund of knowledge concerning the human body. For medical practitioners, this has meant increasing subspecialization even within internal medicine. Yet, simultaneously, not only must internists know more, but they have to depend more on other subspecialists, laboratory technicians, records, and so forth in order to diagnose and prescribe.

Hence, the organizational context of residency influences the socialization process primarily through its mediation of larger societal forces. The hospital becomes an arena in which the actual struggles generated in the larger society take place. Doctors, degraded, albeit temporarily, by their own exploitation, are forced to treat people who have been degraded in the larger society. Because the well-being of the lower strata is a low social priority, facilities are maintained at substandard levels, mandating that underpaid, overworked doctors treat patients as quickly as possible and get rid of them expeditiously. Technology, far from reducing the work load, actually increases it and reduces the physician's observations in the calculus of diagnosis, turning it into what house staff calls a "numbers game." It also increases the amount of "scut" work and bureaucratic red tape.

Hence, the power, authority, and autonomy of house officers are ambiguous; they are often put in situations where they are not sure of the proper course of action. While they are powerless with respect to the conditions of labor, they have control over the labor process. This creates for them the ambivalent condition of being forced to perform under poor conditions while simultaneously having to take responsibility for the quality of labor. Many find this situation unfair. The payoff seems to be that, while they may be held responsible for the quality of labor, the system tacitly condones a wide range of errors by maintaining superficial supervision and an almost nonexistent formal sanctioning system.

Thus, the structure and dynamics of the system allow for less than optimal patient care. The main bulwark against gross negligence and misconduct is the normative system of the house staff subculture. Moreover, while social control is maintained by house staff condemnation of those who commit social sins (such as sloughing), normative power is weak. Peers influence but have no authority to demand conformity.

OUTCOMES

Taken as a totality, the allocation of resources, the division of labor, and the distribution of power within the medical profession have a profound effect on the socialization of interns and residents. They are situated in a position in which they are given the poorest resources, the most labor, and ambiguous power. They are also given a clear picture of the actions of their superiors and ancillary personnel. They witness the relative privilege of one, the exploitation of the other, and the consequences of the stratification of the health system in ways from which they were insulated as medical students. What they see for the most part is overall exploitation and apathy and a general disregard of most patients by almost everyone, including themselves.

The medical school graduates came to SAMs, however, to learn how to be competent and confident internists. They generally agreed that they had fulfilled that objective upon the completion of their residency. They assured themselves of that by comparison with the faculty and with the local medical doctors. They felt assured that they were every bit as good as, if not better than, almost anyone they saw in private practice and better than most attendings in general or critical care internal medicine.

At the same time, they also learned negative attitudes and behavior toward some, if not all, patients. They learned to regard some of them as less than human and generally to ignore those aspects of the patient—including the patient's subjectivity—not directly related to diagnosis and treatment. Clearly, the provision of health care by hospital house staff in the public sector is highly deleterious to the doctor–patient relationship in that setting. The use of house staff by hospitals as a source of easily exploitable labor not only undermines the delivery of health care generally (Who wants to be taken care of by an inexperienced intern who has not slept in the past thirty-six hours or an apathetic, disgruntled resident?) but also has implications for the generalized doctor–patient relationship. With the rising public concern about the health care delivery system in the United States, the apathy or even antipathy with which many doctors approach patients is being echoed in the public's attitude toward doctors.

The outcome of this experience seems to affect greatly their career choices and their expectations about future relationships with patients. What emerges is a no-career-is-the-ideal-choice syndrome. They seem to describe their career decisions as based as much on their aversions to aspects of internal medicine practice as on the positive components of the specialty. I found four adaptive responses—becoming system perpetuators, system defenders, system rejectors, or system distorters—each of which in its own way maintained the GROP perspective after training.

FOLLOW-UP

Five and six years after their internship and residency, the SAMs physicians had settled into their careers. The system perpetuators had found their way into academic practice in either general internal medicine or one of its subspecialties. They were disgruntled, primarily because of bureaucratic politics and the pressures exerted upon them. The majority of the former house staffers were clearly system defenders who had entered subspecialty private practice and were doing quite well, although they were working harder than they anticipated. The system rejector (there was only one in the sample) had turned to a specialty that was removed from prolonged patient care— emergency medicine. Finally, there were three system distorters who saw themselves pursuing medicine to the point of financial independence, at which time they would retire or pursue other interests.

Five years is a long time psychically. The doctors in the follow-up sample remembered the stresses and strains of their internship and residency years in attenuated form. Most remembered sleep deprivation as the most significant problem. Those in private practice felt that their patients were closer to the "ideal" patient than those they faced in residency. Although they did not work as grueling a schedule as the house staff, they still averaged sixty to eighty hours a week in their practice. Their emphasis on the abuses of the system had lessened considerably. Most thought that internship and residency, as they had experienced it, was a necessary if not efficient way to learn to practice medicine. When I asked about changes in the training process, none advocated drastic overhauling of the system.

With the exception of a few doctors having some difficulties with their career trajectories, the former SAMs doctors were self-satisfied. They perceived themselves as delivering good health care for their patients; they bridled at their being labeled "LMDs" by the contemporary house staff and complained that present house staffs, while technically sophisticated, did not deliver optimal health care, which included the PSE factors they themselves had denigrated as house officers. They had redefined optimal health care by decreasing the relative importance of technical and academic virtuosity and increasing the importance of the "whole" patient. The emphasis on the inclusion of the PSE factors was especially strong among the doctors who had to compete for patients in the fee-for-practice marketplace. The academically employed SAMs doctors regarded their relations with patients as improved because they had a much smaller patient load, more control over the types of patients they treated, and greater leisure than during residency.

The term *trade-offs* was used by the doctors as both house officers and practitioners. The trade-off for learning the medical "trade" was being subject to degradation, poor facilities, and a lower-class patient population. The ultimate trade-off was that at the end of this temporary degradation, a doctor was guaranteed—unless one was unusually greedy or had severe character defects—a life of high income and reasonably high public esteem. At the end of residency, a substantial number of the doctors came to believe that the trade-off was not worth the investment. The psychic costs of dehumanization were disillusionment, cynicism, and a disregard for the patient. The follow-up study pointed out, however, that such a calculus was premature. After five years of elevated social privilege and professional identification, most of the doctors had become convinced that the trade-offs were worth the investment.

Cognition derives from experience and cannot easily be divorced from interest. It appears to be in the interests of practicing physicians to uphold the value and downplay the deleterious aspects of graduate medical training because it provides the gateway to their own social privilege, just as it is in the interests of house officers to attempt to control and ease the conditions under which they practice. The attitudes toward patients that are engendered are a direct result of structural factors. Private practitioners are concerned about PSE factors and the "whole" patient because they are competing in what they perceive to be a highly competitive marketplace. Their outlook is more humanistic than that of house staff because for the most part their patients pay them directly or indirectly for their services, are closer to them in social rank, and share a similar value system. Academic practitioners treat their patients more humanistically than house staff because they have little responsibility for primary care, leaving that to the new house staff, and can choose their own patients more carefully. Still, they do not pay much attention to PSE factors because they are still fundamentally interested in the patient as an object for research or teaching.

Work conditions have the opposite effect on house staff; they cause them to avoid and objectify patients. To consider PSE factors or the "whole" patient would be tantamount to disaster in training, for if they did, they would literally never be able to sleep. Moreover, their client population consists primarily of the poor and degraded, who are designated by the profession as those instrumentalities upon which young doctors learn. The house staff is systematically prevented from considering PSE factors whether it wants to or not. Most of the physician socialization literature poses the question: Will physicians-in-training regain their humanism, if not idealism, in their permanent, "real" career settings? While the answer to that question for the physicians in this study is, from their perspective, a qualified yes, that answer is no help to the thousands of patients across this country under the collective care of house staff. For those patients, the training institutions are their "real" setting.

Thus it is obvious that if the medical profession is to be reformed to provide more humanistic health care, the fundamental structures of social privilege within the profession must be altered. As this study amply shows, the profession simply has too much invested in its own system of professional prerogative. The rewards for sacrificing seven to ten years of one's life are very high. Once on the other side, the practitioners are ready and willing to defend the necessity of gratuituous sacrifice from a position of high income, social status, and (to a lesser degree) patient gratitude.

The potential for change in the profession is beyond the scope of this book. Change can come from conflict between fractionations within the profession, for example, unionization of house staff, or from change in the context of medical practice, for example, saturated markets. If patient care is to be changed for the good of the patients, however, the consumers and their allies must struggle to pressure hospitals and medical practitioners to accede to their interests. Fundamental to the improvement of the delivery of health care in America is the necessity of altering the training of doctors, which is intrinsically caught up in a two-tier system of medical delivery in which those who cannot pay are abused and those who can pay get less than what they pay for.

Appendix A

Research Methodology

My interest in physician training and the doctor–patient relationship resulted from my background in health care policy and the consumer health movement (Madison 1978a, 1978b). I wanted to understand more about the dynamics of the so-called health crisis and in particular to understand the role of physicians in shaping and perpetuating the American health system. I chose to scrutinize internal medicine because it is the largest and one of the most prestigious specialties. I undertook a multi-method study using participant observation and open-ended interviews as the principle techniques. Advantages and disadvantages of qualitative research have been discussed in the literature (Glaser and Strauss 1968; Schwartz and Jacobs 1979), so I only highlight them here.

PARTICIPANT OBSERVATION

Many researchers (Becker et al. 1961; Becker 1970; Blum 1970; Bruyn 1970; Filstead 1970; Hadden and Long 1978; Schatzman and Strauss 1973) have summarized the advantages of the observational method: observation opens to scientific investigation a considerable number of areas inaccessible through other methods. For example, it permits the researcher to see what people actually do as opposed to what they say. It permits action to be understood in the context of its physical and organization setting, its surrounding sequence of events, and the participants who share in its observation. Observation over a period of time yields a breadth of understanding not possible through measurement at a single point, and it provides a basis for comparison of related action in different contexts.

In addition, observation provides a factual check on what subjects report in questionnaires and interviews, and it aids in interpreting meaning and significance of differences over time as measured by these other methods. This is not at all to imply that

173

a discrepancy between word and deed means the word is to be discredited; it merely identifies a "reality disjuncture" (Pollner, in Schwartz and Jacobs 1979:47) the meaning of which needs to be analyzed more carefully. For example, the significance of the iatrogenesis in shaping the house staff orientation to patients would never have been discovered through interviews alone, whereas I almost daily observed house officers and attendings expressing their fears of harming patients, directly or indirectly.

Negotiating Entry

I accepted the generous support of Dr. G., the chairman of one of the divisions of internal medicine, a man who had a genuine interest in social science research but never intruded in nor restricted the process once I began. He provided me with some secretarial help for a limited time and with office space in a building adjoining one of the SAMs hospitals; there I conducted some of my interviews and dictated and stored my work (in a locked cabinet). Overall I believe this sponsorship facilitated rather than impeded my acceptance and progress. It also gave me credibility and status in the system.

I realize that an identification with the department of medicine could have had some adverse consequences if the house staff had not believed that my research was totally independent despite official approval. I did encounter occasional questions or comments about that affiliation, but it never seemed to prevent my establishing my independence with the house staff.

Because of the interest of Dr. G., I was given permission to interview and to circulate self-administered questionnaires to the house staff and to attend the orientation for new interns each June. My formal introduction to the new interns by the internal medicine chief residents was crucial in establishing my legitimacy because one of the traditional perceived functions of chief resident is to serve as role model for younger recruits (Chaiklin [1960] also mentions how important the chief residents were in obtaining access to his subjects). To insure introductions, I formally interviewed all three prospective chiefs.

Gaining formal permission from the department heads and chief residents was only the beginning of the process. Given the autonomy of the house staff, I had to negotiate individually with each member on each new medical service. I would usually call the resident in charge the day before, and when I arrived I would introduce myself to him or her and to the other members of the house staff team as unobtrusively as possible. When the opportunity presented itself, I would also introduce myself to the attending, although I quickly realized that I did not need the attending's permission to observe. This fact contributed to my discovery of the dual dimensions of power—influence and authority—in the training hierarchy. Faculty may have formal authority, but they have very little informal influence over the daily events on the ward.

Field Notes

In note-taking, I took the middle ground between total concealment and openness. I took notes openly during those occasions when it seemed natural (for example, on rounds or during other more structured or formal interaction). Some house officers would remark or joke about what I might be writing, but their casualness seemed to indicate that they felt no need to alter their discussion because I was writing (aspects of the upcoming section on reliability and validity are pertinent here). I never took notes, however, when I was observing informally on a service or when I was following specific house officers around. In the latter circumstances, I made extensive use of unused rooms to jot down notes at intervals of an hour or two, depending on the intensity and extensiveness of the observation. This practice I was successful in keeping entirely to myself.[1]

I dictated my day's observations (reconstructed from notes aided by memory) into a tape recorder each evening, or the next morning, in so far as possible, trying never to go more then forty-eight hours without dictating. The recording technique I used was similar to the one described by Mumford (1970): I described what happened verbatum according to the sequence of events. I then attempted to separate out subjective interpretations and analysis from the "objective" observations by setting off the former with parentheses and labeling them "observer's comments" (OC). The tapes were later transcribed in triplicate. At the end of eight months I had more than seven hundred pages of single-spaced typed field notes with three-inch margins to provide space for coding and other comments.

For one year I conducted intensive and comprehensive participant observation in all three hospitals on all the required services: inpatient, intensive care, ER, and outpatient. Because of the organization of rotations, I observed at least two entirely different groups of interns, residents, and attendings during the approximately two months I spent on each service.

During the first five months I spent the equivalent of five days a week (including time on weekends and evenings) observing house staff interaction. For this first stint I attached myself to a team and a service. A three-month break followed during which I had a baby. During the break I did some preliminary data analysis, and as a result of those findings I structured my observation upon returning to the field according to the gaps and unanswered questions I had identified. For example, before the hiatus I had spent most of the time observing structured and formal group interaction. Therefore, upon returning to the field, I attached myself instead to a specific house officer each day, with his or her permission, and followed that officer around as much as possible. The rapport that developed let me observe personal and private reactions and made additional informal interviewing constantly possible. Thus, in the course of the year I was able to develop a feel both for the structure and organization of the various services and for how individual house officers experienced them.

While all members of the house staff were subjects of the study, I scrutinized some more intensely than others. Table A.1 summarizes the extensiveness of the house staff participation. During the field year, 86 percent (N = 88) of the interns and residents were observed one or more times. As the table shows, more than 90 percent of the interns and JRs and more than 70 percent of the SRs were observed at least once. I also attended special events such as the weekly informal resident gatherings with the department of medicine chairman and the variety of rounds. Table A.2 summarizes the structured interaction I observed during the field year.

175

TABLE A.1. House Staff Participation in the Study

	Observed during one year						Interviewed			Observed and formally interviewed	
	Number of times				Total number of subjects	Percentage of total cohort	Formal	Informal	Total	Number	Percentage of cohort
	1	2	3	4							
Interns	12	7	13	2	34	94	22	2	24	10	26
Junior residents	12	16	3	—	31	91	27[a]	9	36	12	34
Senior residents	11	10	2	—	23	71	34[b]	2	36	7	20
Total					88		83	13	96	29	

[a]Includes interviews with one beginning and one ending JR informant and the ten JRs who had already been interviewed as interns.
[b]Includes eight ending SRs who had already been interviewed as ending interns and three chief residents.

TABLE A.2. Structured Interaction Observed

Formal Sessions	Number attended	Total number	Percentage attended
Task rounds	70	312[b]	22
Resident rounds	57	260[c]	22
Attending rounds	99	260	38
Grand rounds	9	50	18
Resident gatherings	9	27	33
Others[a]	9		
Total	253	899	

[a]Social work rounds, subspecialty conferences, etc.
[b]Task rounds are held approximately six times a week.
[c]Resident rounds are held five times a week.

INTERVIEWS

Table A.1 also includes a breakdown of the interviews I conducted. I interviewed approximately one-third of two different cohorts of house staff formally over a three-year period. I obtained longitudinal data by reinterviewing as ending residents eight interns I had interviewed at the end of their first year and by reinterviewing as JRs ten interns I had interviewed in their first year. The interview instruments I used included both original questions and questions adopted from relevant studies (Bucher and Stelling 1977; Chaiklin 1960; Duff and Hollinghead 1968; Knafl and Burkett 1975; Miller 1970; Mumford 1970; Roberts 1977) so that it would be possible to make some comparisons with other professional socialization and doctor–patient studies.

With a small grant from my educational institution, I was able to pay interviewees for lengthy interviews, the sums varying from twelve to twenty dollars. I believe (for I was often told so directly) that the interview response rate was much greater as a result of that stipend, and receiving a payment also seemed to make subjects less inclined to turn down my requests to observe them. I never found any evidence that offering a payment for participation distorted the process or results of the interviews. Rather, payment served as a token of appreciation and a proof that the study was important. Some researchers no doubt contend that payment may contaminate the motivation for and hence bias the outcome of participation. I believe it possible to offer enough incentive to insure cooperation but little enough to leave participants unconcerned about their responses.

All the new interns each year were interviewed within the first two months (Bucher and Stelling [1977] conducted theirs within a similar time period). By the time most interns were interviewed, they had already completed their first rotation. No doubt these early encounters with the system had already influenced their responses. Had they been questioned before they began, their responses would have been only projections and ideations about internship and lacking in a relativistic perspective on medical school. But, the early comparisons between medical school and internship and the views of the "crisis" of beginnings that I did elicit were also important to understand. It was clearly a trade-off, for I could not tap both perspectives.

Interviews with randomly selected house officers provided some important data about their past experiences in medical school and about expectations after completion of training. They also revealed actual and anticipated perspectives on patients and the doctor–patient relationship, major changes that occurred from beginning to ending internship, and differences in perspective between interns and ending residents. Moreover, the interviews provided clues as to which events and processes I should concentrate on observing or follow up by informal interviewing.

For example, I might not have discovered by observation alone the conflicting norms that affected house staff behavior. It was the house staff's own collective articulation of these norms in interviews that prompted the insight that there was no one uncontradicted way to behave; that is, norms of professional conduct were, at least partially, in contention with each other.

ON RELIABILITY AND VALIDITY

Qualitative interviewing and observing have certain limitations. Because of the non-standardized way in which data are collected, they are generally not useful in establishing quantitative relationships. McCall and Simmons (1969) suggest that, in the long run, social sciences will have to rest on rigorously established generalizations. Furthermore, the researcher's use of personal relationships and contacts and the consequent likelihood of bias is a potential limitation. Based on emergent data, hunches, or hypotheses arising from early discussion or observation, the researcher frequently changes both what is studied and how it is studied. These changes may then steer the researcher away from other potential sources of data that are inconsistent with the initial findings or viewpoints. To counteract this possibility, and the related tendency to congregate with those who are the friendliest or most open (Geer 1976), a field researcher has to be self-aware and alert to these possibilities.

Glaser and Strauss (1968) maintain that qualitative methods are not designed to guarantee that two analysts working independently with the same data will achieve the same results. They also believe that qualitative research requires relaxation of rigorous rules of accuracy, evidence, verification, and tests of significance. Schwartz and Jacobs (1979:126–127) speak to a "science of the inside" and suggest that sociologists pursue understanding instead of prediction and control.

To assure some reliability of the interviews, I pretested all items in each instrument for comprehensiveness and clarity. To check the reliability of the coding schema, I employed an outside coder, who independently coded about one-quarter of the eighty-three interviews. Since the coding categories were emerging throughout the study, we discussed differences in interpretation between her results and mine, occasionally refining or adding categories. Then we would reread and recode all the previous interviews as necessary.

As a result of early observations and interviews, I discovered how totally insulated the world of the house staff is from any outsiders and, more significantly, how little overall impact the faculty seem to have on that house staff culture. The overwhelming importance of collegial relationships emerged unequivocally. It became patently clear from observations that they spent most time with and learned most from their peers and from colleagues one and two steps ahead of them. From direct questioning I confirmed that indeed it was the house staff (as a group) to whom they owed their allegiance and to whom they felt most accountable. I therefore included many more questions about and observations of the relationship between junior and senior house staff, and I also focused some attention on the interaction of medical students and house staff in order to comprehend better the beginning processes of socialization for the doctor–patient relationship.

I paid particular attention to the following aspects of the medical culture and its organization: what the socializing agents showed to residents with respect to the doctor–patient relationship; how they showed it to them; and how house staff responded to what they were shown. I closely observed the formal and informal sanctioning and certifying activities of members with respect to relationship with patients, peer culture perspectives on doctor–patient-relations, and house staff expressions of self-concepts as they interacted with or discussed patients.

As to the issue of validity in questioning participants, one can never be certain that respondents are telling the truth; they may offer socially desirable responses. Some of my questions were sensitive ones that conceivably could cause subjects, intentionally or otherwise, to distort or conceal behavior or verbal responses they thought I might construe negatively or misconstrue.

Two circumstances seemed to work against that sort of distortion. First, socially acceptable shading of responses is less apt to emerge if, as in this study, rapport has been established between interviewer and respondent and if the interviewer has been on the scene. Second, and perhaps more important, even allowing for the likelihood of the socially acceptable response, any negative or unpopular findings would thus clearly err on the conservative or understated side. In other words, it is much more likely that personal admissions of socially undesirable attitudes or conduct would be underestimated than the converse. For example, the house staff would be more likely to downplay than exaggerate their extensive use of pejorative slang; they would be more likely to conceal serious errors than to reveal them. If one adapts here the adage about field observation in anthropology, namely, that the observer admits to his or her *second* worst error, then clearly house staff confessions of misconduct and violations of norms—of which there were plenty—can only have been undercounted.

This is not to say that distortions in self-reporting did not occur at both extremes in some instances, for I observed evidence of them. Here lies the importance of the multimethod approach. I was able to observe violations in everyday practice of principles verbally conveyed during interviews; for example, actual behavior to patients was sometimes worse than self-reported behavior. Conversely, I observed behavior to patients that was sometimes better (for example, more polite) than respondents' verbal comments would have indicated; that is, the verbal abuse of patients was sometimes more pronounced out of their presence than in it.

Since my research was time limited, I made every effort to ascertain from those familiar with house staff interaction and the training environment whether events or situations I observed were typical or atypical. Informants emerged from among the ancillary personnel and from the house staff as well. Informants as both representative respondents and as observer's observer can help extend data collection or analysis and improve reliability and validity (Zelditch 1970). Three such persons—an intern, a JR, and a social worker—consulted with me periodically.

Furthermore, the most significant independent validation of my findings came from a small group of family practice interns who were rotating through the internal medicine services (for four of the twelve months) but who were not training to be internists. They were "among them" but not "of them." They were expected to carry the same responsibilities as internal medicine interns, so they experienced the training system from inside while simultaneously evaluating its effects on themselves and others. Accordingly, they were in an excellent position to corroborate, refute, or explain my findings and interpretations.

I used the principle of saturation (Glaser and Strauss 1968) in deciding when to stop observing an event or series of activities; that is, observation ceased when I found no additional data with which to identify or develop properties or categories and when I found myself repeating in my field notes, "It was a typical day . . ." etc. As Becker (1970) suggests, I also used a framework for deriving inferences from field work by quantifying the frequency and intensity of selected observations and responses.

These techniques were employed in the analyses of the data gathered in this study. The use of direct quotations from both interviews and field notes is for the purpose of establishing proof. Terms such as "typical," "overwhelming number," "majority," "exceptional," "spontaneously offered," "virtually unanimous" are intended to convey the extensiveness as well as the intensity of the findings.

POSTTRAINING FOLLOW-UP

The main limitation of most sociological research is that it is time limited. While comparative perspectives are prevalent in qualitative studies, longitudinal perspectives are infrequent. Rarer are those studies that follow a cohort from one setting or status to the next, across thresholds.

There are few in-depth studies of physicians in practice, almost none in internal medicine, that follow the same group from professional education to permanent career setting or to a subsequent phase of advanced training. The major longitudinal studies of physicians primarily use quantitative data obtained almost exclusively from self-administered questionnaires. Given the increasing attention being paid to physician impairment and consumer dissatisfaction with medical care, I consider it important to investigate causes of physician and patient malaise.

Because of my ongoing contact with Dr. G. on the SAMs faculty, I was in the unusual position of having access to the addresses of the former house staff in my study, the twenty-six I had interviewed at the end of their training. This represented a random sample of approximately one-third of each of two cohorts from two consecutive years in the late 1970s. I eventually located all twenty-six, and all but one agreed to be interviewed. The reaction of the former house staff to being recontacted, first by letter and then by telephone, was overwhelmingly positive. A few even went out of their way to reach out to me. These interviews, like those at the end of residency training, seemed to have a cathartic effect. I was able to travel to their locations as a result of a small grant. In every instance they remained for a longer time than we had verbally contracted for; the average interview time was three hours. One interview was conducted by long-distance telephone.

Most of the subjects remembered their initial interview and expressed curiosity about what they said previously as well as how their peers responded. All had lost contact with some or all of their cohort and welcomed the opportunity to hear where others were. I was able to use regards from peers as a rapport builder.

The interview schedule was constructed to include three components: a retrospective look at their training five or so years later; a current examination of their experiences since training including their present professional life, and their own projections for their future career. The questions included original ones and ones taken or adapted from Erdmann, Jones, and Toneski 1978; Gerber 1983; E. Gross 1985; L. Harris et al. 1981; Mawardi 1979; and McCue 1981, 1982, among others. Those pertaining to the period of training included several that were identical to questions asked five years earlier and several that I constructed as a result of findings in the original research. I also asked the subjects to recall, corroborate, refute, or explain my observations and analysis.

Appendix B

Notes from the Field
Roles of the Observer

During the course of this research, I had to play many roles.[1] Some of these have been discussed in the social science literature; others have not yet been adequately covered. I, of course, was affected by the roles I played.

THE PARTICIPATING OBSERVER

The question of when and how much to participate in the everyday work and interaction of the subjects has been discussed in the literature, usually in the context of gaining access to the subjects and their world. Both Bosk (1979) and Scully (1977) believe that playing the helper role with surgical residents contributed to the rapport they developed with their subjects. Assumption of a participatory role is also an honest acknowledgment of the impossibility, if not inadvisability, of attempting to maintain a posture of total unobtrusiveness and noninvolvement in field research.

The nature of internal medicine as a discipline did, however, limit active participation in this study. Internists act less and think more than other physicians such as surgeons. Indeed, the situations in which I was asked to assist the house staff were precisely those that involved invasive procedures with patients. Like other sociologists, I felt more comfortable and accepted on those few occasions when performing a useful task. The role of participant raises the issue, so easily dispatched by positivist methodology, of the artificial division between the researcher and the data. Positivism merely assumes the division is not artificial even though the questions are composed and the categories of discourse are determined a priori by the researcher. When a researcher becomes directly involved in the day-to-day activities of his or her subjects, it becomes extremely difficult to make that differentiation, since he or she is part of the totality of social interaction, like it or not. The researcher does not merely watch but actually engages—necessarily—in social relationships with subjects, achieves an identity, and becomes a repository for sentiments from those "observed."

Additional problems may arise. On occasion I was asked to go beyond the rather innocuous "go-fer" role and witness "informed consent" being obtained by doctors from a patient or a family member when, in my opinion, the contract was not fulfilled.

THE MORAL OBSERVER

Some participant observers have discussed the moral dilemmas they faced when they observed behavior (of omission or commission) that had the potential to (or actuality did) seriously harm somebody they were observing (Sjoberg 1967). If an observer's goal is to attempt to reconstruct the reality from the subject's perspective, then understanding and sympathy can easily emerge. The term "going native" describes that process in the extreme. Scully (1980) addresses some of the ethical issues involved when studying physicians and justifies her overall stance of noninterference by asserting, "It is my hope that the report of what I found will justify my silence" (9). Rare is a researcher's admission of active intervention to prevent or rectify a mishap. Bosk (1979) candidly acknowledges breaking his stance of nonintervention when he reminded his surgeons to discuss their findings with patients and their families. Light (1980) mentions his commission of what could be construed as a serious breech of professional ethics; he also admits that he suffered from an intense moral dilemma when he observed errors of commission by the psychiatric residents he studied. For handling such situations, Jones (1973) suggests naturalness rather than pretense; the observer should do what is comfortable as well as what is right. This approach seems inadequate, however; the if-it-feels-good-do-it ethic does not solve moral dilemmas in anthropological and sociological research.

Since social groups usually do engage in some collective deviance, all participant observation research must, sooner or later, confront the issue of collusion. Collusion occurs at the point where the group being studied attempts to advance its interest over the conflicting interest of another group. In the above example, the doctors, by denying patients' rights in front of me and asking me to certify that the rights had been protected, forced me into a position of colluding with them or else inserting myself into the politics of a doctor–patient relationship on the side of the patient.

The house staff often used me conspiratorily to elicit sympathy for their anger or frustration (usually toward a patient) as well as to justify adverse behavior. Repeatedly a house officer would explain to me why he or she resorted to a particularly negative comment or action. Sometimes, among a group of house officers, someone would turn to me and present a rationalization or justification for a colleague's deviant conduct, seemingly out of embarrassment or to distance themselves from it. Sometimes they were quite self-conscious with me about the possible adverse effects on patients of some attitudes or behavior, but most of the time they either ignored me or implicitly included me. No doubt most of the house staff thought I would be in sympathy with their responses to difficult patients and the oppressive constraints of the system.

Goffman (1959) makes an important point that collusion engenders shared secrets. The paradox of deviant behavior is that those who share a person's secret have a means of control over that deviant behavior by virtue of threat of exposure. There is no guarantee that a group of "observed" will not attempt to gain control over the "observer" in such a way. Light (1980) suggests that dealing with secrets of those observed is a fundamental problem not easily resolvable in field research. Loyalties and trust only complicate the contradiction between insider and outsider that the researcher must face. The canons of social science inquiry demand of the researcher a position of at least some measure of marginality relative to the collectivity under study, the core of that marginality being the "sociological imagination" (Mills, 1959), which is composed of orientations, categories of meaning, ethical standards, and tools of research derived from social sciences. My field notes served me in this way, allowing me to justify nonintervention and silence when I observed questionable or objectional behavior by my subjects. Nevertheless, in comparing my experiences with those of other sociological observers of physician socialization, I cannot help but speculate about why I did not more often experience a sense of outrage at so much brutally indifferent and sometimes callous treatment of patients.

Two possible reasons come to mind, especially given my previous criticism of the entire American medical system (Madison 1978a and b): first, the observed examples of apathetic and at times rude behavior toward patients were so much a part of the house staff culture that what should have been considered aberrant or deviant behavior came to be accepted as normal and rational interaction under the circumstances. Second, it became increasingly clear that the overwhelming convergence of factors discussed in this book precluded much possibility of implementing a more humanistic doctor–patient relationship. The whole system of medical care functioned to prohibit extensive involvement of the house staff with patients, notwithstanding any possible individual actions to the contrary. This is not to suggest endorsement of the passive-vessel theory of socialization but to assert that, given the obstacles to establishing a decent doctor–patient relationship, it seems perfectly plausible that it does not develop.

Finally, there is no question that I came to identify to some degree with the plight of the house staff. The frustrating and difficult circumstances of their daily lives were easy for a social science graduate student to sympathize with. While my initial intent in this study was to examine the impact of medical training on the formation of the doctor–patient relationship, by the time I had conducted my second set of interviews and initiated the participant observation, I began to realize how destructive the system could be for many house officers as well.

THE INVISIBLE OBSERVER

A participant observer is not always an active participant in the interaction. There were times when I was treated as absent. For example, the greeting I received from many house officers upon returning to the field after an absence of three months (owing to the birth of my son) indicated that up until the moment of reencounter, they had not noticed that I had even been gone (Light [1980] notes a similar phenomenon upon his return to observing psychiatric residents after an absence). Many expressed complete surprise to hear I had left temporarily to have a baby and told me explicitly that they were never aware of my pregnancy—this in spite of my presence on the wards and at rounds through my eighth month! There were some exceptions to those statements of real or feigned obliviousness to my absence. Almost all the women, and a few of the male house officers who had children, noticed my physical state, and their comments and questions indicated interest in the process and outcome of the pregnancy.

Also attesting to my invisibility would be occasional comments by house officers when I would appear during nontraditional working hours including weekends and holidays: "Are you still here?" "Are you 'on-call'?" "Do you have to be here?" My appearances at these unexpected times not only made them notice me however, but helped establish rapport and camaraderie with the house staff. For example, I was more likely to be included in informal interaction or in events such as the sharing of food during the "odd" hours.

My reaction to this level of invisibility was mixed, not unlike Light's (1980), who writes of the tension between intimacy and impartiality the participant observer would experience in relation to his or her subjects. Indeed Light (1980) and Daniels (1967) are quite candid in admitting how intrusive they have been with their subjects. While Geer (1976) advocates making oneself as much of a nonentity as possible (presumably so as not to alter the natural processes and outcome of the situation), I had difficulty both accepting and maintaining that stance. The combination of my assertive and enthusiastic personality and professional background made it hard for me to remain completely silent while subjects were either reacting to a situation or demanding a "real" response from me.

More important, I found that those who took a personal interest in my welfare or who actively attempted to engage me in social conversation also provided me with some of the richest and most insightful data. Many of those house officers were the ones I felt freest to use as "sociological collaborators" (Millman 1977) or as informants. Those who seemed the most accepting of my presence as an observer also seemed to be the most candid, sometimes painfully so.

To account partially for any bias introduced as a result of my participation, I identified in my field notes all those occasions when I was aware of either interfering with natural processes or simply meeting my own need for acceptance and recognition. I also tried to hold in check and limit my responses to both personal questions and questions about the findings.

THE WOMAN OBSERVER

Beginning to be identified in the literature is the unique perspective feminism brings to the social research role (Millman and Kantor 1976). While mention is made that women are sensitized to issues of status and insider–outsider positions in the professional world of sociology, as in the large world, there is little discussion available about the impact of gender on the data-gathering process itself. The intimacy and friendship that males Bosk (1979) and Light (1980) described in their relationships with most of their physician subjects was not shared by Scully (1980), Daniels (1967), or myself—all women studying predominantly male environments. It seems important to speculate about the role of gender differences in distancing the observer from the subject and about whether the male subject is inclined to withhold or even negatively express feelings or thoughts about a woman observer. Wiseman (1970), in her study of skid row alcoholics, mentions the use of escorts and inside informants to observe in those settings inaccessible to a woman researcher, but she does not draw out any other implication of that social fact or further discuss her role as woman observer. Daniels (1967) is one sociologist who specifically indicates that she encountered refusal, denial, or avoidance largely based on gender alone.

Geer (1976) uses the concept of "sociological rudeness," meaning the necessity for participant observers to intrude into the more inaccessible and private individual and collective experiences of subjects. She suggests that persistence and boldness in interacting with subjects are among the necessary characteristics of a researcher. Yet, these traits of assertiveness or aggressiveness have traditionally been associated in the larger society with the male personality. Indeed, she might not even have raised the issue had she been a male researcher.

My relationships with house officers (with a few notable exceptions) ranged from tolerance to cordiality. There were very few outright refusals of interview requests and even fewer denials of direct observation. Like Millman (1977) I found most of the house staff to be friendly and cooperative in allowing me to observe their world. While some were clearly indifferent, I found that others went to considerable lengths to interpret events I witnessed.

One sex-linked aspect of the interaction I encountered as an observer was paternalism, not unlike that reported by Roberts (1977) when she studied physicians. Occasionally I was courted or the object of flirtation and macho behavior. Daniels (1967) mentions that she experienced this as well. Women researchers immersing themselves in male-dominated cultures have to be aware of the possibilities of some differences in process and or outcome because of gender. Whether they are viewed suspiciously or chauvinistically, these differential dynamics need to be recognized. Women may need to work harder to overcome or compensate for that inherent difference. A strong ego and support from other women and sympathetic male sociologists (for example, Scully's empathetic response to my reticence to intrude was invaluable in helping to lessen it) are helpful indeed.

The issue of the sensitivity that a woman may bring to the observation process is evident in the following discussion of the therapeutic observer. It may well be that in certain situations women may obtain richer, more comprehensive data because, in the traditional nurturing role, they may be easier to talk to—especially if expressions of caring and concern are cultivated.

THE THERAPEUTIC OBSERVER

Millman (1977) observed that some of her subjects became special allies and sociological collaborators. While this happened in the sams study as well, my presence also provoked a variety of self-protective responses and self-conscious reactions. For example, Intern Nelley and others asked me if I thought them all compulsive, paranoid, and crazy. Nelley asked me how long I was going to follow him, and Resident Brinkley chimed in, "Oh, about one or two years. She'll always be around. She's doing an expose of our pathology" (Field notes, VAH). Bosk (1979) briefly describes a similar set of reactions from his physician subjects, identifying his own role as that of "The Sounding Board." Ironically, the fact that he found himself assuming a quasi-therapeutic role with so many of his residents is not reflected in the body of his finding. That is, his interpretation of the coping mechanisms the surgical residents used to handle mistakes and other tension-filled activities—the main theme of his study—does not include any such presentation of their doubts or ambivalence as described in his field appendix. Discontent with the injustices or oppressiveness of the training system was pervasive among the internal medicine house staff at SAMs. Beyond cathartic recitations of their frustrations (even by those who stated that they were satisfied overall with their training), my presence or my questions often precipitated spontaneous expressions of self-deprecation. Countless unprompted comments addressed to me unmistakably portrayed their world as bizarre, crazy, and pathological.

There is no evidence that the house staff actually believed that I was a muckraking journalist, which would have called for circumspection. Rather, their use of self-mocking humor, derision, and sarcasm seemed to be for the purposes of belittling their training. Since they characterized their world as a comedy of the absurd, they appeared to have a need (publicly and privately) to let an outsider know that they, too, understood what was "really happening." Without relying too heavily on psychological metaphors, perhaps one way to cope with an insane situation is to distance oneself from it. By openly acknowledging it or anticipating someone else's like conclusion one divorces oneself from it and simultaneously disarms the observer. Additionally, if an outsider can corroborate one's impressions, it reduces feelings of vulnerability and isolation because the observer is perceived to be in collusion.

Furthermore, as Bosk (1979) has also found, a few house officers wanted to play the role of confessor or confidante and sought me out. They were usually among the most malcontent. Others seemed genuinely interested in the findings or were impressed with my provocative questions. Many of the interviews seemed to serve a therapeutic and self-reflective purpose. Once engaged in an interview, most of them continued beyond the time allotted. I was often more self-conscious about imposing on their time than they were conscious of protecting it. When interruptions were unavoidable, several returned for a second session. All but one of those interviewed as ending residents consented five years later to even lengthier interviews than at the conclusion of formal training.

Such openness and candidness during (and beyond) training might also go beyond the "therapeutic" need to confess. They certainly were not afraid of any repercussions of their attitudes and behavior. This points up a major difference between observing graduate medical training and undergraduate medical education. House staff have already been certified as physicians (analogous to tenure provisions in academia) and can only be dismissed (or more likely, redirected) for "cause." Since that so infrequently occurs, they may not feel vulnerable to outside scrutiny. Indeed, the third-year medical students seemed to be the most curious and self-conscious about my presence, as Geer (1976) and Bloom (1973) also found.

My presence seemed to provide the opportunity for house staff to state their case when confronted with what they perceived as injustices. The assumption underlying the research process is that it can be a possible mechanism of improvement. As a representative of the "outside," I may have been perceived as someone through whom to communicate with the higher-ups and outsiders. The research conducted would sooner or later be available to all interested parties. Thus, my presence may have presented a rare opportunity for even such a privileged collectivity to present their side of the "case."

Finally, I cannot ignore the fact that in spite of their disgruntlement or disillusionment, internal medicine house officers were still being socialized into an elite and highly prestigious specialty. Therefore, they also may have been exhibiting their invulnerability because of their perception of their collective power in the eyes of the public. Moreover, since many were indeed experiencing a degree of dissonance between their expectations and their experiences, they may also have adopted an indifferent attitude toward outsiders. Perhaps as far as they were concerned I could see and hear whatever I wanted.

CONCLUSION

Serious epistemological questions are raised by participant observer research. Unlike positivist sociology, which imposes sociological constructs upon the study prior to the actual data-gathering process, thereby deflecting issues of observer bias, participant observers enter a system of social relations in which they are identified by the various categories in which they maintain membership. Significant are those major social categories of social status, class, age, gender, and sexual status in addition to those that are more inimical (e.g., somatic norm image or ideological orientations). Therefore, the identity of the researcher will influence the nature of the data. Women will most likely have access to different kinds of data than men. Among doctors, women, who have higher morbidity rates than men, are more likely to be identified with patients and may be treated thus.

Therefore, participant observation unhinges the positivistic assumption of the separation of data from researcher, making the relationship problematic. Notions of "objectivity" are removed from the absolute to the relative category. That is, in the words of ethnomethodologists, "All realities are created equal." It is impossible, however, to study a reality system using a method that demands the imposition of ideological constructs prior to the data collection and rejects all responses not in conformance with the method (e.g., "uncodable responses"). In this kind of research, what becomes objective is the social identity of the researchers and the ideological constructs through which the data is filtered upon analysis.

Participant observation research in the medical field has demonstrated its usefulness in plumbing areas of inquiry inaccessible to positivistic types of inquiry. As in all such research, however, which seeks access to the actors' interpretation of reality, it produces dilemmas of social identity and categorization for the researcher and raises issues of subject reflexivity. This produces difficult methodological and moral quandaries for the researcher, which must be resolved in light of ethical constraints and the canons of research method.

Notes

CHAPTER 1: INTRODUCTION

1. See Jonas 1978; Starr 1982; and Stevens 1971, 1978 for histories of medical education and medical specialization.

2. These recent studies of graduate medical training have made important contributions to understanding aspects of the socialization process or outcomes for select groups of physicians. See Bosk 1979 on surgical residency training; Light 1980 on residency training of psychiatrists, Scully 1977 on obstetrician/gynecologist residency training, Knafl and Burkett 1975 and Burkett and Knafl 1974 on the training of orthopedic residents, Werner and Korsch 1979 on the pediatric internship, and Bucher and Stelling 1977 for a comparative study of four graduate programs including internal medicine.

3. As of 1977 there was a total of 62,138 internists in the United States out of approximately 340,000 physicians (32,000 of whom were board certified). They constitute the single largest group of certified physicians ("Annual Report on Medical Education" 1977). As of 1983 there were 17,703 residents in 440 internal medicine training programs representing about one-quarter of all residencies (Crowley 1983). During the early part of 1970s subspecialization by internists increased to nearly 80 percent, decreasing to 75 percent by 1978. At the same time, the number of fellowship training programs decreased from 1,512 in 1976/1977 to 1,318 in 1980/1981, a fact no doubt related to the above decline (Schleiter, Tarlov, and Weil 1981).

4. As of 1983 there were within internal medicine ten distinct subspecialties offering postresidency fellowships: cardiology, critical care, endocrinology, gastroenterology, hematology, infectious disease, medical oncology, nephrology, pulmonary disease, and rheumatology. All were offered at the site of this study.

5. Bucher and Stelling's (1977) sample consisted only of two cohorts of seven residents each, and they largely ignored the patient care implications of those elements of

professional training that they identified. Another major study that includes internal medicine is Roberts 1977. While it describes important doctor–patient perspectives in a university hospital environment it does not specifically focus on the socialization component. The recent studies that have examined the patient relationships of internal medicine house officers in clinic settings mostly pointed to deficiencies in interpersonal skills but rarely deal with the larger structural and situational variables affecting the orientation of the house staff (see, for example, Duffy, Hamerman, and Cohen 1980; Linn and Wilson 1980; Platt and McMath 1979; Robbins et al. 1979). Yet, internal medicine house staff across the country will continue to provide the major amount of medical care to outpatients in hospitals (Shipp 1977; Stoeckle 1975).

6. Some residency programs have done away with the term *intern* and call the first year of graduate medical training postgraduate year (PGY) 1, the subsequent years PGY 2 and so forth. Because the historical connotations of the term *intern* are important, I use that term here. All names in the book have been disguised to protect confidentiality.

7. As of 1983 about 24 percent of all trainees and 40 percent of those in internal medicine and pediatric specialties (Crowley 1983) and residencies were women. Although I did not include behavioral differences between men and women house staff in this study, my impressions were not unlike the findings of Scully (1977): that there were few appreciable differences between them. Over the range of house staff behavior toward patients, the women were as evenly distributed as the men. This is not to say, however, that there were no biases against female house staff. The male house officers I interviewed identified their male colleagues' and their own negative attitudes toward many, if not all, female house staff as well as female patients. Some of the women house staff felt discriminated against. See recent studies by Lesserman (1981) and Heins (1979) and articles in the *Journal of the American Medical Women's Association* where these issues are raised.

8. Wigton and Steinmann (1984) identified seventy-two procedures with which house staff is expected to be familiar.

9. The limitations of a static, one-dimensional approach, one that often correlates personality or social background with attitudes or outcomes, have been discussed by Hadden and Long (1978) and by Olsen and Whittaker (1970), among others.

10. See also Rezler 1974 for a major literature review.

11. Moody, Gray, and Elton Newman (1965) almost twenty years ago conducted a small study of one group of physicians before and after they entered practice, but the study did not examine background or socialization aspects of the sample. Kantor and Giner, (1981) surveyed by questionnaire a group of alumni from an internal medicine training program about their educational experiences. These cohorts had not been questioned during training.

12. Both found that students (1) enter with idealistic views and strong motivation, (2) experience problems of uncertainty in mastering the scope of medical knowledge but develop ways of dealing with these problems, and (3) develop some preferences for types of patients based on their interest in and perception of the degree to which they can develop expertise. Both also found an increasing preference for specialization stemming from students' concern about coping with medical knowledge (Hadden and Long 1978).

CHAPTER 2: CAREER AND CULTURE OF THE HOUSE STAFF

1. The National Board of Medical Examiners (NBME) gives examinations required by all state licensing boards for physician licensure. Part One is usually given after the first two years of medical school, and Part Two is given at the end of the fourth year.

2. The Association of American Medical Colleges has developed a national system of licensing for residency programs. Medical students choose a specialty and several graduate medical programs, while the programs in turn choose the students they want. For many of the house staff SAMs was among their first three choices; for others it was further down on their list. No one interviewed was totally unhappy with the selection process, and almost all had been accepted to other residency programs as well. They contrasted the SAMs internal medicine training program both with smaller community hospital–based residency programs and with the more research-oriented university-affiliated tertiary care centers (those institutions where most patients were referred by community practitioners and other hospitals for further diagnosis and treatment). The SAMs program combined aspects of those two contrasting training settings, which Mumford (1970) describes.

3. This finding is at variance with Miller (1970), who found that it took the interns at Boston City Hospital several months to redefine the service component as educational, and with Chaiklin (1960), who found that the house staff assessed their entire experience in educational terms.

4. Studies of medical students have uncovered negative outcomes of medical school socialization, especially those that affect adversely the beginning physician and his or her patients (Becker et al. 1961; Bloom 1973). For example, Coombs (1978) discusses certain depersonalizing techniques used by medical students—such as the objectification of death, the suppression of personal anxieties, and the avoidance of certain patients—none of which were discussed fully and openly by their mentors. Of Coombs's sample, 38 percent left medical school with conflicted, rather than positive, attitudes toward patients. Thus it may be inferred that medical school predisposes interns to objectified and alienated relations with patients. Rosenberg (1979) concludes that "the environment in today's medical schools—technically oriented, highly structured, time pressured, competitive, and unrealistically demanding . . . may destroy the humanitarian orientation of the entering medical student" (81). The responses to the many conflicts she identified were cynicism, lowered self-image, apathy, and concern about the preciousness of time. Klein and Mumford (1973) argue that the important shaping of the physician occurs before entry into medical school. According to their "bent twig" hypothesis, the medical school selection process that identifies smart, achievement-oriented, somewhat aloof persons who know how to get good grades, indirectly gives preference to qualities that frequently accompany a strong premedical background: intense competitiveness, intellectual narrowness, and occasional difficulty in getting along with others. With this general background, new medical students enter a climate that provides limited opportunities for developing sensitivity and caring.

5. According to Jonas (1978), "Hospital house staff are significant contributors to the educational process: they spent about ten percent of their time teaching medical students, and provide forty percent of all medical student contact with teachers. House

staff are, of course, the least experienced teachers, not trained to teach, not paid to teach, not hired to teach, and have as their major responsibility patient care, at the same time, they are supposed to be learning themselves" (293–294).

6. Moore (1970) identifies the concept of the "fellowship of suffering" as part of his discussion of a "punishment centered" type of socialization, a major component of which is the prominence of desocialization in which trainees are isolated and share the difficult experiences with one another. Light (1980) comments that Moore does not explain how one progresses beyond suffering to become a member of the profession. Yet the fellowship of suffering was perhaps the most humanizing aspect of the entire socialization of interns and residents at SAMs as patients were objectified, other staff were alienated, and social lives atrophied.

7. Bucher and Stelling (1977) discuss at length the ways in which faculty evaluation of residents was discounted—an unexpected finding in their research. Coser (1961) concludes that the insularity of subordinate groups in a hospital is functional for both in that it serves to protect both superiors and subordinates in their respective role performance. She also quoted Homans (1946) as commenting that not having to know is not having to act and that not acting may be as important in crucial situations as acting. Neither one discusses any of the possible negative repercussions of this distancing.

8. This term is often used by house staff to depict unworthy patients. The pervasiveness of this disparaging patient description is evidenced by a lengthy article on the subject by George and Dundes (1978).

9. Viewing their practice as veterinary medicine was an obvious way of casting aspersions on the patients, likening them to animals with whom they could not communicate.

10. It is important to note that I resisted the Catch-22–like portrayal of their circumstances after reading the book because the latter seemed a much more chaotic and callous characterization of the everyday world of the house staff than I was observing. A. Strauss (1975a) describes the differences between an insider's and outsider's perspective with respect to a similar situation: "Because the definition of each [hospital] ward arises from daily activity rather than solely from administrative fiat, the definition is characterized by flexibility and ambiguity. Observers like ourselves [outsiders] are amazed at first to find personnel grumbling that a ward is out of shape when, to our untutored eyes, it is not very noticeably out of shape, when conversely, what seems to laymen to be a badly misshapen ward is scarcely remarked upon by its personnel. . . . Unquestionably this apparent inconsistency is related to subjective perspectives" (183).

11. The first of my hundreds of observations of a GROP orientation and the combative expressions used to describe the training process occurred during my first day in the field. These included a reluctance to admit patients from the ER to the inpatient floors. For example, when I arrived in the SAMs ER there was a "code" in process. Later on, SR Ryder talked about the patient to the others in the er office and on the phone. The patient apparently was about to die. SR Ryder met with opposition to admitting her and had to negotiate with a resident on the phone to do so.

CHAPTER 3: GROP DYNAMICS

1. This derives from a widely held belief that American health care is delivered inequitably (see Duff and Hollingshead 1968; Ehrenreich and Ehrenreich 1970; Kosa and Zola 1975; Krause 1977; Rosner 1982; Waitzkin 1983; among others).

2. It should be noted that the concept of "private" is a misnomer since, increasingly, public funds directly and indirectly support the private system. Such programs and policies as Medicare and Medicaid, tax-exempt status, Hill-Burton facilities construction, among others, have blurred the distinction. Nevertheless both in the profit-making and nonprofit sectors (e.g., group practices, hospitals, nursing homes) private, self-perpetuating boards of trustees, owner-operators, or both have had sole control over the policies of those institutions.

3. See Merton (1968:261–278) for a general discussion of the conflicts between intellectuals in public bureaucracies. Also, H. Cohen (1965) and Wiseman (1970) discuss the ways in which supervisory-level and professional workers outside of medicine attempt to control their work by manipulating clients.

4. Iatrogenic diseases may be caused by physical, chemical (drug), nutritional, or infectious elements or by such occurrences as unnecessary surgery, psychological problems, or psychosomatic reactions. Articles appear frequently in the professional and popular literature about the harm done to patients by the medical system profession. For example, Steel et al. (1981) found 36 percent of 815 consecutive patients on a general medical service of a university hospital had an iatrogenic illness. Sartwell (1974) analyzed iatrogenic disease from an epidemiological perspective. The concept of iatrogenesis has been expanded by Illich (1976) to include a variety of cultural and social as well as clinical deficiencies in modern medical care.

5. Bosk (1979) and Light (1980) also identify this means/ends inversion among surgical and psychiatric residents, respectively.

6. The concept of norms as used in the traditional sociological sense is useful here because of the salience of norms in house staff thinking. Norms here are "blueprints of social action" (Mumford 1970) or rules of conduct and standards by which behavior is judged. They are conceptualized as cultural (shared) definitions of desirable behavior (Williams 1968).

7. The concept of dialectical contradiction seems useful as a heuristic device if it is defined as the nature of those conflicting elemental processes that are believed to constitute the essence of the reality itself (Heilbroner 1980). This perspective views reality as shifting because it consists in its very innermost being of unstable coexistence and successful resolution of incompatible forces. As Heilbroner suggests, however, while the dialectical orientation tries to find real essences and can include ambiguities, metaphorical references, and Janus-like meanings, it does not shed light on an actual sequence of events through which contradictory tendencies work themselves out. It is even difficult to attempt to describe these contradictory norms logically in linear sequence. What emerges from this dialectical perspective is a comprehension of existence that is of necessity more complex and ambiguous than a nondialectical approach. It is also important to note that the existence of the conflicting principles governing the practice of internal medicine does not mean that either chaos or inertia results. The

house staff moves, changes, and grows in spite of, as well as because of, these inherent dilemmas. It does imply, however, that these contradictions must continuously be confronted as they shape their situational reality and long-range perspectives on their profession as well as on patients.

Merton (with Barber 1976) uses the concept of "sociological ambivalence" to describe normative conflicts.

8. I discovered another set of contending norms that was tangentially related to the grop conflicts engendered by the norms of compulsiveness and efficiency. This second set I called the norms of self-reliance and humility. The former manifests itself in a "trust-no-one-but-yourself" attitude, which can be in contention with the latter, which manifests itself in a "you-can't-know-it-all-and-do-it-alone" attitude. Merton (with Barber 1976) identifies these norms as the dual values of autonomy and humility. See Mizrahi (1983) for a full discussion of how the norms of self-reliance and humility manifested themselves in the house staff culture.

CHAPTER 4: GROP CRITERIA

1. According to Becker et al. (1961) the sources of the categorization are located in the student, medical, or lay cultures. From the student culture came, first, a dislike for patients without physical pathology; second a preference for patients with whom they have a chance to exercise some real measure of medical responsibility; third, a view of patients as persons who may either help or hinder their attempts to impress the faculty; and fourth, the notion that patients should not take up a student's time without providing something worthwhile in return. Clearly, these multiple and contradictory sets of classifications cover many, if not all, patients.

2. To take one social evaluation measure—race—one can identify how racism in the lay, medical, and student cultures all converge to affect the house staff's patient perspective, although class was certainly a confounding or intervening variable, and not all blacks were automatically disparaged. First, institutional racism is evident both in the nature of the two-class American health care system and in the once *de jure* and now *de facto* segregated hospital network in which house staff function (Duff and Hollingshead 1968; Seham 1973). Second, in the larger medical culture, racism has been documented both in the training of medical professionals and in the delivery of patient care at the health institution and individual practitioner levels (B. Roth 1974; Singer 1967; Yamamoto, Dixon, and Bloombaum 1972; and Yamamoto et al. 1967). Scully (1980), for example, in tracing the evolution of the specialty of obstetrics and gynecology, describes the widespread experimentation conducted on slave women prior to the use of anesthesia. A second example occurred more recently. It was revealed that black men who were part of a federally funded medical experiment on the effects of syphilis had penicillin deliberately withheld from them after it was discovered to be a cure for the disease. Third, with respect to student culture, Moser (1978), in pleading for house staff to help rectify the social schism between blacks and whites in American society, identified the rampant problems existing between a largely black lower-class patient population and an overwhelmingly white upper-class male group of health care providers.

3. Chaiklin (1960), among others, found these attitudes in the house staff he studied.

4. Roberts (1977) also found that to be among the most prized patient traits.

5. Scully (1977) found that the ideal female patient was similarly characterized by the obstetrician/gynecologist residents she studied.

6. The classification of "washed" and "unwashed" poor was made by physicians in the study by Duff and Hollingshead (1968). Glaser and Strauss (1964) found that vague notions of "personality" were one of the major characteristics upon which the social value of a patient was calculated. See Wiseman (1970) for an excellent discussion of the concepts of gratitude and trust in the relationship between rehabilitation counselors and alcoholics. Ford, Ort, and Denton (1967) found the characteristic of "niceness" to be of major importance in the practicing doctor's assessment of patients, but it was clearly one sided. The study by Jeffery (1979) in British casualty departments (ERs) demonstrated that moral evaluation of patients by physicians is prominent in other Western cultures as well.

CHAPTER 5: GROP STRATEGIES

1. There is, of course, much psychological literature on mechanisms of defense, adaptation, and coping (Coelho, Hamburg, and Adams 1974; Freud 1966; Haan 1965; Kroeber 1963). Coping mechanisms are usually defined as adaptation mechanisms under relatively difficult or stressful situations (Haan 1965; White 1974), whereas defense mechanisms are commonly viewed as unconscious pathological mechanisms of behavior, or as adaptive devices gone wrong (White 1974). A sociological definition of these mechanisms—which seems appropriate here— would include a greater emphasis on interactional, learned, and situational elements and would not present them as necessarily a natural and permanent part of the self (Mechanic 1974).

2. Examination of coping and defense mechanisms among physicians has been rare. For example, Spitz and Block (1981), in their literature review, found no studies of normal physician mechanisms of denial, disavowal, and minimization; yet, the family physicians in their study constantly employed those techniques in telephone contacts with patients, and the result was distorted diagnosis and treatment plans. Coombs and Goldman (1973) identified the following coping mechanisms employed by medical personnel: humor, escape into work, language alteration, and rationalization. Physical as well as psychological avoidance techniques have been noted in the behavior of medical students (Coombs and Powers 1975; Martin 1957) and psychiatric residents (Coser 1967; Light 1980).

3. There has been a recent surge in the application of negotiation theory to medical practice, led by Freidson (1961, 1975), Maines (1982), and A. Strauss (1963, 1978a). The primary focus of this application, developing as it did out of the concerns of symbolic interaction, is on analyzing the development of social structure within the confines of the organization and profession. Maines (1982:275) has referred to this emergent structure as "mesostructure," that arena in which "interaction" and "structure" form a unity. Thus, what is being negotiated is "reality" in the forms of roles, imputations of intentionality, status, ideology, and so forth. In any process of negotiation,

contextual factors (called the "negotiation context") provide important constraints on the process. For example, Drass (1982) has indicated that, while a medical consultation between patient and doctor is negotiated, the doctor, by virtue of his superior status has greater leverage with which to shape the negotiated order than does the patient. A similar example was documented by Sugrue (1982) in her analysis of a patient who refused to negotiate on the terms of the medical staff. As a consequence of her refusal, the staff slipped tranquilizers into her IV in an attempt to calm her and enforce hospital discipline upon her.

Theories of negotiated order have been an important addition to understanding hierarchical and peer relations in medical practice, yet they create problems when used to deal with interaction in which there is an actual physical medium of exchange. The work of Blau (1964), who works from a neo-Weberian position, provides a welcome connective, even though the work was done nearly two decades ago. To summarize Blau: within an organizational context there is an inequality of social resources, which are organized formally (chain of command, strategic positioning, and so forth) and informally (expertise, contacts, and so forth). These social resources are made scarce by virtue of their distribution and constitute the basis of social status and esteem within the organization. Therefore, an informal system of exchange relations develops on the basis of the distribution of these scarce resources. When persons draw upon the resources, they incur obligations—often unspecified—that result in the obligated conferring esteem and status upon the owners of the resources.

The problem in my study is that the medium of exchange is not "esteem" nor "reality" but patients, who are so numerous that their value is negative and they are continually being passed from doctor to doctor, moving down or across the social hierarchy. The fate of the patients in the house staff reality system is not difficult to imagine. They suffer the same sort of literal devaluation as any currency in a system of exchnge when inflation sets in. They *are* resources. Otherwise the staff would never learn the practice of medicine. Because there is an oversupply of patients—who are themselves sentient human beings—they enter into a system of social exchange in which they are generally dehumanized and disparaged by the very persons who are supposed to care for them. An additional source of devaluation comes from the fact that many are poor and often suffer from the diseases and gratuitous violence that are endemic to poverty.

4. Attempts by workers to control client flow through rather intransient people-processing bureaucracies (Hasenfeld 1974) have been discussed elsewhere in the organizational literature (see H. Cohen 1965; Lipsky 1980). Among physicians, Scully (1977) identified a similar process occurring among obstetrician/gynecologist residents. She attributed it principally to educational factors, in other words, to how much they needed to learn, whereas in my study a constellation of variables contributed to it, making it both more complex and more fundamental to the culture and social organization of internists' training. J. Roth (1974b) described a similar process observed in an ER. On exchanging and negotiating psychiatric patients, see Lang (1981) and Mishler and Waxler (1963) among others.

5. References to sloughing are made in passing by Freidson (1975:211, 231) in his analyses of physician relationships in a group practice setting. Sloughing was considered a deviant action rather than a normal mistake. Bosk (1979) likewise found that

surgical residents distinguished among normative, judgmental, and technical mistakes, only the first of which they considered serious.

6. Reference to the former TV series *Marcus Welby* appeared several times in the interviews, always in the context of a discrepancy between the public's and the house staff's expectations about physician–patient interaction. House officers indicated that the contrast between the reality of internal medicine practice and society's image of it was striking. How much this dissonance contributed to their feelings of disillusionment is an important question, which Huntington (1981), raises with respect to physicians in Great Britain and Australia.

7. In her discussion of the importance of the medical record, Mumford (1970) makes only passing reference in a footnote to the possibility that an instrumental value may become an end value, meaning that the chart may become an end in itself or that goal displacement might occur. Freidson (1975) has demonstrated how doctors in practice discount the appropriateness of the chart to evaluate their performance, while at the same time recognizing it contained the only "objective" assessment of their work. Hence his characterization of it as tool, weapon, and cover. Unlike the house staff in this study, those doctors, according to Freidson, saw the work experience and not the chart as the reality. For the house staff at SAMs, the chart had symbolic and existential meaning, while its use for political purposes was limited principally to the informal system of social control: that is, for unofficial assessments of each other's work.

8. Roberts (1977) presents a functional explanation for physician behavior that focuses on the case instead of the person. By describing the symptoms, as in "The 'burn' is doing fine," she asserts the doctors are probably transmitting a much more precisely coded message than by using names in that they do not mix people up. Given the fear of mistakes and the occasional instances of mistaken orders and identities I observed, this interpretation is not entirely satisfactory.

9. A. Cohen (1966), Goffman (1961), and Sykes and Matza (1957) describe mechanisms that deviants use to cope with and control a variety of restrictive and oppressive environments. For analytical purposes, protective house staff behavior can be compared to the behavior of deviant groups. For example, Sykes and Matza enumerate a variety of neutralization techniques used by juvenile delinquents within their subculture to rationalize their offenses against their victims: denial of responsibility, denial of injury, denial of the victim, condemnation of the condemners, and appeal to higher loyalties. I saw varying degrees of analogous behavior in the house staff in this study. They asserted that negative behavior toward patients was due to forces beyond their control; stated that no great harm was done (i.e., they redefined many errors of omission and commission as normal or understandable behavior); implied that the patient was the wrongdoer; complained that no one cared or that others did worse things to patients (e.g., the faculty in the former instance and "LMDs," or local medical doctors, in the latter case); and they maintained that house staff must survive.

Sykes and Matza (1957:667) make two points relevant to this study: First, deviance occurs not because societal (read: professional) norms are neglected but because other norms are more pressing and (presumably) immediate. This was true for the house staff, who defined their behavior in survival terms. Second, "interpretations of responsibility are cultural constructs and not just merely idiosyncratic behavior, although from a psychodynamic viewpoint, this orientation toward one's own actions may represent a profound alienation from self." What is evident from the findings in my study is that indeed there was a constant interplay between social structure and personal adaptation that has been neglected in much of the medical socialization literature.

CHAPTER 6: BARRIERS TO DOCTOR–PATIENT RELATIONSHIPS

1. A. Strauss (1975b) has discussed the complexities involved in establishing collegial relationships as a result of various combinations of different levels of trainees and trainers moving around at different periods, but he does not discuss the effects on the doctor-patient relationship.

2. The complicated system of rotation and coverage not only precluded any meaningful house staff–patient relationships but had further repercussions for the issue of responsibility and accountability for patient management decisions. More than occasionally, the issues of boundaries, belonging, and responsibility surfaced, usually when a patient management error occurred. There were times when the question Whose patient is this? had significant meaning in attempting to identify those house officers responsible for a set of decisions made about a patient. While formal responsibility for a patient terminated at the end of a rotation (that is, once a house officer left the service, his or her remaining patients were formally transferred to an incoming one), on-call and coverage responsibilities during the month presented many potential problems. Miscommunication among house staff could occur, and did, infrequently, as did breaches of house staff protocol or norms of professional conduct. A house officer's observations of the decisions made by a colleague covering for him or for her contributed to his or her assessment of that doctor's competence. They also caused occasional strain when a patient management decision was made or implemented by that covering house officer when he or she did not concur, about which he or she was not consulted, or which resulted in the deterioration or demise of the patient.

An additional complicating factor derived from the diseases of the adult patients on internal medicine services. Problems that were the result of either iatrogenesis or natural complications would sometimes not surface until days, weeks, or even months after the original intervention. Therefore it sometimes was difficult to identify and track down those responsible since so many different physicians were involved in patient management. This situation could become an issue both for the patient and for the various members of the team. The discussion of "norms of relay learning" by Mumford (1970) begins to touch on this issue. She admits the possibility that patients may "fall between the cracks" vertically because of the hierarchical division of labor, but she does not identify the horizontal permutations that can also adversely affect patient responsibility and continuity of care.

3. Since this study focuses solely on the graduate medical training of internists, the information obtained about the house staff's beginning acquisition of doctor–patient skills during medical school was of necessity indirect. I obtained it principally through interviews during the first two months on internship, although house staff continued to refer to those early experiences at every stage of training.

4. The JR responses to the teaching and supervising of medical students ranged from apathy to active dislike. A few house staff asserted that they liked the more formal teaching role, but during the occasional times when I observed them engaged in that activity, it was hardly with any enthusiasm. Moreover, most of them detested the chore of writing medical work-ups. The JR relationship with medical students largely depended upon their assessment of how willing and able the student was to assist in the daily work of the team. Yet house staff provide at least 40 percent of the formal teaching to medical students (Jonas 1978). Becker et al. (1961) discuss medical students' perspectives on their relationship with residents.

5. Poor relationships between house staff and patient in OPC settings have also been identified by Duffy, Hamerman, and Cohen (1980); Linn and Wilson (1980); Plaja, Cohen and Samora (1968); Platt and McMath (1979); Robbins et al. (1979); and Scully (1977), among others.

CHAPTER 7: OUTCOMES OF INTERNAL MEDICINE TRAINING

1. Hadden and Long (1978) note: "Only by sustaining the assumption of knowledge, skill and commitment can members be confident that their fellow members will live up to the requirement of their world in practice. . . . Though necessary tools of commitment, knowledge and skill leave open questions of their utility and appropriateness for action. . . . Of the two classic conditions for moral responsibility, willingness and ability, knowledge and skill signify capability while commitment validates willingness. . . . *Commitment is clearly more significant for membership and hence for socialization* [emphasis added] (109–110).

2. While by no means a perfect fit, this typology was inspired by the framework developed by Merton (1968) in conceptualizing anomie and deviant behavior at a societal level. The types of adaptation with respect to goals and means, conformity, innovation, ritualism, retreatism, rebellion, and resentment correspond in a gross way to the way many house officers characterized their world and their choices within it.

3. Analogies to fraternity or military life have been noted by Mumford (1970) and more recently by Cousins (1981). Cousins's commentary elicited an outpouring of emotional responses from physicians both supporting and rejecting such a characterization.

APPENDIX A: RESEARCH METHODOLOGY

1. On the issue of note-taking in the field, opposite viewpoints can be found in the literature. Mumford (1970:11) apparently took open notes all of the time, which she says aided her by serving as a self-protective device. She comments, "At times it would have been more difficult to stand by, with no apparent function to perform, in the face of fear and death or pain. I sometimes felt protected by being able to take notes." I am not sure hers is a valid (albeit honest) reason for doing it that way. She also comments that her consistent reporting of what people said seemed to encourage some interns to add comments or begin discussions. She makes no mention of the pos-

sibility of a contrary outcome, namely, that openly taking notes might inhibit some people from speaking out. Daniels (1967), however, admits that her public note-taking inhibited interaction among her subjects as well as between her and them. Nevertheless, she indicates with hindsight that she persisted too long before giving it up, thus damaging the relationship she had with the subjects. Geer (1976) specifically reported on the amount of suspicion she encountered when she began her study of the medical students (Becker et al. 1961). She believes, therefore, in absolutely no note-taking in public and even advocates not carrying around any instrument such as a clipboard that might suggest that possibility to the subjects. She recommends waiting to record findings until one leaves the field for the day.

APPENDIX B: NOTES FROM THE FIELD

1. Bosk (1979) identifies six roles he either assumed or was assigned by surgical house staff, only some of which I experienced: (1) helper ("go-fer"), (2) emissary from the outside world, (3) fellow sufferer of the indignities of adult studenthood, (4) sounding board for disputes and disagreement, (5) conflict referee, and (6) historian about patients or the service—not all of which, he says, he accepted with equal ease or assumed with equal frequency. He was also used as advisee by attendings and as a referee of conflicts between them and the house staff, indicating to him that even with their senior status, their faculty role remained disturbing to them.

Bibliography

Adams, P., and N. McDonald. 1968. "Clinical Cooling-Out of Poor People." *American Journal of Orthopsychiatry* 38:457–463.

Alford, R. 1975. *Health Care Politics: Ideological and Interest Group Barriers to Reform*. Chicago: University of Chicago.

American Board of Internal Medicine. 1979. "Clinical Competence in Internal Medicine." *Annals of Internal Medicine* 90:402–411.

American Medical Association. 1977. *Proceedings of the AMA Conference. The Impaired Physician: Answering the Challenge*. Chicago: AMA.

American Medical Association, Council on Mental Health. 1973. "The Sick Physician: Impairment by Psychiatric Disorders." *Journal of the American Medical Association* 223:684–687.

Annas, G. 1975. *The Rights of Hospital Patients*. New York: Avon.

"Annual Report on Medical Education in the United States." 1977. *Journal of the American Medical Association* 238:2781–2808.

Becker, H.S. 1970. "Problems of Inference and Proof in Participant Observation." In W. Filstead, ed., *Qualitative Methodology*, 189–200. Chicago: Markham.

Becker, H.S., B. Geer, E. C. Hughes, and A. L. Strauss. 1961. *Boys in White*. Chicago: University of Chicago.

Blau, P. 1963. *Dynamics of Bureaucracy*. Chicago: University of Chicago Press.

——.1964. *Exchange and Power in Social Life*. New York: Wiley.

Blau, P., and R. W. Scott. 1962. *Formal Organizations*. San Francisco: Chandler.

Bloom, S. W. 1963. "The Process of Becoming a Physician." *Annals of AAPSS* 346:87–99. Reprint Edition.

——.1965. "The Sociology of Medical Education: Some Comments on the State of a Field." *Milbank Memorial Fund Quarterly* 43:143–173.

——.1973. *Power and Dissent in Medical School*. New York: Free Press.

——.1979. "Socialization for the Physician's Role: A Review of Some Contributions of Research to Theory." In E. C. Shapiro and L. M. Lowenstein, eds., *Becoming a Physician: Development of Values in Medicine*, 3–49. Cambridge, Mass.: Ballinger.

Bloom, S.W., and R. N. Wilson. 1972. "Patient–Practitioner Relationships." In H. E. Freeman, S. Levine, and L. G. Reeder, eds., *Handbook of Medical Sociology*, 315–339. Englewood Cliffs, N.J.: Prentice-Hall.

Bloomfield, A. L. 1959. "The Origin of the Term 'Internal Medicine.'" *Journal of the American Medical Association* 169:1628–1629.

Blum, F. 1970. "Getting Individuals to Give Information to the Outsider." In W. Filstead, ed., *Qualitative Methodology*, 83–91. Chicago: Markham.

Bosk, C. 1979. *Forgive and Remember: Managing Medical Failure*. Chicago: University of Chicago Press.

Brandt, C. S., and B. Kutner. 1957. "Physician–Patient Relationship in a Teaching Hospital." *Journal of Medical Education* 32:703–707.

Braverman, H. 1974. *Labor and Monopoly Capital*. New York: Monthly Review Press.

Bruyn, S. T. 1970. "The Methodology of Participant Observation." In W. Filstead, ed., *Qualitative Methodology*, 305–327. Chicago: Markham.

Bucher, R., and J. Stelling. 1969. "Characteristics of Professional Organizations." *Journal of Health and Social Behavior* 10:3–15.

———. 1977. *Becoming Professional*. Beverly Hills, Calif.: Sage.

Burkett, G., and K. Knafl. 1974. "Judgment and Decision-Making in a Medical Specialty." *Sociology of Work and Occupations* 1:82–109.

Butler, R. M. 1970. "Geriatrics and Internal Medicine." *Annals of Internal Medicine* 91:903–908.

Cambridge Research Institute. 1975. Trends Affecting the U.S. Health Care System. Washington, D.C.: U.S. Department of Health, Education and Welfare.

Caplovitz, D. 1980. *Student–Faculty Relations in Medical School: A Study of Professional Socialization*. New York: Arno.

Cassell, E. 1975. *The Healer's Art*. Philadelphia: Lippincott.

Chaiklin, H. 1960. "The House Staff of a University Teaching Hospital: A Study of Conflicting Norms." Ph.D. diss., Yale University.

Cloward, R., and F. Piven. 1973. *Regulating the Poor: The Functions of Public Welfare*. New York: Random House, Vintage.

Coe, R. M., M. Pepper, and M. Mattis. 1977. "Is There a 'New' Medical Student: Another View." *Journal of Medical Education* 52:89–98.

Coelho, G.V., D. A. Hamburg, and J. E. Adams, eds. 1974. *Coping and Adaptation*. New York: Basic Books.

Cohen, A. 1966. *Deviance and Control*. Englewood Cliffs, N.J.: Prentice-Hall.

Cohen, H. 1965. *Demonics of Bureaucracy*. Ames: Iowa State University Press.

Coombs, R. N. 1978. *Mastering Medicine*. New York: Free Press.

Coombs, R. N., and L. J. Goldman. 1973. "Maintenance and Discontinuity of Coping Mechanisms in an Intensive Care Unit." *Social Problems* 20:342–355.

Coombs, R. N., and P. S. Powers. 1975. "Socialization for Death: The Physician's Role." *Urban Life* 4:250–271.

Coser, R. L. 1959. "Some Social Functions of Laughter." *Human Relations* 12:171–182.

———.1960. "Laughter among Colleagues." *Psychiatry* 23:81–95.

———. 1961. "Insulation from Observability and Types of Social Conformity." *American Sociological Review* 26:28–39.

———. 1962. *Life in the Ward.* East Lansing: Michigan State University Press.

———. 1967. "Evasiveness as a Response to Structural Ambivalence." *Social Science and Medicine* 1:203–218.

Countiss, R. B., and E. R. Dienst. 1981. "A Comparative Survey of Former Residents' Professional Activities and Retrospective Ratings of Training Program Effectiveness." In *Research in Medical Education, 1981,* Proceedings of the Twentieth Annual Conference. Washington, D.C.; Association of American Medical Colleges.

Cousins, N. 1981. "Internship: Preparation or Hazing?" *Journal of the American Medical Association* 246:377.

Crane, D. 1975. *The Sanctity of Social Life: Physicians' Treatment of Critically Ill Patients.* New York: Russell Sage Foundation.

Crowley, A. E. 1983. "Graduate Medical Education in the United States." *Journal of the American Medical Association* 250:1541–1553.

Dana, B., H. D. Banta, and K. W. Deuschle. 1974. "An Agenda for the Future of Interprofessionalism." In H. Rehr, ed., *Medicine and Social Work,* 77–88. New York: Watson Academic Publications, Prodist.

Daniels, A. K. 1967. "The Low-Caste Stranger in Social Research." In G. Sjoberg, ed., *Ethics, Politics, and Social Research,* 267–296. Cambridge, Mass.: Schenkman.

———. 1971. "How Free Should Professions Be?" In E. Freidson, ed., *Professions and Their Prospects,* 39–58. Beverly Hills, Calif.: Sage.

Davis, F. 1972. "Uncertainty in Medical Prognosis: Clinical and Functional." In E. Freidson and J. Lorber, eds., *Medical Men and Their Work,* 239–248. Chicago: Aldine-Atherton.

Davis, M. 1968a. "Attitudinal and Behavioral Aspects of the Doctor–Patient Relationship as Expressed and Exhibited by Medical Students and Their Mentors." *Journal of Medical Education* 43:337–343.

———. 1968b. "Variations in Patients' Compliance with Doctors' Orders: An Empirical Analysis of Patterns of Communication." *American Journal of Public Health* 58:274–288.

———. 1971. "Patient Compliance and Doctor/Patient Communication." *Psychiatry and Medicine* 2:31–39.

Donabedian, A. 1978. *Needed Research in the Assessment and Monitoring of the Quality of Medical Care.* Washington, D.C.: National Center for Health Services Research, Department of Health, Education, and Welfare.

Dowling, H. 1982. *City Hospitals: The Undercare of the Underprivileged.* Cambridge, Mass.: Harvard University Press.

Drass, K. A. 1982. "Negotiation and the Structure of Discourse in Medical Consultation." *Sociology of Health and Illness.* 4:320–341.

Duff, R. 1975. "Patient Care, the Poor, and Medical Education." In J. Kosa and I. K. Zola, eds., *Sociological Analysis,* 2d ed., *Poverty and Health*: 335–350. Cambridge: Harvard University Press.

Duff, R., and A. Hollingshead. 1968. *Sickness and Society*. New Haven, Conn.: Yale University Press.

Duffy, D. L., D. Hammerman, and M. A. Cohen. 1980. "Communication Skills of House Officers: A Study of a Medical Clinic." *Annals of Internal Medicine* 93:354–357.

Durkheim, E. 1938. *The Rules of Sociological Method*. Glencoe, Ill. Free Press.

Ehrenreich, B., and J. Ehrenreich. 1970. *American Health Empires*. New York: Random House, Vintage.

Emerson, J. P. 1963. "Social Functions of Humor in Hospital Settings." Ph.D. diss., University of California.

Erdmann, J. B., R. F. Jones, and X. Toneski, 1978. *aamc Longitudinal Study of Medical School Graduates of 1960*. Washington, D.C.: Association of American Medical Colleges.

Etzioni, A. 1964. *Modern Organizations*. Englewood Cliffs, N.J.: Prentice-Hall.

Fabricant, M. 1975. "Administering Juvenile Justice in an Urban Setting." Ph.D. diss., Brandeis University.

Filstead, W. 1970. "Introduction." In W. Filstead, ed., *Qualitative Methodology,* 1–15. Chicago: Markham.

Ford, A., R. E. Ort, and J. C. Denton. 1967. *Doctors' Perspective: Physicians View Their Patients and Practice*. Cleveland: Case Western Reserve.

Fox, R. C. 1957. "Training for Uncertainty." In R. K. Merton, G. G. Reader, and P. L. Kendall, eds., *The Student-Physician*, 207–243. Cambridge: Harvard University Press.

———. 1959. *Experiment Perilous*. Glencoe, Ill.: Free Press.

———. 1975. "Is There a 'New' Medical Student?" *Key Reporter* (Summer): 2–4.

———. 1977. "The Medicalization and Demedicalization of American Society." *Daedalus* 106:9–19.

———. 1980. The Human Conditions of Health Professionals. Durham, N.H.: University of New Hampshire.

Fredericks, M. A., and P. Mundy. 1976. *The Making of a Physician: A Ten Year Longitudinal Study of Social Class, Academic Achievement and Changing Attitudes of a Medical School Class*. Chicago: Loyola University Press.

Fredericks, M.A., P. Mundy, and J. J. Lennon. 1971. "The Student-Physician and the Poor: A Study of Expressed Willingness to Serve the Indigent Patient." *Journal of the National Medical Assocation* 63:332–339.

Freidson, E. 1961. *Patients' Views of Medical Practice*. New York: Russell Sage Foundation.

———. 1970a. *Professional Dominance: The Structure of Medical Care*. Chicago: Aldine-Atherton.

———. 1970b. *The Profession of Medicine*. New York: Dodd, Mead.

———. 1973. "Prepaid Group Practice and the New Demanding Patient." *Milbank Memorial Fund Quarterly/Health and Society* 51:473–488.

———. 1975. *Doctoring Together*. New York: Elsevier.

Freud, A. 1966. *The Ego and the Mechanisms of Defense*. New York: International Universities Press.

Gaylin, W., I. Glasser, S. Marcus, and D. Rothman. 1978. *Doing Good: The Limits of Benevolence*. New York: Pantheon.

Geer, B. 1976. "Field Research." Lecture to the University of Virginia Medical Sociology Seminar, Charlottesville.

Geertsma, R., and R. Stoller. 1966a. "Changes in Medical Students' Conceptions of the Ideal Patient." *Journal of Medical Education* 41:45–48.

———. 1966b. "Student–Patient Orientations." *Journal of the Kansas Medical Society* 67:141–146.

George, V., and A. Dundes. 1978. "The Gomer: A Figure of American Hospital Folk Speech." *Journal of American Folklore* 91:568–581.

Gerber, L. A. 1983. *Married to Their Careers: Career and Family Dilemmas in Doctors' Lives*. London: Tavistock.

Glaser, B. G., and A. L. Strauss. 1964. "The Social Loss of Dying Patients." *American Journal of Nursing* 64:119–121.

———. 1968. *The Discovery of Grounded Theory: Strategies for Qualitative Research*. Chicago: Aldine.

Goffman, E. 1959. *The Presentation of Self in Everyday Life*. New York: Doubleday.

———. 1961. *Asylums*. New York: Doubleday, Anchor.

Goldfinger, S. E. 1977. "Continuing Education and General Internal Medicine." *Archives of Internal Medicine* 137:1311–1315.

Goldner, F. H. 1967. "Role Emergence: The Ethics of Ambiguity." In G. Sjoberg, ed., *Ethics, Politics, and Social Research*, 245–266. Cambridge, Mass.: Schenkman.

Goode, W. J. 1957. "Communities with a Community: The Professional." *American Sociological Review* 22:194–200.

Gottheil, E., I. N. Hassenfeld, and E. Gronkiewicz. 1969. "Students' Perceptions of Medical School and Their Attitudes towards Patients." *British Journal of Medical Education* 3:353–358.

Gouldner, A. 1960. "The Norm of Reciprocity: A Preliminary Statement." *American Sociological Review* 25: 161–178.

———. 1973. "The Sociologist as a Partisan: Sociology and the Welfare State." In A. Gouldner, ed., *For Sociology*, 27–68. New York: Basic Books.

Gray, R. M., P. M. Moody, and W. R. Elton Newman. 1965. "Analysis of Physician Attitudes of Cynicism and Humanism before and after Entering Practice." *Journal of Medical Education* 40:760–766.

Greenberg, S. 1965. *The Troubled Calling: Crisis in the Medical Establishment*. New York: Macmillan.

———. 1971. *The Quality of Mercy: A Report on the Critical Conditions of Hospital and Medical Care*. New York: Atheneum.

Greenwood, E. 1957. "Attributes of a Profession." *Social Work*. 2:55–67.

Gross, E. 1985. "Physicians and Their Work: A Study of Strains in Medical Practice. Ph.D. diss., Bryn Mawr College.

Gross, M. 1978. *The Psychological Society.* New York: Random House.

Groves, J. E. 1978. "Taking Care of the Hateful Patient." *New England Journal of Medicine* 298:883–887.

Haan, N. 1965. "Coping and Defense Mechanisms Related to Personality Inventories." *Journal of Consulting Psychology* 29:373–378.

Hadden, J., and T. Long. 1978. "A Study of Physician Socialization." Final report to the U.S. Department of Health, Education, and Welfare.

Hagner, S. B., V. J. LoCicero, and W. A. Steiger. 1968. "Patient Outcome in a Comprehensive Medicine Clinic: Its Retrospective Assessment and Related Variables." *Medical Care* 6:144–156.

Harris, L. and Associates. 1981. *Medical Practice in the 1980's: Physicians Look at Their Changing Profession.* Prepared for Henry J. Kaiser Family Foundation. Menlo Park, Calif.

Harris, R. 1966. *A Sacred Trust.* New York: New American Library.

Hasenfeld, Y. 1974. "People Processing Organizations: An Exchange Approach." In Y. Hasenfeld and R. English, eds., *Human Service Organizations*, 60–71. Ann Arbor: Univeristy of Michigan Press.

Haug, M. 1976. "The Erosion of Professional Autonomy: A Cross-Cultural Inquiry in the Case of the Physician." *Milbank Memorial Fund Quarterly/Health and Society* 54:83–106.

Haug, M., and B. Lavin. 1983. *Consumerism in Medicine: Challenging Physician Authority.* Beverly Hills, Calif.: Sage.

Haug, M., and M. B. Sussman, 1969. "Professional Autonomy and the Revolt of the Client." *Social Problems* 17:153–161.

Heilbroner, R. 1980. *Marxism: For and Against.* New York: Norton.

Heins, M. 1979. "Career and Life Patterns of Women and Men Physicians." In E. C. Shapiro and L. M. Lowenstein, eds., *Becoming a Physician: Development of Values in Medicine*, 217–236. Cambridge, Mass: Ballinger.

Homans, G. 1946. "The Small Warship." *American Sociological Review* 11:294–300.

Howard, J. 1978. "Patient-Centric Technologies: A Case for Soft Science." In E. B. Gallagher, ed., *The Doctor–Patient Relationship in the Changing Health Scene*, 347–361. Washington, D.C.: Department of Health, Education, and Welfare.

Howard, J., and A. L. Strauss. 1975. *Humanizing Health Care: The Implications of Technology, Centralization and Self-Care.* New York: Wiley.

Hulka, B., L. L. Kupper, J. C. Cassel, and F. Mayo. 1975. "Doctor–Patient Communication and Outcomes among Diabetic Patients." *Journal of Community Health* 1:15–22.

Hulka, B., and A. B. Roberts. 1975. "Practice Characteristics and Quality of Primary Medical Care: The Doctor–Patient Relationship." *Medical Care* 13:808–820.

Huntington, J. 1981. *Social Work and General Medical Practice: Collaboration or Conflict.* London: Allen and Unwin.

Hyman, H. H., and E. Singer, eds. 1968. *Readings in Reference Group Theory and Research.* Glencoe, Ill. Free Press.

Illich, I. 1976. *Medical Nemesis.* New York: Bantam.

Ima, K., D. M. Tagliacozzo, and J. C. Lashof. 1970. "Physician Orientation and Behavior: A Study of Outpatient Clinic Physicians." *Medical Care* 3:189–199.

Jacoby, R. 1976. *Social Amnesia*. Boston: Beacon.

Jeffery, R. 1979. "Normal Rubbish: Deviant Patients in Casualty Departments." *Sociology of Health and Illness* 1:90–107.

Jonas, S. 1978. *Medical Mystery and the Training of Doctors in the United States*. New York: Norton.

Jones, D. 1973. "Culture Fatigue: The Results of Role-Playing in Anthropological Research." *Anthropological Quarterly* 46:30–37.

Kadushin, C. 1962. "Social Distance between Client and Professional." *American Journal of Sociology* 62:517–531.

Kahn-Hut, R. 1974. "Psychiatric Theory: A Professional Ideology." Ph.D. diss., Brandeis University.

Kantor, S.M., and P. F. Giner. 1981. "Educational Needs in General Internal Medicine as Perceived by Prior Residents." *Journal of Medical Education* 56:748–756.

Kendall, P. L. 1961. "The Impact of Training Programs on the Young Physicians' Attitudes and Experiences." *Journal of the American Medical Association* 176: 992–997.

———. 1965. *The Relationship between Medical Educators and Medical Practitioners: Sources of Strain and Occasions for Cooperation*. Evanston, Ill.: Association of American Medical Colleges.

Kennedy, E. 1972. *In Critical Condition: American Health Care*. New York: Simon and Schuster.

Kirsch, A., and L. G. Reeder. 1969. "Client Evaluation of Physician Performance." *Journal of Health and Social Behavior* 10:51–57.

Klein, H., and E. Mumford. 1973. "The Bent Twig: Psychiatry and Medical Education." *American Journal of Psychiatry* 78:587–593.

Knafl, K., and G. Burkett. 1975. "Professional Socialization in a Surgical Specialty: Acquiring Medical Judgment." *Social Science and Medicine* 9:397–404.

Korsch, B. M., E. K. Gozzi, and V. Francis. 1968. "Gaps in Doctor–Patient Communication: I. Doctor–Patient Interaction and Patient Satisfaction." *Pediatrics* 42:855–871.

Korsch, B. M., and V. Negrete. 1972. "Doctor–Patient Communication." *Scientific American* 227:66–75.

Kosa, J. 1970. "Entrepreneurship and Charisma in the Medical Profession." *Social Science and Medicine* 4:25–40.

Kosa, J., and I. K. Zola, eds. 1975. *Poverty and Health: A Sociological Analysis*. 2nd ed. Cambridge, Mass.: Harvard University Press.

Kotelchuck, R. 1984. "Baring Costs: How the DRG System Works." *Health PAC Bulletin* 15:7–12.

Krause, E. 1977. *Power and Illness*. New York: Elsevier.

Krauss, D. R., A. S. Robbins, I. Abrass, R. F. Bataitis, and L. A. Anderson. 1980. "The Long Term Effectiveness of Interpersonal Skills Training in Medical School." *Journal of Medical Education* 55:595–601.

Kroeber, T. C. 1963. "The Coping Functions of the Ego Mechanisms." In R. W. White, ed., *The Study of Lives*, 179–198. New York: Atherton.

Lang, C. L. 1981. "Good Cases—Bad Cases: Client Selection and Professional Prerogative in a Community Mental Health Clinic." *Urban Life* 10:289–309.

Langwell, K. M. 1980. "Career Path of First Year Resident Physicians: A Seven Year Study." *Journal of Medical Education* 55:897–905.

Lesserman, J. 1981. *Men and Women in Medical School: How They Change and How They Compare*. New York: Praeger.

Levin, T. 1974. *American Health: Professional Privilege vs. Public Need*. New York: Praeger.

Levine, D. M., A. J. Barsky III, R. C. Fox, R. B. Fredin, S. R. Williams, and J. A. Wysong. 1974. "Trends in Medical Education Research: Past, Present and Future." *Journal of Medical Education* 49:129–136.

Levine, S., and P. E. White. 1974. "Exchange as a Conceptual Framework for the Study of Interorganizational Relationships." In Y. Hasenfeld and R. English, eds., *Human Service Organizations*, 545–560. Ann Arbor: University of Michigan Press.

Light, D. 1980. *Becoming Psychiatrists: The Professional Transformation of Self*. New York: Norton.

Linn, L., and R. N. Wilson. 1980. "Factors Related to a Communication Style among Medical Housestaff." *Medical Care* 18:1013–1019.

Lipp, M. 1980. *The Bitter Pill*. New York: Harper and Row.

Lipsky, M. 1980. *Street Level Bureaucracy: Dilemmas of Individuals in Public Services*. New York: Russell Sage Foundation.

Lowenstein, L. M. 1979. "The Structure and Function of Graduate Medical Education." In E. C. Shapiro and L. M. Lowenstein, eds., *Becoming a Physician: Development of Values in Medicine*, 95–112, Cambridge, Mass.: Ballinger.

Lyden, F. J., H. J. Geiger, and O. L. Peterson, 1968. *The Training of Good Physicians*. Cambridge, Mass.: Harvard University Press.

Madison, T. M. 1978a. *Organizing for Better Community Health*. 2nd ed. Chicago: National Clearinghouse for Legal Services.

———. 1978b. *The People's Right to Good Health*. 2nd ed. Chicago: National Clearinghouse for Legal Services.

Maguire, G. P., D. L. Julier, K. E. Hawton, and J. H. J. Bancroft. 1982. "Psychiatric Morbidity and Referral on Two General Medical Wards." *British Medical Journal* 1:268–270.

Maguire, G. P., and D. Rutter. 1976. "Training Medical Students to Communicate." In A. E. Bennett, ed., *Communication between Doctors and Patients*, 45–74. Oxford: Oxford University Press.

Maines, D. R. 1982. "In Search of Mesostructure: Studies in the Negotiated Order." *Urban Life* 11:267–279.

Martin, W. 1957. "Preference for Types of Patients." In R. K. Merton, G. G. Reader, and P. L. Kendall, eds., *The Student-Physician*, 189–206. Cambridge: Harvard University Press.

Mauksch, H. O. 1973. "Ideology, Interaction and Patient Care in Hospitals." *Social Science and Medicine* 7:817–830.

Mawardi, B. H. 1965. "A Career Study of Physicians." *Journal of Medical Education* 40:658–666.

———. 1979. "Satisfactions, Dissatisfactions and Causes of Stress in Internal Practice." *Journal of the American Medical Association* 241:1483–1486.

———. 1980. "Physician Career Satisfaction: Another Look." In *Research in Medical Education, 1980*. Proceedings of the Nineteenth Annual Conference. Washington, D.C.: Association of American Medical Colleges.

McCall, G. J., and J. L. Simmons, eds. 1969. "Issues in Participant Observation. London: Addison-Wesley.

McCue, J. D. 1981. "Training Internists: Insights from Private Practice." *American Journal of Medicine* 71:475–479.

———. 1982. "The Effects of Stress on Physicians and Their Medical Practice." *New England Journal of Medicine* 306:458–463.

McGovern, J. P., and C. R. Burns. 1970. *Humanism in Medicine*. Springfield, Ill.: Thomas.

McKinlay, J. B. 1975. "Who Is Really Ignorant—Physician or Patient?" *Journal of Health and Social Behavior* 16:3–11

———. 1978. "The Changing Political and Economic Context of the Patient–Physician Encounter." In E. B. Gallagher, ed., *The Doctor–Patient Relationship in the Changing Health Scene*, 155–188. Washington, D.C.: Department of Health, Education, and Welfare.

McKnight, J. 1977. "The Professional Service Business." *Social Policy* 8:100–117.

Mechanic, D. 1968. *Medical Sociology*. Glencoe, Ill.: Free Press.

———. 1974. "Social Structure and Personal Adaptation: Some Neglected Dimensions." In C. V. Coelho, D. A. Hamburg, and J. E. Adams, eds., *Coping and Adaptation*, 133–44. New York: Basic Books.

Meltzer, B. 1975. *Symbolic Interactionism: Genesis, Varieties and Criticism*. London: Routledge and Kegan Paul.

Merton, R. K. 1968. *Social Theory and Social Structure*. Enlarged ed. Glencoe, Ill.: Free Press.

Merton, R. K., with E. Barber. 1976. "Sociological Ambivalence," In R. K. Merton, ed., *Social Ambivalence and Other Essays*, 3–31. New York: Free Press.

Merton, R. K., G. G. Reader, and P. L. Kendall. 1957. *The Student Physician*, Cambridge, Mass.: Harvard University Press.

Miller, S. 1970. *Prescription for Leadership*. Chicago: Aldine.

Millman, M. 1977. *The Unkindest Cut: Life in the Backroom of Medicine*. New York: Morrow.

Millman, M., and R. M. Kantor. 1976. *Another Voice: Feminist Perspectives on Social Life and Social Sciences*. New York: Octagon.

Mills, C. W. 1959. *The Sociological Imagination*. New York: Oxford University Press.

Milner, M., Jr. 1980. *Unequal Care: A Case Study of Interorganizational Relations*. New York: Columbia University Press.

Mishler, E., and N. Waxler. 1963. "Decision Processes in Psychiatric Hospitalization: Patients Referred, Accepted and Admitted to a Psychiatric Hospital." *American Sociological Review* 28:576–587.

Mizrahi, T. 1983. "The Impact of Graduate Medical Education of Internists on the Doctor–Patient Relationship." Ph.D. diss. University of Virginia.

―――. 1984a. "Managing Medical Mistakes: Ideology, Insularity and Accountability among Internists-in-Training." *Social Science and Medicine* 19:135–146.

―――. 1984b. "The Out-Patient Clinic: The Crucible of the Doctor–Patient Relationship in Graduate Medical Education." *Journal of Ambulatory Care Management* 7:51–68.

Mizrahi, T., and J. Abramson. 1985. "Sources of Strain between Physicians and Social Workers: Implications for Social Workers in Health Care Settings." *Social Work in Health Care* 10:33–51.

Moore, W. E. 1970. *The Professions: Roles and Rules*. New York: Sage.

Moore, W. E. and M. Tumin. 1949. "Some Social Functions of Ignorance." *American Sociological Review* 14:788–796.

Moser, S. 1978. "House Staff and the Indigent Black Patient." *Forum on Medicine* 1:21–27.

Mumford, E. 1970. *Interns: From Students to Physicians*. Cambridge,: Mass. Harvard University Press.

Myers, J. D. 1981. "Preventing Iatrogenic Complications." *New England Journal of Medicine* 304:664–665.

Nadelson, C. C., and M. T. Notman. 1979. "Adaptation to Stress in Physicians." In E. C. Shapiro and L. M. Lowenstein, eds., *Becoming a Physician: Development of Values in Medicine*, 201–215. Cambridge, Mass.: Ballinger.

Navarro, V. 1976. *Medicine under Capitalism*. New York: Watson Academic Publications, Prodist.

Olsen, V., and E. Whittaker. 1968. *The Silent Dialogue: A Study in the Social Psychology of Professional Education*. San Francisco: Jossey-Bass.

―――. 1970. "Critical Notes on Sociological Studies of Professional Socialization." In J. A. Jackson, ed., *Professions and Professionalization*, 179–221. New York: Cambridge University Press.

Osofsky, H. J. 1968. "The Walls Are Within: An Exploration of Barriers between Middle-Class Physicians and Poor Patients." In I. Deutscher and E. J. Thompson, eds., *Among the Poor*, 239–258. New York: Basic Books.

Papper, S. 1970. "The Undesirable Patient." *Journal of Chronic Disease* 22:777–779.

Parker, S. 1960. "The Attitudes of Medical Students toward Their Patients: An Exploratory Study." *Journal of Medical Education* 35:849–854.

Parsons, T. 1951. *The Social System*. Glencoe, Ill: Free Press.

―――. 1975. "The Sick Role and the Role of the Physician Reconsidered." *Milbank Memorial Fund Quarterly/Health and Society* 53:257–258.

Pellegrino, E. D. 1974. "The Identity of an Ideal." In J. Ingelfinger, R. V. Ebert, M. Finland, and A. S. Pelman, eds., *Controversies in Internal Medicine*, vol. 2, 41–58. Philadelphia: Saunders.

Perkoff, G. 1978. "General Internal Medicine, Family Practice or Something Better." *New England Journal of Medicine* 299:849–854.

Perrow, C. 1979. *Complex Organizations: A Critical Essay*. 2nd ed. Glenview, Ill. Scott, Foresman.

Petersdorf, R. G. 1975a. "Internal Medicine and Family Practice: Controversies, Conflict and Compromise." *New England Journal of Medicine* 293:326–332.

———. 1975b. "Issues in Primary Care: The Academic Perspective." *Journal of Medical Education* 50:5–13.

———. 1976. "Internal Medicine 1976: Consequences of Sub-Specialization and Technology." *Annals of Internal Medicine* 84:92–94.

———. 1977. "Evaluation of the General Internist." *Archives of Internal Medicine* 137:1305–1310.

———. 1978. "The Doctor's Dilemma." *New England Journal of Medicine* 299:628–634.

Pfifferling, J. H. 1978. "Risks Factors for Physician Impairment and the Promotion of Physician Well-Being." Paper delivered to Department of Medicine of the Medical College of Virginia, Richmond.

———. 1983. *The Impaired Physician: An Overview*. Durham, N.C.: Center for Professional Well-Being.

Plaja, A. O., L. M. Cohen, and J. Samora. 1968. "Communication between Physician and Patient in Out-Patient Clinics: Social and Cultural Factors." *Milbank Memorial Fund Quarterly* 46:161–175.

Platt, F. W., and J. McMath. 1979. "Clinical Hypocompetence: The Interview." *Annals of Internal Medicine* 91:898–902.

Pratt, L., A. Seligmann, and G. G. Reader. 1957. "Physicians' View on the Level of Medical Information on Patients." *American Journal of Public Health* 47:1277–1286.

———. 1978. "Reshaping the Consumer's Posture in Health Care." In E. B. Gallagher, ed., *The Doctor–Patient Relationship in the Changing Health Scene*, 197–214. Washington, D.C.: Department of Health, Education, and Welfare.

Preston, T. 1981. *The Clay Pedestal*. Seattle: Madrona Publishers.

Rayack, E. 1967. *Professional Power and American Medicine: The Economics of the American Medical Association*. Cleveland: World.

Reeder, L. 1972. "The Patient-Client as Consumer: Some Observations on the Changing Professional–Client Relationship." *Journal of Health and Social Behavior* 3:406–412.

Regelson, W. 1978. "The Weakening of the Oslerian Tradition." *Journal of the American Medical Association* 239:317–319.

Reynolds, R., and T. Bice. 1971. "Attitudes of Medical Interns towards Patients and Health Professionals." *Journal of Health and Social Behavior* 12:307–311.

Rezler, A. 1974. "Attitude Changes in Medical School: A Review of the Literature." *Journal of Medical Education* 49:1023–1030.

Ries, R. K., J. A. Bokan, W. J. Katon, and A. Kleinman. 1981. "The Medical Care Abuser: Differential Diagnosis and Management." *Journal of Family Practice* 13:257–265.

Robbins, A. S., D. R. Krauss, R. Heinrich, I. Abrass, J. Dreyer, and B. Clyman. 1979. "Interpersonal Skills Training: Evaluation in an Internal Medicine Residency." *Journal of Medical Education* 54:885–894.

Roberts, C. M. 1977. *Doctor–Patient in the Teaching Hospital: A Tale of Two Life-Worlds*. Lexington, Mass.: Heath.

Robinson, V. M. 1977. *Humor and the Health Professions*. Thorofare, N.J.: Slack.
Rosenberg, P. 1979. "Catch-22: The Medical Model." In E. C. Shapiro and L. M.
Lowenstein, eds., *Becoming a Physician: Development of Values in Medicine*,
81–92. Cambridge, Mass.: Ballinger.
Rosner, D. 1982. *A Once Charitable Enterprise: Hospitals and Health Care in Brook-
lyn and New Cambridge*. New York: Cambridge University Press.
Roth, B. 1974. "Patient Dumping." *Health PAC Bulletin* 5:3–7.
Roth, J. 1963. *Timetables*. Indianapolis: Bobbs-Merrill.
———. 1970. "The Public Hospital: Refuge for Damaged Humans." In A. L.
Strauss, ed., *Where Medicine Fails*, 53–66. Chicago-Aldine.
———. 1972. "Staff and Client Control Strategies in Urban Hospitals' Emergency
Services." *Urban Life and Culture* 1:39–60.
———. 1974a. "Professionalism: A Sociologist's Decoy." *Sociology of Work and
Occupations* 1:6–23.
———. 1974b. "Some Contingencies of the Moral Evaluation and Control of Clientele: The Case of the Hospital Emergency Service." *American Journal of Sociology* 77:839–856.
———. 1975. "The Treatment of the Sick. In J. Kosa and I. K. Zola, eds., *Poverty
and Health: A Sociological Analysis*, 2d ed., 274–302. Cambridge: Harvard University Press.
Ryan, W. 1970. *Blaming the Victim*. New York: Random House, Vintage.
Sartwell, P. E. 1974. "Iatrogenic Disease: An Epidemiological Perspective." *International Journal of Health Services* 4:89–93.
Schatzman, L., and A. L. Strauss. 1973. *Field Research: Studies for a Natural Sociology*. Englewood Cliffs, N.J.: Prenctice-Hall.
Scheff, T. J. 1972. "Decision Rules, Types of Error, and Their Consequences in Medi-
cal Diagnosis." In E. Freidson and J. Lorber, eds., *Medical Men and Their Work*,
308–323. Chicago: Aldine-Atherton.
Scheiber, S. C., and B. B. Doyle, eds. 1983. *The Impaired Physician*. New York:
Plenum.
Schleiter, M. K., A. R. Tarlov, and P. A. Weil. 1981. "National Study of Internal
Medicine Manpower: VII. Residency and Fellowship Training 1976–1977
through 1980–1981." *Annals of Internal Medicine* 95:762–768.
Schmalenberg, C., and M. Kramer. 1979. *Coping with Reality Shock*. Wakefield,
Mass.: Nursing Resources.
Schwartz, N., and J. Jacobs, 1979. *Qualitative Sociology: A Method to the Madness*.
New York: Free Press.
Scully, D. H. 1977. "Skill Acquisition in Obstetrics and Gynecology: Social Processes
and Implications for Patient Care." Ph.D. diss., University of Illinois.
———. 1980. *Men Who Control Women's Health*. Boston: Houghton Mifflin.
Seham, M. 1973. *Blacks and American Medical Care*. Minneapolis: University of
Minnesota Press.
Shapiro, E. C., and S. G. Driscoll. 1979. "Training for Commitment: Effects of the
Time-Intensive Nature of Graduate Medical Education." In E. C. Shapiro and
L. M. Lowenstein, eds., *Becoming a Physician: Development of Values in Medi-
cine*, 187–201. Cambridge, Mass.: Ballinger.

Shapiro, E. C., and L. M. Lowenstein, eds. 1979. *Becoming a Physician: Development of Values in Medicine*. Cambridge, Mass.: Ballinger.

Shem, S. 1978. *The House of God*. New York: Marek.

Shipp, J. C. 1977. "Ambulatory Care and Teaching Hospitals." *Annals of Internal Medicine* 86:237–241.

Shuval, J. 1975. "From 'Boy' to 'Colleague': Process of Role Transformation in Professional Socialization." *Social Science and Medicine* 9:413–420.

———. 1980. "The Role and Models in Professional Socialization." *Social Science and Medicine* 14A:5–14.

Singer, B. D. 1967. "Some Implications of Differential Psychiatric Treatment of Negro and White Patients." *Social Science and Medicine* 1:77–83.

Sjoberg, G., ed. 1967. *Ethics, Politics, and Social Research*. Cambridge: Mass.: Schenkman.

Solon J. 1966. "Patterns of Medical Care: Socioculture and Variations among Hospitals' Outpatients." *American Journal of Public Health* 56: 884–894.

Sorenson, J. 1974. "Bio-Medical Innovation, Uncertainty and Doctor–Patient Interaction." *Journal of Health and Social Behavior* 15:366–380.

Spitz, L., and E. Block. 1981. "Denial and Minimization in Telephone Contacts with Patients." *Journal of Family Practice* 12:93–98.

Starr, P. 1982. *The Social Transformation of American Medicine*. New York: Basic Books.

Steel, K. P., P. M. Gertman, C. Crescenzi, and J. Anderson. 1981. "Iatrogenic Illness on a General Medical Service." *New England Journal of Medicine* 304:638–641.

Stelling, J., and R. Bucher. 1973. "Vocabularies of Realism in Professional Socialization." *Social Science and Medicine* 7:661–675.

Stevens, R. 1971. *American Medicine and the Public Interest*. New Haven, Conn.: Yale University Press.

———. 1978. "Graduate Medical Education: A Continuing History." *Journal of Medical Education* 53:1–18.

Stewart, A., and C. Buck. 1977. "Physicians' Knowledge of and Response to Patients' Problems." *Medical Care* 25:578–585.

Stimson, G. V. 1976. "General Practitioners' Trouble and Type of Patients." In M. Stacey, ed., *Sociology of the National Health Service* 43–59. Staffordshire: University of Keele Press.

———. 1978. "Interaction Between Patients and General Practitioners in the United Kingdom." In E. B. Gallagher, ed., *The Doctor–Patient Relationship in the Changing Health Scene*, 69–84. Washington, D.C.: Department of Health, Education, and Welfare.

Stoeckle, J. D. 1975. "The Outpatient Department–Ambulatory Care at the Hospital." *New England Journal of Medicine* 293:775–781.

Stokes, J. III, N. Cliff, C. V. Riche, and D. D. Rudstein. 1963. "The Effect of a Course on Family Medicine on Medical Students' Skills and Attitudes." *Journal of Medical Education* 38:547–555.

Strauss, A. L. 1963. "The Hospital as a Negotiated Order." In E. Freidson, ed., *The Hospital in Modern Society*, 147–169. Glencoe, Ill.: Free Press.

Strauss, A. L. 1975a. "Negotiated Order and the Coordination of Work." In A. L.

Strauss, ed., *Professions, Work and Careers*, 175–202. New Brunswick, N. J.: Transaction Books.

———. 1975b. "Rotational System: Its Impact upon Teaching, Learning, and the Medical Service." In A. L. Strauss, ed., *Professions, Work and Careers*, 275–313. New Brunswick, N.J.: Transaction Books.

———. 1978. *Negotiations: Varieties, Contexts, Processes and Social Order*. San Francisco: Jossey-Bass.

Strauss, R. 1978. "Medical Education and the Doctor–Patient Relationship." In E. B. Gallagher, ed., *The Doctor–Patient Relationship in the Changing Health Scene*, 413–422. Washington, D.C.: Department of Health, Education, and Welfare.

Strelnick, H., with R. Younge. 1980. *Double Indemnity: A Health pac Special Report*. New York: Health Policy Advisory Center.

Stub, H. 1972. *Status Communities in Modern Society: Alternative to Class Analysis*. Hinsdale, Ill.: Dryden.

Sudnow, D. 1964. "Normal Crimes." *Social Problems* 12:255–275.

———. 1967. *Passing On*. Englewood Cliffs, N.J.: Prentice-Hall.

———. 1970. "Dead on Arrival." In A. L. Strauss, ed., *Where Medicine Fails*, 111–130. Chicago: Aldine.

Sugrue, N.M. 1982. "Emotions as Property and Context for Negotiation." *Urban Life* 11:280–292.

Sykes, G. 1958. *The Society of Captives*. Princeton, N.J.: Princeton University Press.

Sykes, G., and D. Matza. 1957. "Techniques of Neutralization: A Theory of Delinquency." *American Sociological Review* 22:664–670.

Szasz, T. S. 1972. "Malingering: Diagnosis or Social Condemnation." In E. Freidson and J. Lorber, eds., *Medical Men and Their Work. 353–368*. Chicago: Aldine-Atherton.

Szasz, T. S., and M. H. Hollander. 1975. "A Contribution to the Philosophy of Medicine: The Basic Model of the Doctor–Patient Relationship." *Archives of Internal Medicine* 97:585–597.

Tokarz, J. P., W. Bremer, and K. Peters. 1979. *Beyond Survival*. Chicago: American Medical Association.

Valiant, C. E. 1972. "Some Psychological Vulnerabilities of Physicians." *New England Journal of Medicine* 287:372–375.

Vladeck, B. C. 1984. "Medicare Hospital Payment by Diagnosis-Related Groups." *Annals of Internal Medicine* 100:576–582.

Waitzkin, H. 1983. *The Second Sickness*. New York: Free Press.

Waitzkin, H., and J. D. Stoeckle, 1972. "The Communication of Information about Illness." *Advanced Psychosomatic Medicine* 8:180–215.

Waitzkin, H., and B. Waterman. 1974. *The Exploitation of Illness in a Capitalist Society*. Indianapolis: Bobbs-Merrill.

Waring, E.M. 1974. "Psychiatric Illness in Physicians." *Comprehensive Psychiatry* 15:519–530.

Wartman, S. A., L. L. Morlock, F. E. Malitz, and E. Palm. 1981. "Do Prescriptions Adversely Affect Doctor–Patient Interactions?" *American Journal of Public Health* 71:1358–1361.

Wechler, H. 1976. *Handbook of Medical Specialities*. New York: Human Sciences.

Werner, E. R., and B. M. Korsch. 1979. "Professionalization during Pediatric Internship: Attitudes, Adaptations and Interpersonal Skills." In E. C. Shapiro and
L. M. Lowenstein, eds., *Becoming a Physician: Development of Values in Medicine*, 113–137. Cambridge, Mass.: Ballinger.

White, R. W. 1974. "Strategies of Adaptation: An Attempt at Systematic Description." In G. V. Coelho, D. A. Hamburg, and J. E. Adams, eds., *Coping and Adaptation*, 47–68. New York: Basic Books.

Wigton, R. S., and W. C. Steinmann. 1984. "Procedural Skills Training in Internal
Medicine Residency." *Journal of Medical Education* 59:392–398.

Williams, R. 1968. "Norms." *International Encyclopedia of Social Sciences*. Vol. 2.
New York: Macmillan.

Williamson, P. B., B. D. Beitman, and W. Katon. 1981. "Beliefs That Foster Physician Avoidance of Psychosocial Aspects of Health Care." *Journal of Family
Practice* 13:999–1003.

Wiseman, J. 1970. *Stations of the Lost*. Englewood Cliffs, N.J.: Prentice-Hall.

Yamamoto, J., F. Dixon, and M. Bloombaum. 1972. "White Therapists and Negro
Patients." *Journal of the National Medical Assocation* 312–316.

Yamamoto, J., Q. C. James, M. Bloombaum, and J. Hattem. 1967. "Racial Factors in
Patient Selection." *American Journal of Psychiatry* 124:84–90.

Young, R.E. 1975. "Changes in the Post-Doctoral Education of Internists." *Annals of
Internal Medicine* 83:728–730.

Zelditch, M., Jr. 1970. "Some Methodological Problems of Field Studies." In W.
Filstead, ed., *Qualitative Methodology*, 217–234. Chicago: Markham.

Zola, I. K. 1963. "Problems of Communication, Diagnosis, and Patient Care: The Interplay of Patient, Physician and Clinic Organization." *Journal of Medicine Education* 38:829–838.

———. 1972. "Medicine as an Institution of Social Control. *Sociological Review*
20:487–504.

———. 1977. "Taking Your Medication: Problem for Doctor or Patient." In I.
Barofsky, ed., *Medication Compliance*, 3–8. Thorofare, N.Y.: Slack.

Zola, I. K., and S. Miller. 1971. "Erosion of Medicine from Within." In E. Freidson,
ed., *Professions and Their Prospects*, 153–172. Beverly Hills, Calif.: Sage.

Index

*(Page numbers in italics
indicate tabular material.)*